Dr. Bob Sheets is the former director of the National Hurricane Center in Miami, Florida, and a veteran of many hurricanes.

Jack Williams is one of the founders of the *USA TODAY* Weather Page, and the author of *The USA TODAY Weather Book* and *The USA TODAY Weather Almanac*.

The USA TODAY Weather Book:
An Easy-to-Understand Guide to the USA's Weather

The USA TODAY Weather Almanac:
The Most Complete, Up-to-Date Look
at the USA's Weather

HURRICANE
WATCH

HURRICANE WATCH

FORECASTING THE DEADLIEST STORMS ON EARTH

DR. BOB SHEETS

and

JACK WILLIAMS

VINTAGE BOOKS

A DIVISION OF RANDOM HOUSE, INC.

NEW YORK

A VINTAGE BOOKS ORIGINAL, SEPTEMBER 2001
First Edition

Library of Congress Cataloging-in-Publication Data
Williams, Jack, 1936–
Hurricane watch : forecasting the deadliest storms on earth /
Jack Williams and Bob Sheets.— 1st ed.
p.   cm.
"A Vintage original."
ISBN 0-375-70390-X
1. Hurricanes.   2. Cyclone forecasting   I. Sheets, Bob.   II. Title.

QC944.W55 2001
551.64'52 — dc21
2001026102

Book design by Jo Anne Metsch

www.vintagebooks.com

Printed in the United States of America
10 9 8 7 6 5 4 3 2 1

ACKNOWLEDGMENTS

I N MY NEARLY forty years of study and experience in the field of meteorology, specializing for the past thirty-six years in the study and forecasting of hurricanes, many individuals have contributed directly or indirectly to the material presented in this book. First and foremost would be my teacher and friend Professor Yoshikazu Sasaki at the University of Oklahoma; Dr. Robert Cecil Gentry, who gave me my start at the National Hurricane Research Laboratory; and Dr. Neil L. Frank, under whom I served at the National Hurricane Center. Others include Dr. Robert H. Simpson and the late Gordon E. Dunn, former directors of the National Hurricane Center; professors Noel E. LaSuer of Florida State University and William Gray of Colorado State University; along with several hurricane forecasters, including Raymond Kraft, Gil Clark, John Hope, and Paul Hebert—with whom I have enjoyed many exchanges and from whom I learned much. Some specific material for this book was provided by Dr. Frank Marks and Dr. Hugh Willoughby of NOAA's Hurricane Research Division; Richard Decker of NOAA's Aircraft Operations Center; and others too numerous to mention individually.

Also, I wish to acknowledge the numerous Hurricane Hunter crews and technicians from NOAA and its predecessors—the U.S. Air Force and Navy—with whom I had the pleasure of flying over a period of sixteen years; and the numerous Local, State, and Federal Emergency Managers with whom I had the pleasure of working over many years in an effort to protect life and property when hurricanes threatened. I would also like to thank the individuals and families who shared the personal Hurricane Andrew experiences with me that I related in this book so that others may learn from them.

Finally, I wish to thank my spouse, Mary Jane, and my children, Mark, Robin and Kimberly, for the sacrifices that they have made over the years to support my career, and for enduring my numerous absences from family activities associated with my various positions of responsibility that are partially related in this book.

—Dr. Bob Sheets

Growing up in Florida in the 1940s and 1950s, when every year seemed to bring hurricanes, planted the seeds of my fascination with what I later learned are the world's deadliest storms. My interest blossomed during the 1980s and 1990s when, as weather editor of *USA TODAY*, I reported on hurricanes, sometimes from the National Hurricane Center and a few times from airplanes inside hurricanes. When I began thinking about a book on hurricanes, I realized that I wanted Bob Sheets to join me as an author. Bob is not only an experienced hurricane forecaster and scientist, but is skilled at communicating his work to nonscientists. Perhaps even more important, in August 1992 I spent four days as a reporter at the National Hurricane Center during Hurricane Andrew. Before, during and after the early morning hours when Andrew damaged Bob's home and destroyed the homes of some of his colleagues, Bob stayed calm, clearly explaining the storm during one live television interview after another, while making forecasting decisions that could have meant life or death for hundreds of Americans. I concluded that anyone who could stay so cool during Hurricane Andrew was ready for the challenge of working with a journalist on a book.

Bob more than lived up to my expectations, never losing his patience as he led me to a deeper understanding of the science and history of hurricanes. I want to acknowledge the many others who have taught me about hurricanes over the years, going back to my first visit to the Hurricane Center in the early 1980s. They include forecasters, research scientists, and crew members I was privileged to meet on hurricane flights. I want to especially thank Bob and Joanne Simpson, who shared their memories of the creation of modern hurricane science; Bill Gray, who helped me see how hurricanes and other tropical cyclones fit into the global climate picture; and Hugh Willoughby, who doesn't let his job as head of the government's hurricane research program get in the way of his wit and way with words.

I want to offer special thanks to Mike Bryan, who led this book back to the light after I had let all of the information that Bob and I had collected bury the story we had to tell. J. Edward Kastenmeier, our Vintage Books editor, is one of those rare editors who closely examines every word, raising questions an author might find tiresome at the time, but which he later appreciates. I want to thank our agent, Joe Spieler, for making the business side of the book work well.

Finally, without the love and encouragement of my wife, Darlene, I would be able to accomplish little. Being able to share any success we might enjoy with her makes all of the work worthwhile.

— Jack Williams

CONTENTS

PREFACE

I N THE WHISPERING PINES neighborhood about twenty miles southwest of downtown Miami, Tom Ochmanski and his wife, Laurie, have put their one-year old son, Ryan, and two-year-old daughter, Caitlyn, to bed early in the evening. Whispering Pines is not in an evacuation zone and the Ochmanski house is a strong one—they think. Around midnight, Tom and Laurie and Laurie's mother, Lee Bolander, finally try to get some rest, but the howling winds wake them two hours later. As the adults sit in the living room, watching reports on their battery-operated television set, squalls of heavy rain and high winds became stronger and more and more frequent. By 4:45 a.m., winds are probably gusting to over 150 or 160 mph, and debris slamming into the house creates an almost deafening roar. Above this roar, parents and grandmother hear breaking glass in Ryan's bedroom. Tom rushes in to find the window shattered by flying debris and scattered around the room, but, remarkably, Ryan is not cut or hurt. Tom grabs him and Laurie gets Caitlyn from her bedroom and the entire family huddles in the living room, close to the hallway entrance. They hear the other windows breaking on the north end of the house. As Hurricane Andrew's eye wall moves directly over them, the screaming wind becomes even more terrifying. The Ochmanskis know when the wind shifts direction because the loud thumps of striking debris now come from the east side of the house.

Tom shines a large flashlight at the top of the front wall and sees it pulling away from the ceiling. This is a reinforced concrete tie beam connecting the walls to the roof, and these winds are doing their best to lift it right off the house. The family moves closer to the hallway door and starts praying. Suddenly, and with a tremendous crash, the entire front of their house slams inward, while the front half of the roof is ripped away. A large blunt object strikes Tom in the back, knocking him across the room. Laurie quickly crawls through the debris to the hallway, taking the two terrified children with her. She places Ryan and Caitlyn on shelves in the linen closet off the hallway and crouches in the open doorway to protect them with her own body.

Where is Tom now? Where is her mother? Are they alive or dead? Laurie has only her fears and her prayers.

———

Great tropical cyclones are the largest and most destructive storms on the face of this planet; collective memory never forgets the passage of a powerful, deadly storm, such as Hurricane Andrew in South Florida in 1992. In the past, these typhoons and hurricanes struck without warning. Today, this never happens. We can forecast the great storms with increasing, often remarkable, accuracy. We can save lives and property—some lives, some property. However, we will never be able to stop these storms. The residents of shorelines of the world exposed to storms from the tropics, and the tourists who flock to these sandy paradises will always prick their ears when they hear the words, "A hurricane watch has been posted for. . . ."

HURRICANE

WATCH

This cross section shows the major features of a mature hurricane. Most of today's scientific understanding of what happens inside these monster storms is based on hurricane flights that scientists have been making since the 1950s. Note that the vertical scale has been enlarged with respect to the horizontal scale for illustrative purposes.

Cool air flows up and near the top of the hurricane, flows out from center in a clockwise spiral in the Northern Hemisphere.

Warm, moist air flows into the hurricane near the surface.

Condensed water vapor left in the air becomes ice crystals and forms a canopy of cirrostratus clouds over the storm.

The nearly calm eye.
The eye wall is generally the area of greatest wind speed.

Rainbands are the thunderstorms that spiral in toward the center, and are typically 3 to 30 miles wide and 50 to 300 miles long.

The air speeds up as it approaches the center.

The storm surge develops in front and to the right of the storm's eye.

Air cools as it rises, but generally remains warmer than surrounding air.

CHAPTER 1

EARLY HISTORY AND SCIENCE

FROM HIS ACCUSTOMED perch high on the slant stern castle, Christopher Columbus eyed the cirrus clouds drifting overhead from the southeast, and he felt the exceptionally long ocean swell rolling in from the same direction. The *Capitana* dipped and bobbed on the anchor. Columbus noted the large number of dolphins leaping from the water at the mouth of the Ozama River, just outside the excellent harbor at Santo Domingo, the new capital of Espanola. It was a beautiful sight, a beautiful day—but not a beautiful forecast; the Admiral of the Ocean Sea had learned a great deal about tropical weather during his four journeys of exploration in the New World. On his first voyage, in 1492, he had observed similar clouds and a deep swell from the southeast without understanding their portent. On his second trip, three years later, he had encountered the same signs yet again off Espanola, and then later on the same trip the correlation between portent and weather became self-evident when his fleet was struck full force by a heavenly blast. Two of his three ships went to the bottom: thus did Columbus and his crews have the honor of being the first Europeans known to have experienced a real tropical storm.

And now, in July 1502, he saw these ominous signs again. Moreover, his rheumatic, fifty-one-year-old joints were sore, and these creaky things had never lied to him. With Espanola once again in harm's way, Columbus dispatched his captain to approach Don Nicholas de Ovando, the new governor of the Spanish colony, advising him to hold in harbor the thirty ships ready to sail for the homeland and requesting permission for Columbus's four ships to join them for safekeeping.

Permission denied. The new governor and Columbus were rivals for the Crown's affection, and the Admiral's stock in this regard had fallen drastically since his triumph a decade earlier. Ferdinand and Isabella had been wary of granting permission for this final voyage, and when they finally relented, they stipulated that Columbus could land in Santo Domingo only on his way home. The politically secure new governor now felt comfortable in denying the great man any anchorage at all. Chastened but heeding the skies, Columbus sailed off to the west in search of safety. Gloating and ignoring the skies, the governor wished his fleet of thirty sails Godspeed as they set forth for Spain. This was a grave mistake. When the storm did indeed strike two days later, these ships were caught in the Mona Passage between Espanola and Puerto Rico. Within hours, twenty-one of them were lost, and at least 500 sailors had died. A handful of beleaguered ships returned to a battered Santo Domingo, while one plowed ahead and somehow made it to Spain.

Meanwhile, Columbus had anchored his four ships in a sheltered lee on the south coast of the island, hard under a bank of high cliffs. Only the *Capitana* stayed snug beneath these cliffs, but the three ships whose anchors had failed nevertheless rode out the storm and met Columbus the following day at a prearranged rendezvous, with all hands safe. The incensed Columbus later wrote to his sovereigns, "What man ever born, not excepting Job, who would not have died of despair when in such weather, seeking safety for my son, brother, shipmates, and myself, we were forbidden the land and the harbors that I, by God's will and sweating blood, had won for Spain?"

We now know that Columbus's hurricane prediction that July is the first in recorded history. In this way, too, the Admiral of the Ocean Sea led the way in the New World. Of course, Europeans had experienced damaging winds and waters, and Mediterranean seafarers had sailed through heavy storms, but the eastern Atlantic Ocean and the Mediterranean rarely produce winds stronger than 100 miles per hour. The monster winds of the western Atlantic, the Caribbean Sea, and the Gulf of Mexico—often reaching speeds of 140 to 150 miles per hour—were a different matter altogether. Their scale,

A fanciful image by Theodore de Bry of the hurricane of July 1502, destroying the ships of Don Nicholas de Ovando, the governor of Hispaniola, after Columbus had warned of the storm.

ferocity, and path of movement were completely beyond the bounds of understanding. Columbus and other precocious veterans of the New World—not including the governor of Hispaniola, as the colony of Espanola came to be called—had come to recognize the ominous signs of an impending storm, but they had no knowledge of the causes of these leviathans of the atmosphere.

The *effects* in damage and death were understood all too well though—and they had been understood for as long as humankind had lived by the shorelines of these warm western seas. The Mayans, who flourished in the lowlands of modern-day Guatemala, Honduras, and southern Mexico for more than 1,000 years, until about A.D. 900, recorded hurricanes in their hieroglyphics. Is it accidental that none of the great Mayan cities was on the Caribbean coast? Not likely. Today's "Mayan Riviera" was the Mayans' own no-man's-land. Their only port city discovered to date is the modestly sized Tulum, on the east coast of the Yucatán Peninsula south of Cancun. Tulum was still occupied when the Spanish arrived in the sixteenth century, and its citizens were more prepared for the storms than for the Spanish. As the tens of thousands of visitors to the ruins can easily see, the ceremonial buildings and grounds of the city, so ably constructed that many remain today, are well above sea level.

We shouldn't be surprised to learn that the Spanish and English words for the great tropical storms of the Atlantic Basin have their origins in the indigenous religions of the old civilizations. The Mayans' storm god was named *hunraken*. The storm god of the Taino people living on the islands of the Caribbean when the Spanish arrived was *harakan*. Variations of these words made their way into the languages of the early European conquerors: the Spanish *huracan* and the English *hurricane*. The English word seems to have entered the language first as *furacane*, in a 1555 translation of a Spanish history of Columbus's voyages. Various spellings were used until *hurricane* was settled on. The first recorded use of this word was by John Winthrop, who wrote about the "Great Colonial Hurricane" of August 1635.

Clearly, the earliest civilizations in the tropics were shaped in part by the terrible storms that battered the coastlines, and so was the first European presence in the New World. There was no predicting or escaping these *huracans*. Just half a century after Columbus's voyages, Spain had amassed a huge colonial empire in Mexico, Central America, parts of South America, and all around the Caribbean Sea, but the few Spanish attempts to settle in what is now the United States had failed. In May 1564, French Huguenots gave it a try, sailing up the St. Johns River to what is now an eastern suburb of Jacksonville and establishing a small fort. They named the new settlement *la Caroline* (or "the colony" of Charles, King of France). Small though it was, this French encroachment was considered a threat to the Spanish shipping routes on their return trips to Europe, which adhered closely to the peninsular coastline. And the French Huguenots were Protestant, of course, not Catholic, which didn't help relations. Quickly the Spanish established a countervailing fort and small settlement about forty miles south of Fort Caroline. This was St. Augustine, commanded by Pedro Menendez de Aviles.

On September 8, 1565, Jean Ribaut, who had brought reinforcements and supplies to the Huguenot settlement, sailed from Fort Caroline with 200 sailors and 400 soldiers for the purpose of attacking St. Augustine. He left behind about 240 people, mostly women and children, some ill men, and a few healthy soldiers. On September 20, Menendez marched overland from St. Augustine with 500 men in heavy rain and attacked the now severely outnumbered Huguenots at Fort Caroline, killing 132 of them, with no Spanish deaths. Fearing that Ribaut, in turn, was about to attack the now undermanned St. Augustine, the victorious Menendez started back to St. Augustine with about half of his force. Of course, he had no way of knowing that the rain that had soaked his troops was the mild manifestation of the storm that had scattered the French ships, dashing many of them against the southern coast. The Spaniards on foot captured and killed those French sailors and soldiers, including Jean Ribaut, who had survived the shipwrecks.

This French defeat gave undisputed control of Florida to Spain. The contemporary accounts of the Spanish march to Fort Caroline mention two or more days of heavy rain but say little about the wind. Such weather doesn't sound like a hurricane, but Jose Carlos Millas isn't so sure. This Cuban scientist devoted much of his career to the study of the historical record and wrote the definitive *Hurricanes of the Caribbean and Adjacent Regions, 1492–1800*, which was published after his death in 1965. Millas cites an account by a Spanish army chaplain who had written in his own journal, "A hurricane and a tempest came, and it was so great that [the French ships] must have been lost."

The French and the Spanish didn't know nor care whether this had been a tropical storm or a weak hurricane that stalled with steady rain along the northeastern Florida coast. They only knew and cared that the weather had precipitated a disaster for the French and a triumph for the Spanish, whose economy in the New World empire was based on the strictest control of trade. By law, residents of the colonies could buy manufactured goods only from the fleets that sailed from Spain twice a year. Safely across the Atlantic, these fleets then split up and spread out to visit all the ports around the Caribbean and Gulf of Mexico, exchanging European goods for gold and other treasure and products. After a few months, the ships would rendezvous in Havana for the return journey home. The best route for this journey was to sail from Havana toward the Florida Keys to catch the east-flowing Florida Current, which becomes the Gulf Stream as it heads north along the east coast of Florida. The Gulf Stream then hoisted the trading ships northward until they were off the coast of what is now North Carolina, where they caught the more or less steady westerlies of the middle latitudes and sailed directly for Europe.

This was the *best* route, but it was not necessarily the *safest* one, because it directed the ships around Florida's southern tip, where hurricanes are likely anytime from June through November, and where, as the historical records prove, hurricanes are more likely to hit than anywhere else along the coast of what is now the United States. The fleets were protected from English and Dutch raiders by Spanish warships, but the hurricanes were as much a threat as Fort Caroline or any French encampment in Florida might have been.

For almost two centuries, Spanish seamen were bedeviled by hurricanes in these narrow seas between Florida and Cuba, and between Florida and the Bahamas. Just three storms that hit the peninsula—in 1622, 1715, and 1733—were the cause of most of the shipwrecks that now yield their booty to modern-day treasure hunters. In the last few decades, these resourceful as well as lucky students of history have hauled up millions of dollars' worth of gold, jewelry, and artifacts from the wrecks of Spanish ships off Florida's east coast and the Keys. The loss of these treasure fleets was not the chief reason Great Britain eventually supplanted Spain as the New World's—and the entire world's—leading maritime power, but those three disasters at sea, especially the ones in 1715 and 1733, were undoubtedly major economic blows to the Spanish crown. If an equivalent disaster struck any society today, the press would be in full cry, hearings would be held, and measures would be taken to prevent similar disasters in the future. But as far as we know, the Spanish treated the loss of their all-important fleets as the will of God, who had always worked his wonders in mysterious ways indeed.

From the arrival of Columbus at the end of the fifteenth century well into the eighteenth century, a scientific understanding of the atmosphere to forecast the weather did not exist. There was no scientific meteorology as we understand it today. What was called "meteorology" consisted of arguments about Aristotle's ideas from the fourth century B.C., arguments about how the four elements of fire, air, earth, and water combine to create various phenomena of the world. Aristotle's meteorology allowed subsequent thinkers to believe that comets, lightning, winds, and earthquakes all belonged in a single category: "dry exhalations" of the Earth. Observing the real weather and trying to make sense of it was left to practical forecasters, such as Columbus. While the best of these "amateurs" learned the warning signs at sea and many of their inferiors in this regard perished at sea, they had no ability to predict the movement of the dangerous storms. With the technological and scientific tools we have at our disposal today, it's hard for us to imagine how earlier peoples were confined to experiencing weather *in the moment.* They had no mental pictures of what storms really are. Until the nineteenth century, most people believed that even the greatest storms developed and then dissipated in one place, more or less. Storms were viewed as chaotic maelstroms whose winds shift direction willy-nilly. No one clearly understood that they move from place to place, and that the winds follow an organized pattern. When practical forecasters such as Columbus saw a storm's winds and swells approaching from the southeast, they apparently did not realize that the winds of the same storm could be blowing from the northeast less than fifty miles away.

In the tropics, specifically, the early sailors had no mental picture of the way the atmosphere circulates in general, although they certainly did know about the *alisios,* or trade winds. These were the prevailing easterlies that made the trip west from Europe a relatively simple matter of running before the wind, but the fortunate mariners had no idea what caused them. In fact, they are caused by large-scale movements of the tropical atmosphere. Each day at noon throughout the year, the sun is almost directly overhead in the tropics, which stretch 3,243 miles, from the tropic of Cancer, latitude 23.5 degrees north, across the equator to the tropic of Capricorn, 23.5 degrees south. In the tropics, day and night are almost equally long in all seasons, unlike the middle latitudes, which have long days in the summer and short days in the winter. In the tropics, the seasons themselves are poorly differentiated. With the sun climbing higher in the sky than over other parts of the Earth, it is always warm, with more solar energy reaching the surface of the planet.

Most of the time, the tropical oceans and their islands and coastlines have the Earth's most placid day-to-day weather. Temperature extremes are unknown, with lowest temperatures rarely below 70 degrees Fahrenheit. A record low temperature would be in the 60s. While inland areas in the tropics contain some of the world's hottest deserts, such as the Sahara in Africa, where temperatures routinely soar above 110 degrees, the islands of the tropical oceans rarely see a day in the high 90s, because of the cooling winds passing over the surrounding seas. Those seas are extensive, to say the least. Ocean waters cover about 75 percent of the tropics, and this water reflects only about 5 percent of the solar energy reaching it. The rest is absorbed—a vast quantity of energy that both warms the water and evaporates large amounts of it to create the typically warm and humid tropical climate, with steady breezes to blow away much of the discomfort. Puffy, cumulus clouds usually dot the sky, and on many days they build into larger clouds that bring brief rain showers and sometimes lightning and thunder.

Tropical oceans have been soaking up the sun's energy and heat since water first covered the young Earth. Yet the oceans have not gotten warmer and warmer. Even the warmest parts of the oceans generally stay below 90 degrees Fahrenheit because ocean currents and the weather in the atmosphere, including hurricanes, are always working to equalize the Earth's heat budget by distributing heat away from the tropics and toward the poles.

Although hurricanes do help transfer tropical heat and moisture to the more northerly and southerly latitudes, the atmosphere's share in this process is more benign most of the time. On normal days in the tropics, the larger cumulus clouds that produce showers are pumping upward huge amounts of air. A satellite photo of the planet almost always shows these white bands of thunderstorms near the equator. At 30,000 feet or higher, this air begins flowing north in the Northern Hemisphere, or south in the Southern Hemisphere, toward the middle latitudes, where it sinks back to the surface. At the surface, this air now naturally flows *back* toward the equator to replace, in effect, the air that's rising in the thunderstorms. If the Earth were not rotating, these return winds would blow from the north straight to the south, in the Northern Hemisphere. But the Earth is rotating to the east, of course, which adds an easterly component to the flow. This is why the Intertropical Convergence Zone is blessed in the Northern Hemisphere with steady northeasterlies, and in the Southern Hemisphere with steady southeasterlies.

These steady, generally reliable winds occur in the Atlantic, the Pacific, and the Indian Oceans. They came to be called the "trade winds" in English from the now obsolete use of "trade" to mean a steady course. Soon the phrase took on another sense as well: these reliable, beneficent breezes almost guaranteed sufficient power for the sails that ferried goods from the Old World to the New. The trades are also the reason that the eastern sides of mountainous tropical islands are wetter than the western sides, as the humid breezes spawn showers and thunderstorms as they are lifted uphill.

The broad picture of this atmospheric circulation system in the tropics was first developed with some accuracy and published in 1735 by George Hadley, an English barrister, not a professional scientist at all. But this was a time when gentlemen amateurs could still make important scientific contributions. Hadley's theory held that air heated in the tropics becomes lighter and rises, with cooler air flowing toward the tropics to replace it. The rising air flows north and south toward the poles, before sinking back to Earth. In Hadley's system, the air flowed almost all of the way to the poles before descending. Today, we know that there are three "cells" in each hemisphere, each cell covering about thirty degrees of latitude. In the one that circulates above the tropics—"Hadley's cell"—the rising air near the equator descends around thirty degrees north and south. In addition to understanding that rising air in the tropics is one of the major engines that drives the Earth's atmosphere, Hadley also recognized that the Earth's rotation "turns" the winds blowing toward the tropics so that they blow from the northeast in the Northern Hemisphere, or from the southeast in the Southern Hemisphere. Many of the details of the large-scale systems of atmospheric circulation had to wait until well into the nineteenth century to be worked out, but Hadley did demonstrate that the answers were within our mental reach.

The next step in our ability to forecast hurricanes depended on the realization that the storms are bodies of swirling winds moving *within* this overall pattern. One of the first individuals who had even the most rudimentary mental picture of hurricanes and other tropical cyclones was William Dampier, a late-seventeenth-century British explorer and privateer—that is, a freelancing pirate with permission from his government to prey on the ships of his nation's enemies. In an age when most people never ventured more than twenty miles from home (even though this was almost 200 years after Columbus's incredible career), Dampier sailed around the world three times, keeping journals that are still admired for the detail and precision of their natural history observations. His *Discourse on Trade-Winds* was the seminal text on the subject at the time. His description of a typhoon in the China Sea in 1687 illustrates his power of observation:

> Typhoons are a sort of violent whirlwinds. Before these whirlwinds come on . . . there appears a heavy cloud to the northeast which is very black near the horizon, but toward the upper part is a dull reddish color. [This heavy cloud and the onset of stronger winds later became known as the "bar" of the hurricane.] The tempest came with great violence, but after a while, the winds ceased all at once and a calm succeeded. This lasted . . . an hour, more or less, then the gales were turned around, blowing with great fury from the southwest.

With its implication that storms somehow *move*, rather than remain stationary, this observation represents a quantum leap in understanding. So does the hunch that storms were some sort of whirlwind. There's no record that anyone had that correct idea before. The world, however, was not spending a lot of time mulling the situation. Going all the way back to Columbus, most sailors had neither the time, the interest, nor the means to think a great deal about storms. Or if they did, they kept those thoughts to themselves, because they are not in the historical record. It was more than sixty years after Dampier's insight when Benjamin Franklin, in Philadelphia, a devoted student of the weather, took the budding theory a step further. On October 22, 1743, this man destined to be a revered founding father was looking forward to an eclipse of the moon that evening, but a storm settled over Philadelphia, blocking the view. Since the wind was from the northeast, and since Boston is northeast of Philadelphia, Franklin quite naturally assumed that the storm with its clouds had come from the direction of Boston and had blocked the eclipse for his friends in that colonial town. But weeks later, when newspapers from Boston finally reached him in Philadelphia, Franklin read accounts such as one in the October 24 issue of the *Boston Evening Post:* "Last Friday night, soon after a total and visible eclipse of the Moon (which began about nine and ended past one o'clock) came on a storm of wind and rain, which continued all the following day with great violence." But how had the storm coming *from* Boston hit Boston *later* than it hit Philadelphia, allowing Boston residents to enjoy the eclipse? The contradiction led to Franklin's conclusion that a storm does not necessarily travel in the same direction as the wind it carries; it might even move *toward* the direction from which the wind was *coming*—the northeast, in this case. Exactly how and when Franklin unraveled the puzzle we don't know, because his voluminous correspondence (or at least the large portion that survives) includes not a word about his thinking until 1750, seven years later, when he proposed a theory of storms in a letter to his friend Jared Eliot. Franklin concluded correctly that storms were entities of atmospheric disturbance that move independently across the face of the planet.

Franklin knew that warm air rises, and in this letter he pictures warm air rising over the Gulf of Mexico. As this occurred, air from the north (channeled by the mountains of eastern North America, he incorrectly assumed) would flow south to replace the rising air. Franklin describes the air as moving somewhat like water in a canal controlled by a sluice gate. When the gate is lifted, the immediately adjacent water starts flowing, pulling after it the water upstream until eventually all the water in the entire canal is flowing. While Franklin was correct that a storm's winds often come from a direction opposite the movement of the storm itself, he did not recognize the whirlwind nature of storms. If the northerly winds of a storm envisioned by Franklin ripped a page out of *Poor Richard's Almanac* and held it aloft, he believed that page would flutter down somewhere to the south, maybe even the Gulf of Mexico. He had no way of knowing that the page would spiral around the storm and drop to Earth in the Canadian Maritimes, or maybe in the cold North Atlantic.

The storm of October 22, 1743, was more than just a storm—it was a hurricane, which brushed Philadelphia and other cities with its rainy, gusty outer fringes and caused flooding around Boston Bay—and it holds not one but two important distinctions. It not only encouraged Benjamin Franklin to think about the nature of storms, it was also the first American storm that we know for certain was measured by scientific instruments. John Winthrop, a professor of natural history at Harvard College, had started keeping weather records the year before. He was thus one of the few individuals anywhere in the world who was recording weather observations, and one of fewer still recording the readings of scientific instruments. On October 22, he measured a low barometric pressure in Boston of 29.35 inches of mercury and winds from the north-northeast.

All this was definite progress, but even though Dampier's and Franklin's ideas and Winthrop's habit of scientific observation were to prove vital for an eventual understanding of storms, such knowledge was too scattered and hit-or-miss to constitute a unified theory of the great storms and the science of forecasting remained unexplored—which was unfortunate, because the most brutal hurricane season on record occurred in 1780. Although the American Revolution amounted to a world war at the time—with warships, transports, and merchant ships from England, France, Spain, and Holland plying the waters of the western Atlantic, the Caribbean, and the Gulf of Mexico in support of the warring parties—hurricanes took a toll greater than the bullets and bayonets of the armies and the boarding parties of the navies. During the eight years of the American Revolution, fewer than 10,000 soldiers fighting on the American or the

British sides died on the battlefield. The storms of 1780 cost at least 22,000 deaths.

The first of these hit Louisiana on August 24, almost exactly a year after a powerful storm had hit the same coastline. This tempest in 1780 was more powerful, although deaths were put at less than twenty-five people. The Spanish colonial official in charge of Louisiana issued a pronouncement of sympathy that also said, in effect, that people had no reason to complain since he knew of no countries "which are not occasionally devastated by the fury of storms and hurricanes." He asked the people "to put their faith in divine providence" and the Spanish government. They might as well have, because there could be no help from forecasters.

September was quiet in the tropics; the warring parties in the Revolution had to contend only with each other. But on October 3, a hurricane smashed into Savanna-la-Mar, near the southwestern corner of Jamaica, destroying every building in this busy seaport. Crossing Jamaica, the storm seriously damaged Lucea and Montego Bay, then skipped north across central Cuba and the Bahamas before striking a British fleet about 500 miles east of what is now Daytona Beach, Florida. Most of the ships lost their mainmasts, but apparently none were sunk. Proceeding north, the hurricane then struck another British fleet off the coast of Virginia, where it seriously damaged five more ships and forced the fleet into port for repairs. Total deaths from this hurricane, mostly in Jamaica, were estimated at more than 1,000.

One of the vessels caught in that storm was the British frigate *Phoenix.* Its captain was Sir Hyde Parker; its second in command, Lieutenant Archer. We are fortunate to have a letter—a remarkable letter—from Lieutenant Archer describing the plight of his ship:

> At eight o'clock a hurricane; the sea roaring, but the wind still steady to a point [blowing from the same direction]; did not ship a spoonful of water. However, got the hatchways all secured, expected what would be the consequences, should the wind shift; placed the carpenters by the mainmast, with broad axes, knowing from experience, that at the moment you may want to cut it away to save the ship an axe may not be found. Went to supper—bread,

cheese, and porter . . . the two marine-officers as white as sheets, not understanding the ship's working so much. . . . It seemed as if the whole ship's side was going at each roll.

At midnight, Archer writes, he approached Captain Parker on deck, who said, "It blows damned hard, Archer. . . . I don't know that I ever remember it blowing so hard before, but the ship makes a very good weather of it upon this tack . . . but we must wear [turn] her, as the wind has shifted to the south-east, and we are drawing right upon Cuba." At the time, Archer explains in the letter, all of the ship's sails except a few small ones had been furled, because the wind would have ripped them apart. When the captain suggested setting one of the larger sails in order to turn the *Phoenix*, Archer replied, "Sir, there is no canvass can stand against this a moment; if we attempt to loose [the sail] he will fly into ribbons in an instant, and we may lose three or four of our people; she'll wear by manning the fore shrouds." The fore shrouds are the lines running from the top and middle of the forward mast down to the sides of the ship, holding the mast in place. Horizontal lines attached to the shrouds create rope ladders that the sailors climb when they go aloft to set sails. Archer was suggesting that the bodies of the men hanging on to those shrouds would catch enough of the hurricane's wind to turn the ship!

"No," the captain said. "I don't think she will."

"I'll answer for it, sir; I have seen it tried several times on the coast of America with success."

"Well, try it; if she does not wear, we can only loose the foresail afterwards."

Archer sent 200 men into the forward rigging, and "after a hard struggle, she wore." He doesn't bother to describe these men clinging to ropes in a howling wind as the ship pitched and rolled in the darkness, squeezing them against the lines, which went taut, threatening to rip out of the deck or the masthead. He only notes laconically that the rigging held, so did the men, and the ship turned. The new course kept the *Phoenix* off the Cuban coast for a while, but "she did not make so good weather on this tack as on the other; for as the sea began to run across she had not time to rise from one sea before another lashed against her. Began to think we should lose our masts, as the ship lay very much along, by the pressure of the wind constantly upon the yards and masts alone. . . . My God! To think that the wind could have such force!"

Despite the crew's efforts, the wind finally blew the *Phoenix* onto the Cuban shore where it was destroyed in the surf, but only after all but about twenty of the crew of 260 made it safely to shore.

Before the storm, the *Phoenix* had been in port in Montego Bay with three other British warships, where, Archer writes, "we had a strong party for kicking up a dust on shore. . . . Dancing &c. &c till two o'clock every morning, little thinking of what was to happen in three days' time." When Archer returned to Montego Bay after the storm, he learned the other three ships had also been lost, but with all hands lost as well. "Many of our houses, where we had been so merry, were so completely destroyed that scarcely a vestige remained to mark where they stood. Thy works are wonderful O God! Praised be thy holy name!"

Then came the second storm in October, which struck Barbados on the morning of October 10 and then slowly carved a path of unheard-of death and destruction across the islands of the eastern and northern Caribbean. John Poyer, a historian who survived the storm damage on Barbados, wrote that by the morning of October 11, "far as the eye could reach one general scene of devastation presented itself to the sight." Poyer describes himself as "among the midnight wanderers, who traversed the dreary waste in search of an uncertain place of shelter and repose. The fairest female forms stripped of their drapery by the ruthless blast, passed the dismal night exposed, almost in a state of perfect nudity to the inclemency of contending elements, while their weeping parents and affectionate husbands, in all the agonies of sympathizing tenderness, ineffectually strove to shield them from the pelting of the pitiless storm."

William Senhouse, another survivor, wrote that "the very tone or sound of the wind was wound up to a pitch almost bordering upon a whistle; rain fell like a deluge, which added great weight to the wind, and when driven in our faces felt like hail or small shot; the thunder and lightning was tremendous and incessant." The hurricane destroyed the government house, a structure with walls three feet thick. It leveled the armory, scattering the weapons stored there.

Inland, the wind and waves pushed a 12-pounder cannon (one that fired cannonballs weighing twelve pounds) about 140 yards. The British *Annual Register* for 1780 states that on the island of St. Lucia, "all the barracks and huts for His Majesty's troops, and other buildings on the island were blown down, and the ships driven to sea. At St. Vincent, every building was blown down, and the town destroyed. At Grenada, nineteen of loaded Dutch ships were stranded and beat to pieces. At St. Eustatius, the loss was very great, with seven ships driven on shore near North Point, and their crews perished. Between 4,000 and 5,000 persons are supposed to have lost their lives in St. Eustatius."

The French island of Martinique suffered as much as the British and Dutch islands. A government report said that four ships sank, killing all aboard, in Fort Royal Bay. The cathedral, seven churches, other public buildings, and all the houses were destroyed; the hospital was decimated, burying most of those inside. More than 1,000 people died in St. Pierre, where every house was leveled. The death toll on this island alone was estimated at 9,000 by the French government. Yet the hurricane was not finished. After leveling Martinique, the storm followed a common track for Caribbean hurricanes by turning northwesterly, passing near Puerto Rico and east of Grand Turk Island, where it turned back toward the northeast and its center passed about fifty miles southeast of Bermuda, driving fifty British Navy ships aground, including some that had been hit by the month's first hurricane east of present-day Daytona Beach.

In all, the "Great Hurricane of 1780" was estimated to have killed 22,000 people, on land and sea. Of course no one knows the strength of those winds, but they were certainly in the 135-mile-per-hour range, maybe higher. Moreover, the damage recorded indicates that the storm moved exceedingly slowly, probably at less than ten miles per hour across the eastern Caribbean, subjecting every structure to winds, rains, and high water for many hours. And there was still more to come: that year's hurricane season wasn't over yet. Just a week after the Great Hurricane, a third storm, this one in the Gulf of Mexico, hit sixty-four Spanish sails on their way to attack Pensacola, Florida, which was held by the British. The storm scattered this fleet across much of the eastern Gulf, sinking a number of the ships and killing perhaps half of the 4,000 sailors in the force. (The disaster stalled the Spanish campaign for the year, but the following year they did manage to capture Pensacola and reclaim Florida from Britain. This time Spain held the valuable peninsula until 1821, when it was ceded to the United States.)

The fourth storm in October 1780 hit St. Lucia on the 25th, but apparently it was the weak sister of the family, doing little damage and causing few deaths before moving into the Atlantic. Finally, on November 17, one last storm hit and scattered British warships that were blockading American ports in the Northeast. Damage records aren't complete enough to determine whether this storm was a full-fledged hurricane.

From our perspective, more than 200 years later, we want to ask what might have been the key factors behind the deadliness of the famous hurricanes of 1780. There were several, surely, beginning with the fact that the first two in October, the one that hit Jamaica initially and the Great Hurricane that struck Barbados first, were undoubtedly quite strong. The storm that hit the Spanish fleet in the Gulf of Mexico might not have been as strong, but even a weaker storm would be damaging and deadly to sailing ships. The great number of ships scattered all across the waters of the western tropics, thanks to the American Revolution, also helps account for the death toll. In their 1997 National Hurricane Center study of hurricane deaths in the Northern Hemisphere since Columbus, Edward N. Rappaport and Jose Fernandez-Partages write: "Available records . . . suggest that the population on the Atlantic was the most vulnerable to storms through the 18th century. . . . These ship-borne explorers, emigrants, combatants, fishermen, traders, pirates, privateers, slaves, and tourists made up the crews and passengers on an uncounted but enormous number of local and transatlantic sailings. Most of the ships traveled to or from the ports of Spain, France, Great Britain, and the Netherlands. They usually proved no match for the intense inner core of a tropical cyclone."

In 1780, at least half of the 22,000 who lost their lives in hurricanes were on board ships.

It was a terrible year—and it became a terrible decade. Hurricanes in the next nine years killed another 6,000 people, making the 1780s by far the deadliest decade in the five centuries of recorded hurricane history, with an estimated 31,000 deaths. With the many millions of people living on these islands and the mainland shorelines today, the equivalent percentage of fatalities would surely be in the hundreds of thousands—simply unthinkable. In fact, storms as strong as the Great Hurricane of 1780 have hit the Caribbean in recent years with few deaths, thanks to early warnings and stronger structures. Nor was anyone trapped on eighteenth-century sailing ships.

The numbers for 1780 might even have been *larger* than estimated. The records surviving from that era are far from complete, and the accuracy of newspaper and magazine reports has to be doubted. Many of the ships were carrying Africans destined for the slave markets of the Caribbean and North America. Sometimes these men and women were counted among shipwreck victims, sometimes they were not. We also have reason to believe that officials underreported deaths in at least some cases. One British magazine, regarding reports about a hurricane that struck Martinique in the eighteenth century, said, "The number of persons who have lost their lives is so great, that we dare not mention what [the] report estimates it at, for fear of exaggeration."

Jose Carlos Millas, the indefatigable Cuban author of *Hurricanes of the Caribbean and Adjacent Regions, 1492–1800,* was often frustrated by "the scarcity of data and complete descriptions of hurricanes." He had to use all his skills as a historian to find the original records and all his meteorological knowledge to try to determine the likely nature of the storms reported over the previous three centuries. Were they hurricanes or just severe squalls? Another problem he ascribed to "the character of the men and women that came to colonize the Indies; hardy specimens of humanity that they were, they gave little thought to the inclemency of the weather, withstanding the utmost severity as current events in their lives, accepting without any great comment the injuries received and, therefore, easily forgotten. To this can be added the lack of sufficient education in a majority of individuals to be able to narrate readily the events of their lives in the New World."

Times have changed, certainly. Until the middle of the nineteenth century, anyone who boarded a ship for a journey out of sight of land was facing a risk of death that no traveler today would even think about accepting. Poorly built ships, inexact navigation, incompetent captains, and inept crews accounted for many accidents, but storms, most especially hurricanes, were the biggest danger. A suspect vessel inexpertly navigated by an incompetent captain and sailed by an inept crew might safely complete a journey on smooth seas. Then again, a stout vessel expertly navigated and sailed with consummate skill might also sink immediately in a hurricane. In their most graphic illustration of the dangers involved, Rappaport and Fernandez-Partages write, "Near New England, it was estimated that three out of every five sailors drowned during the period 1790 to 1850. Of course, many of these disasters were unrelated to the weather, while others are attributable to the brutal, cold storms of the North Atlantic winter rather than to tropical cyclones."

Rappaport and Fernandez-Partages conclude that hurricanes in the Western Hemisphere have killed between one-third and one-half a million people. A large percentage of these deaths were at sea, and the authors point out that more than 90 percent of all offshore deaths attributable to hurricanes occurred *before* 1790, as did all twelve offshore disasters that cost more than 1,000 lives. After 1790, the hurricane death toll dropped significantly. For the next century, no decade was marred by more than 5,000 deaths. This fortunate happenstance was due to a cyclical decline in hurricane activity as well as to improvements in shipbuilding and navigation. In his book, Millas notes that during the eighteenth century, "the frame or body of the ships was improved, also the tackle and the general equipment comprising chains, ropes, etc., for working and supporting the masts, booms, sails and minor parts of the rigging." Still, he continues, "It can be said that nothing of great importance was developed during this period, compared to the great change that would be found in the next century."

An etching by Currier and Ives, circa 1850, shows a clipper ship caught in a
hurricane.

That change was nothing less than a new scientific understanding
that paved the way for today's modern maritime forecasting. In 1687
William Dampier had put forth the hypothesis that tropical storms
are whirlwinds, and in 1743 Franklin had correctly understood, or at
least intuited, that large storms, including hurricanes, are organized
bodies of wind that somehow move across the continents and the
seas—but it was yet another eighty-seven years before these intima-
tions were codified into what meteorologists now call the "law of
storms." This law would give sea captains, for the first time, some
practical advice on how to maneuver their ships to increase their
chances of surviving a hurricane.

The year was 1831 when William Redfield, a self-taught American scientist, published an article in the *American Journal of Science*
titled "On the Prevailing Storms of the Atlantic Coast." It advanced

and—here's the key—presented hard evidence for the idea that storms are huge whirlwinds, a subject that Redfield had begun considering on a walking trip across New England nearly a decade earlier, when he noted the patterns of trees blown down by the great New England hurricane of September 1821. The damage pattern and the accounts of observers who lived in the southern part of Litchfield County, Connecticut, led Redfield to conclude that the wind had blown from the southwest for several hours at 75 to 100 miles per hour. But just forty miles to the north, in the same state, the damage evidence suggested that the wind was blowing at about the same time and with the same velocity *toward* the south or southeast.

High winds from the southwest in one area but from almost the *opposite* direction in a nearby area? The puzzled Redfield eventually concluded that a tightly spinning whirlwind was the best explanation for the conundrum. But he did nothing with his observations and his hypothesis. Mostly self-educated, brought up in a poor family, he was too involved making money in the new steamship and railroad businesses. But in 1831, a decade after his original findings, while traveling by steamboat from New York City to New Haven, Connecticut, the amateur scientist happened to strike up a conversation with Denison Olmstead, one of the leading professional scientists of the time. Many years later, Olmstead described that meeting in a memorial address before the American Association for the Advancement of Science:

> "A stranger accosted me, and modestly asked leave to make a few inquiries respecting some observations I had recently published in the *American Journal of Science* on the subject of hailstorms. I was soon sensible that the humble inquirer was himself proficient in meteorology. In the course of the conversation, he incidentally brought out his theory of the laws of our Atlantic gales, at the same time stating the leading facts on which his conclusions were founded. This doctrine was quite new to me; it impressed me so favorably that I urged him to communicate it to the world through the medium of the *American Journal of Science*. He manifested

much diffidence at appearing as an author before the scientific world, professing only to be a practical man little versed in scientific discussion, and unaccustomed to write for the press."

Olmstead was persuasive, however, and Redfield set about collecting much more information about the great New England storm of 1821 from amateur weather observers all along the East Coast, as well as from the logs of ships that had been at sea in the Atlantic at the time. In the journal article, he showed that the storm had churned north from Grand Turk Island to the East Coast of the United States. He was able to demonstrate clearly that the winds were circling a calm center as the body of the storm swung north along the coastline, with its eye just offshore, from Maryland to New Jersey, where it went inland in the area of New York City, crossed Connecticut, and then struck Worcester, Massachusetts, three hours after blowing down the Litchfield County trees in the telltale pattern Redfield had observed firsthand. Redfield concludes that "all violent gales or hurricanes are great whirlwinds, in which the wind blows in circuits around an axis; that the winds do not move in horizontal circles, but rather in spirals. That the velocity of rotation increases from the margin toward the center of the storm. That the whole body of air is, at the same time, moving forward in a path, at a variable rate, but always with a velocity much less than its velocity of rotation."

These three sentences are the key that unlocked the secret of hurricanes and the "law of storms." They represent a triumph of the inductive reasoning of scientific research. Redfield also describes the general path of hurricanes in the Atlantic and gives a good general description of a hurricane that knowledgeable seamen could thereafter use in order to avoid sailing into the worst part of a storm.

As it happened, in the same year that Redfield's article appeared, 1831, a fierce hurricane struck Barbados, with tremendous damage and loss of life. The British immediately sent Colonel William Reid of the Royal Engineers to the colony to help with reconstruction. In his book *The Law of Storms*, published in 1841, Reid writes,

My attention was first directed to the subject of storms from having been employed at Barbados in reestablishing the government buildings blown down in the hurricanes of 1831; when from the violence of the wind 1,477 persons lost their lives in the short space of seven hours. I was induced to search everywhere for accounts of previous storms, in the hope of learning something of their causes and mode of action. West Indian histories, however, contain little beyond a record of the losses in lives and property, and the sufferings of the inhabitants, during the period of these tempests. The first paper I met with, which appeared to convey any just opinion on the nature of hurricanes, was one published in the "American Journal of Science," by Mr. W. C. Redfield of New York.

Reid and Redfield initiated a correspondence that continued until Redfield's death. Reid's research confirmed his mentor's views by using data from studies of hurricanes in the West Indies, including an extensive examination of ships' logs and other records from the Great Hurricane of 1780, which had also struck Barbados, and the other storms of that year. Reid also studied any records he could find pertaining to the storms in the southern Indian Ocean, proving what Redfield had hypothesized: that the winds of storms in the Southern Hemisphere circulate in a clockwise direction, as opposed to the counterclockwise direction of storms in the Northern Hemisphere. Neither men knew why, however. That understanding would come later.

In 1844, three years after Reid's first publication, Redfield weighed in with another in-depth account of a single storm, based on his examination of the logbooks of 164 ships. He developed elaborate tables showing where each ship was at any given time, and what winds each experienced at that time. He then correlated all his data on a large marine chart. It was quite a job, but just one of many for Redfield, a Victorian through and through. In addition to his railroad and steamship businesses and his storm studies, he also conducted geological research, including original work on the fossils of fish. Yale College awarded him an honorary master of arts degree in 1839, and in 1848 he helped found the American Association for the Advancement of Science and served as the organization's first president. Commodore Matthew C. Perry, following his epochal 1853–1854 expedition to Japan, wrote that those who venture onto the sea "are mainly indebted [to Redfield and Reid] for the discovery of a law which has already contributed, and will continue to contribute, greatly to the safety of vessels traversing the ocean."

In his memorial address, Olmstead said that, as soon as Redfield had established that storms are whirlwinds, he "commenced the inquiry, which rules may be derived from it, to promote the safety of the immense amount of human life and of property that are afloat on the ocean and exposed continually to the dangers of shipwreck." He compared this contribution to Benjamin Franklin's work with lightning. After discovering that the bolts were in fact electricity, Franklin developed the lightning rod "to disarm the thunderbolt of its terrors. . . . As every building saved from the ravages of lightning by the conducting rod is a token both of the sagacity and the benevolence of Franklin, so every vessel saved from the horrors of shipwreck by rules derived from these laws of storms, is a witness to the sagacity and benevolence of Redfield."

On the other side of the globe, Henry Piddington, a British East India Company ship's captain who served at one time as president of the marine courts in Calcutta, had also taken up the study of hurricanes and typhoons, naturally concentrating his researches on Pacific and Indian Ocean storms. It was Piddington who coined the word "cyclone" for any "circular or highly curved winds"—typhoons and hurricanes. It comes from the Greek word for the coil of a snake. That was an interesting contribution to our subject, but in 1848 Piddington made a much more important one when he published a book with the forbidding title *The sailor's horn-book for the law of storms: being a practical exposition of the theory of the law of storms, and its uses to mariners of all classes in all parts of the world, shown by transparent storm cards and useful lessons.* These forty-two words are usually shortened to *The Sailor's Horn Book,* which proposes "to explain to the seaman, in such language that every man who can work a day's-work can understand it, the Theory and the Practical Use of the Law of Storms in all parts of the world." The author states that his book teaches "how to avoid Storms—teaches how best to manage in Storms when they cannot be avoided—and teaches how to profit by Storms!"

How can a sailor profit from a storm? By using his understanding of storms to catch winds on the storm's fringe blowing in the direction he wants to go. Piddington compares learning the law of storms with learning how to avoid scurvy, which the British Navy had done in the eighteenth century by providing fresh fruit and vegetables, or, if these weren't available, doses of lime juice—hence the nickname "Limey" for a British sailor. (Not until the twentieth century was it understood *why* these foods prevented scurvy: they are rich in vitamin C, a deficiency of which is the cause of the disease.) Piddington explains how the winds of a tropical cyclone rotate around, or spiral into, a center. Since the spinning storm is itself moving over the surface of the ocean, the net effect of the winds depends on one's location relative to the storm, he correctly argues. He took the first truly practical step in helping seamen create a mental picture of what part of a storm they are in and where relative safety lies. To do so they must ignore compass directions and think only in terms of the right and the left sides of a circular storm.

Face in the direction in which the storm is moving, Piddington instructs. In the Northern Hemisphere, where the winds are circling the storm's center in a counterclockwise direction, the winds on the storm's right side are therefore traveling in the same direction as the entire storm; the speed of the winds and the speed of the storm's movement across the sea are added together. For example, if the winds near the center of a storm in the Northern Hemisphere are blowing at 100 miles per hour in a counterclockwise direction around the eye, and the storm is moving west at 20 miles per hour, the winds on the storm's north side would be 120 miles per hour, because the forward motion combines with the force of the wind blowing. On the left side of the storm, however, where the counterclockwise winds are blowing opposite to the forward movement, the forward speed of 20 miles per hour is subtracted from the wind speed of 100 miles per hour, for a total net wind of 80 miles per hour. This is why Piddington called the storm's right side the "dangerous" semicircle and the left side the "safe" semicircle, although "safe" is a relative term, of course.

In a pocket thoughtfully attached to the inside cover of *The Sailor's Horn Book*, Piddington included two transparent "storm cards," with counterclockwise wind arrows on the Northern Hemisphere card and clockwise arrows on the Southern Hemisphere card. The card indicated from which direction the wind would be blowing in any part of the cyclone. A ship's captain placed the appropriate storm card on his chart, correlating the actual wind conditions at the time with wind directions on the card. The card would now indicate on the chart the relative location of the storm's center, the dangerous semicircle, and the safe semicircle. Piddington also describes in detail how a barometer behaves as a storm approaches, giving the captain some idea of how far a ship is from the storm center. He also discusses the paths storms normally follow in different parts of the world.

The general picture of hurricanes described by Colonel William Reid in *The Law of Storms* and the specific seamanship rules of thumb developed by Piddington in *The Sailor's Horn Book* have now served mariners well for 150 years. Their early descriptions and prescriptions are surely one of the reasons the number of deaths at sea caused by hurricanes has decreased precipitously from the mid-nineteenth century onward. The contemporary student of meteorology will discover in those nineteenth-century books the basic elements of our contemporary understanding of the law of storms.

But not all sailors were interested in mastering the new knowledge. Old-school types such as Captain MacWhirr of the steamer

The Southern Hemisphere storm card, which helped ship captains find their position in relation to a storm center. It's from Henry Piddington's *The Sailor's Horn Book.*

Nan-Shan in Joseph Conrad's story "Typhoon," written in 1902, is a case in point—and an accurate one, we can believe, because Conrad had been a master mariner before he took up his second career. He had known the real MacWhirrs of the sailing world.

In "Typhoon," when it becomes obvious that the *Nan-Shan* is heading into a fierce storm, MacWhirr consults the chapter on storms in his seamanship text, very possibly based on Piddington's *Sailor's Horn Book*. But MacWhirr

> lost himself among advancing semicircles, left- and right-hand quadrants, the curves of the tracks, the probable bearing of the centre, the shifts of the wind and the readings of the barometer. He tried to bring all these things into a definite relation to himself, and ended by becoming contemptuously angry with such a lot of words and with so much advice, all headwork and supposition, without a glimmer of certitude. "It's the damnedest thing, Jukes [his first mate]. If a fellow was to believe all what's in there, he would be running most of his time all over the sea trying to be behind the weather. Running to get behind the weather! Do you understand that, Mr. Jukes? It's the maddest thing," ejaculated Captain MacWhirr. . . . "There's just so much dirty weather knocking about the world, and the proper thing is to go through it."

In the end, the sturdy *Nan-Shan* weathers the storm despite its captain's inability to comprehend the more complicated, perhaps, but safer ways of the sea that Piddington, Reid, and Redfield had established. MacWhirr was a seventeenth-century man sailing in the last part of the nineteenth century. He was out of touch with scientific understanding, which was neatly summarized by Denison Olmstead in his memorial address for William Redfield:

> "In no department perhaps of the studies of nature [has] mankind been more surprised to find things governed by fixed laws than in the cast of the winds. It is now rendered in the highest degree probable that every breeze that blows is a part of some great system of aerial circulation and helps to fulfill some grand design. The

inconsistence of the winds has long been a favorite expression to denote the absence of all uniformity or approach to fixed rules; the researches of the meteorologists of our times force on us the conclusion that winds, even in the violent forms of hurricanes and tornadoes, are governed by laws hardly less determinate than those which control the movements of the planets."

CHAPTER 2

BUT WHY DOES every breeze blow? The work of William Red-field, William Reid, and Henry Piddington had established beyond dispute that "every breeze that blows is a part of some great system of aerial circulation," and that in storms this circulation is some kind of whirlwind subject to the law of storms. But what are the causes of the breezes—including hurricanes—in the first place? This is another question entirely, and it could only be resolved with research in the basic sciences. One of the key figures in this work was James Pollard Espy, a professor at the prestigious Franklin Institute in Philadelphia who then became the U.S. government's first meteorologist when he was appointed as a "professor" with the War Department in 1842. At the time, army physicians were making regular weather observations in an attempt to find relationships between weather and disease. Espy's duties included collecting and analyzing this data and expanding the network of contributors in the United States and around the world. William Reid, who had been appointed governor of the British colony of Bermuda, was among those who agreed to send information.

These attempts to relate weather and climate to illness led nowhere at the time. The most basic findings in the field—for example, that conditions that encouraged mosquitoes helped spread diseases such as malaria—were to come later in the century, but Espy began using all the data for a second purpose: to study storms. He also delved into the role of water vapor, and in the course of this research invented the cloud chamber, which he called a "cloud examiner" or "nephelescope." Helped by his cloud chamber in

Philadelphia, Espy contributed greatly to our understanding of the profound meteorological consequences that flow from the simple fact that heat rises (a fact that even our earliest ancestors on the planet realized, as they warmed themselves over fires in caves). With his 1841 book *The Philosophy of Storms*, Espy unlocked the secrets of what we today call "latent heat," the primary source of energy for thunderstorms and hurricanes.

Molecules of H_2O move more slowly and with less energy in water than in vapor. Therefore energy must enter the system in order for water to evaporate into vapor—energy that must come from the ambient environment. This is why evaporation cools the human body on warm days: it draws energy—heat—from the skin. In tropical climates, evaporation of water into vapor (humidity) also pulls heat out of the ambient environment—the atmosphere. However, the energy pulled from the atmosphere during evaporation cannot and does not just disappear. It is absorbed in the water vapor in the form of the more energized molecules of H_2O. Scientists refer to this energy as "latent heat."

As water evaporates, it mixes with the other gasses that make up the air; the vapor is part of the air. Warm air rises and will continue to rise as long as it is warmer and less dense than the surrounding air. But, as scientists had discovered at the beginning of the nineteenth century, rising air cools at a regular rate. At some point on its upward course, the air cools sufficiently and the water vapor in it begins to condense into the tiny drops of water or ice crystals that make up clouds. When conditions are right, these small drops grow into larger drops that fall as rain (or, if they grow cold enough, as snow or ice). This condensation or freezing releases heat, because the molecules of water have less energy than the molecules of vapor. This is the key science for the entire cycle of thunderstorms and hurricanes: At sea level, evaporation of water into a vapor requires a source of heat; at a higher altitude, condensation of that vapor back into liquid water or ice *releases* heat.

When water vapor condenses back into water as cloud droplets or ice crystals, the latent heat *reheats* the cooled air, causing it to continue rising in the atmosphere. Hurricanes form and grow in the humid air over warm water because this air supplies more water vapor than dry air, water vapor that continues to condense as the air rises, supplying still more heat to the system, literally keeping the engine going onward and upward. As the wind in a disturbance blows faster, it starts to blow the tops off the waves, streaking the ocean with white foam. Faster and faster winds increase the amounts of sea spray blown off the tops of waves. This sea spray becomes yet another factor, in addition to the ocean's temperature, that determines how much energy is available to the growing storm. In the early stages, when there is no spray, evaporation is adding moisture only to air in direct contact with the sea surface. Now, with tiny drops of sea spray in the air several feet above the ocean, water is evaporating from the spray droplets as well as the ocean surface. Increased ocean spray might not seem to be much of a factor in the early stages of a cyclone, but over many square miles of ocean it can greatly increase the amount of water vapor available as, little by little, the humidity increases in a layer of air stretching several feet from the ocean's surface. This added humidity, in turn, means the storm has that much more water vapor to release latent heat when it condenses or goes directly to ice (called "sublimation"). The storm's energy storehouse is growing.

The system is almost like a chain reaction that will continue growing as long as warm, humid air flows in at the bottom, rises, and releases more heat as water vapor condenses and cloud droplets freeze or the vapor turns directly into ice. The only limiting factors are the amount of humidity, upper-level air temperatures, and surrounding wind conditions. Conversely, hurricanes weaken and eventually die when they move over cool water or land, where they lose their rich supply of humidity to convert into latent energy.

What gets the heat pump going in the first place, triggering the initial, concentrated upward motion of the warm air? This energy source can be land that's heated by solar energy, or it can be oceans or lakes absorbing solar energy and then warming the lowest layer of air in contact with the water. Upward motion can also be started by a flow of the atmosphere up the sides of mountains, which is why there are so many afternoon thunderstorms in mountainous areas. A low-level convergence of winds can also force air upward, triggering the heat pump.

However it is triggered, this upward flow of air leaves behind it an area of lower pressure than the surrounding air. We measure this air pressure with a barometer, invented in the seventeenth century by Evangelista Torricelli, one of Galileo's assistants. Torricelli's first device used a column of water for the purpose, but it had to be thirty feet tall in order to work. The first truly useful barometer used mercury, which is why air pressure came to be and still is measured in "inches of mercury" in the English system. A mercury barometer is a tube at least thirty-four inches long that's closed at one end and filled with mercury. The tube is then inverted, and the open end is placed within a small container filled with mercury exposed to the air. The atmospheric pressure on the mercury in the dish will hold up about thirty inches of mercury in the upright tube. As the air pressure decreases, thus decreasing the pressure on the mercury in the container, some of the mercury in the tube will push down into the container. When the air pressure increases and presses down on the mercury in the container, the mercury in the tube is pushed back up. Thus, the inches of mercury in the tube is a precise measure of atmospheric pressure. The average sea level air pressure is 29.92 inches of mercury. (The less accurate but more practical aneroid barometer that homeowners mount on the wall is a sealed metallic box with a slight vacuum inside. Atmospheric pressure depresses or expands the surface of the box, and this movement of the surface is then transmitted by means of a set of levers to a pointer on a scale. The scale registers the barometric pressure in the accustomed inches of mercury.)

If the air over a given location on the ground is rising, the pressure on the ground must be lower. This area of lower pressure pulls in air from adjacent areas of higher pressure. This imbalance between air pressures over distance is the basic dynamic that causes winds—any winds—to blow across the surface of the planet, often over distances of hundreds of miles. It is called the Pressure Gradient Force (PGF). The greater the difference in pressures for any given distance, or the shorter the distance between any two pressures, the higher the velocity of the wind as it rushes from higher to lower pressure. For example, and disregarding all other factors, a difference in pressure of 30.00 inches of mercury in one location and 29.00 inches of mercury in another location 500 miles away will accelerate still air to 80 miles per hour in three hours. If the distance is twice as far, 1,000 miles, the wind speed will be only half as much, 40 miles per hour.

Powerful storms are created when rapidly rising air creates great pressure differentials over a small distance—in a tornado, most dramatically, or in a hurricane, on a much larger scale. Since wind speed is a direct reflection of differences in air pressure, the barometric pressure at a hurricane's center is a good measure of its strength. In fact, it's a better measure than wind speed, since air pressure can be accurately measured even after a hurricane's winds have blown away or broken all of the anemometers (which measure wind speed).

James Espy's work in Philadelphia in the early 1800s did much to confirm the basic machinery of the atmospheric heat pump that generates winds and drives thunderstorms and hurricanes. It broadened and deepened the picture developed by William Redfield and others of how the big whirlwinds work. But many basic questions remained unanswered, or misunderstood. Redfield, for one, thought that winds caused the low pressure in the center of a storm. As it turns out, flowing wind can cause low pressure, but we have no indication that Redfield was thinking of such cases. For example, wind flowing over mountains or even roofs or around the corners of buildings or other objects create a localized "lee side" low-pressure area. (This is what makes it possible for heavy airplanes to lift off the ground. Air accelerates over the top of the wing, creating a low-pressure area on top of the wing, which lifts the airplane.) However, Redfield thought that the large low-pressure areas that one might see on a weather map, including hurricanes, were created this way. That is not correct. The low pressures—or, more accurately, the differences between adjacent pressures—cause the winds to blow. He believed that tides in the atmosphere were somehow responsible for the biggest storms, and he pictured storms as whirls in a flowing stream. This is accurate enough, as far as it goes, but he was wrong in his suspicion that hurricanes might be caused by interactions between the trade winds and tropical islands.

Neither Redfield nor Espy nor anyone else understood exactly how the winds blow in hurricanes. Espy understood that the rising air in a storm pulls in air from the "outside," but he believed that these winds were thereby pulled *straight in* toward the center of the storm. If his idea were correct, a weather map would show the winds like the spokes of a wheel. Redfield argued that the winds of a whirl-wind blow in circles *around* the center, not in straight lines toward the center. He developed this picture from his study of hurricanes, the storm system in which the wind does come the closest to circling around the center.

The disagreement between Redfield and Espy became quite con-tentious, perhaps because the modus operandi of the two men were so different. In one corner was the part-time scientist and full-time businessman Redfield, an "observational" scientist, as we would put it today. In the other corner was Espy, an establishment scientist of the highest prestige in America and overseas, a dedicated laboratory researcher whose strength was in the hard sciences. Joseph Henry, a leading nineteenth-century American scientist and the first secre-tary of the Smithsonian Institution, commented: "Indeed, meteo-rology has ever been an apple of contention, as if the violent commotions of the atmosphere induced a sympathetic effect in the minds of those who have attempted to study them." The disagree-ment was also contentious because it wasn't easy to solve, certainly not in the first half of the nineteenth century. Redfield examined the damage caused by several tornadoes and found "evidence" for circular winds, while Espy examined the damage caused by other tornadoes and found "evidence" for straight-line winds. In fact, if you are looking for a particular wind pattern, it's easy to find it in the jumbled wreckage left by a twister. In addition, tornado damage is easy to study compared with the wind patterns in large winter storms, which are much more complicated, especially over land, where wind flowing around hills and mountains is deflected in ways that will fit no simple theory.

Another problem faced by Redfield and Espy stemmed from the fact that both men believed their ideas applied to al' storms—to a tornado that might be just a couple hundred yards across, a tropical hurricane 300 miles in diameter, and to a landlocked winter storm covering 1,000 miles. But "extratropical" storms, of which winter storms are one type, have considerably different large-scale dynamics than tropical storms. Extratropical storms, the most common storms across the United States, are mainly powered by the contrasting air masses that make them up. Imagine a small, two-room building with a wall between the rooms that can be quickly rolled out of the way. If we heat one closed room and cool the other, while allowing air to flow in and out of the rooms but not between them, the air in the chilled room will be heavier than the air in the warm room. With one warm room and one cool room, the situation is somewhat like that along a weather "front," which might stretch 1,000 miles across the continent, except that a front doesn't have a solid wall between the cool and the warm air. To make our two-room building more like the weather, we should put it on a merry-go-round so that it's slowly spinning, making one rotation a day. Now we're ready to create an extratropical storm in a two-room building by rolling the wall out of the way. Immediately, the cooler, heavier air begins flowing beneath and therefore pushing up the warmer, lighter air. Since the room is spinning, the air has a circular motion, creating a swirl. In the real atmosphere, extratropical storms will often spawn thunderstorms around this low pressure, and these thunderstorms then supply some energy to the system by the release of latent heat.

But scientists didn't get a good handle on the different energy sources for extratropical storms until late in the nineteenth century. Espy and Redfield had no idea. Regarding the very important question of how the wind blows in a whirlwind, both men turned out to be a little wrong—but a little right. We now understand that the winds of major storms do not blow straight toward the center, as Espy believed, nor do they circle around the center, as Redfield believed. Rather, they spiral in toward the center, a truth that just about splits the difference between the hypotheses of Redfield and Espy. It's intriguing to note that in his first paper, published in 1831, Redfield had written this about his whirlwinds: "The winds do not move in horizontal circles, but rather in spirals." Either he did not mean with those words what they seem to say, or he changed his mind, because maps he drew years later to illustrate his ideas clearly show the storm winds blowing in *circles* around a center.

However, a pretty accurate depiction of the spiraling circulation of extratropical storms had been put forward in 1843 by Elias

Loomis, a professor of natural philosophy and mathematics at Western Reserve College in Cleveland, Ohio. At a scientific conference, Loomis presented a paper with several maps that followed the careers of two major winter storms. These maps demonstrated a tendency of the wind to *circle* the low pressure center but also to move *toward* the low pressure—that is, to spiral in toward the center. The maps were teasingly close to the truth, but by no means conclusive. At their deaths in 1857 and 1860, respectively, William Redfield and James Pollard Espy were each still convinced that his own position was correct. The spiraling pattern of storm winds wasn't resolved for once and for all until late in the century, when sufficient data for detailed maps left meteorologists with no other conclusion.

Redfield and Espy were also fatally burdened by their ignorance of the vital role played by the Earth's rotation in the development of cyclones. While George Hadley, working in the eighteenth century, had realized that the Earth's rotation helps curve the winds, the real understanding of the dynamic began with the French mathematician Gustave-Gaspard Coriolis. In the 1830s, Coriolis had worked out the mathematics of how the Earth's rotation to the east would act on objects, but he only hinted that his ideas might be applied to meteorology. In fact, Coriolis's ideas would eventually contribute to our understanding of the balance of forces that affect *all* winds, especially those in the strongest cyclones, but in America they had slipped from view until rediscovered by William Ferrel, a self-taught mathematician and schoolteacher in Nashville, Tennessee. It was Ferrel who applied Coriolis's ideas and other principles to work out the first unified theory of winds operative in all weather systems in all parts of the world. He first published his theory in 1856 in the *Nashville Journal of Medicine and Surgery*, a strange platform for the subject. Quite naturally, the leading meteorologists of the day, including Redfield and Espy, missed this tremendously important paper, but the author also sent his essay to Joseph Henry at the Smithsonian Institution, who recognized its importance and sent it to Espy for review.

Espy was in a position to understand that Ferrel's thesis aligned with the growing body of reliable observations, but he disagreed about the role of the Earth's rotation in creating the winds. He argued that this force would be "vanishingly small" in tornadoes and hurricanes. He was right about tornadoes—the spinning motion of these and other small vortices, including water flowing down a drain, is not due to the "Coriolis force." (Many teachers and authors have said the Coriolis effect causes these small swirls, but they are wrong, to the consternation of meteorology professors who have to spend time correcting the error.) Espy was wrong, however, about hurricanes and other large systems. If the Earth were not rotating, winds created by pressure differences would indeed blow straight from high pressure to low pressure, much as Espy imagined, until the pressure equalized and the wind stopped—but the Earth's rotation causes the moving air to begin following a *circular* path. In the Northern Hemisphere, the wind is diverted to the right; in the Southern Hemisphere, to the left. This "Coriolis force," as we call it today, is precisely why hurricanes exist at all, and why there are whirlwinds. While the Coriolis force dictates that, in the Northern Hemisphere, flowing air turns to the right, it combines with the other forces involved to turn the air flowing *into* low pressure in a counterclockwise direction. We call these winds "cyclonic." Likewise, air flowing *out of* high pressure in the Northern Hemisphere is turned clockwise, causing the "anticyclonic" winds around high pressure to spiral in that direction. In the Southern Hemisphere, where the Coriolis force has the opposite effect, the flows are in the opposite directions. As we might imagine, the actual equations that describe this action, equations that also have to take into account friction against the Earth's surface and the role played by centrifugal force, are something to behold.

William Ferrel recognized that the Coriolis force—or the lack of it, more precisely—is also why hurricanes do *not* form on the equator. Here, the Coriolis force is zero and therefore cannot impart storms with the circular winds they need in order to grow. In fact, the Coriolis force is too weak to have a significant effect on winds anywhere within about five degrees either side of the equator. Individual showers and thunderstorms occur in this equatorial band all the time, but the moving air doesn't take on the spiral path required to organize a large, long-lasting storm.

If science truly had a sense of justice, we should probably speak of the "Ferrel force" instead of the Coriolis force when we talk about the winds, because Ferrel applied Coriolis's mathematics to the winds. But sometimes there is a little justice in scientific honors: the flow of surface and high-altitude air in the middle latitudes is called the "Ferrel cell" (while the one over the tropics is the Hadley cell, as previously noted). After Ferrel died in 1891, Cleveland Abbe, one of the first official "weathermen" in the U.S., compared Ferrel's work in meteorology with Isaac Newton's in astronomy: "As Newton's *Principia* arrested all further vain speculations and turned the whole trend of thought toward the true celestial mechanics, so Ferrel's [papers] served to turn all eyes toward the true atmospheric dynamics. . . . Ferrel's [work] will always remain the *principia mete-orologica*."

On November 14, 1854, a powerful storm struck the Russian city of Sevastopol on the Black Sea precisely as the British and French armies were laying siege to this stronghold during the Crimean War. The winds even had the temerity to blow down the tent of the esteemed *Times of London* war correspondent William Howard Russell, who proceeded to transmit an account of "mackintoshes, quilts, india-rubber tubs, bed-clothes, sheets of tent-canvas . . . whirling like leaves in the gale towards Sevastopol. The shingle roofs of the outhouses were torn away and scattered over the camp." Where wooden hospitals and storehouses had been erected by the French, "a few scattered planks alone met the eye." Several hundred wounded men had been in those buildings. The rain then turned to sleet, then to snow, and the winter storm left troops without warm or dry clothing and other supplies, as several British and French warships and supply ships had sunk in the harbor at Balaklava. From the depths of winter, war correspondent Russell later wrote, "The wretched beggar who wandered about the streets of London in the rain 'ed the life of a prince compared with the British soldiers who were fighting for their country."

Now the British public had had enough. The catastrophe of the Black Sea storm was more evidence, on top of much else, that their government was mismanaging the war. While no one really expected the government to be able to forecast storms precisely, this one's devastating impact on the fighting forces led commentators and critics to wonder whether the sailors and soldiers could have been given some kind of warning. One month later, the British Admiralty ordered Navy Captain Robert FitzRoy to begin comprehensive meteorological observations. Forecasting the weather wasn't part of the assignment, but FitzRoy saw weather observation as the first step toward weather forecasting.

Across the English Channel, the French allies were also displeased with the disaster, and the Minister of War asked Urbain Jean Joseph Le Verrier to study the notorious Black Sea storm. Le Verrier's status as the astronomer who had discovered the planet Neptune indicated the importance placed on this commission. He began the job by sending letters all around Europe, asking for weather observations from the days leading up to November 14. He received 250 replies, a deluge of information. In America, William Redfield and his contemporaries compiled their early maps mainly with reports of wind velocity and direction, not barometric pressure. Working just a few years later, Le Verrier had copious information on barometric pressure—a tremendous advantage, because, as we have seen, the differences between areas of low and high pressure drive the powerful winds of major storms. Le Verrier understood this fact, and his study of the Black Sea storm of 1854 led him to create "synoptic maps" showing air-pressure patterns as well as winds.

We now know that Le Verrier was not the first scientist to create a synoptic weather map. That honor goes to Heinrich W. Brandes of the University of Breslau in Prussia, who did so in 1816. Actually, no one has found a single map created by Brandes, or a copy of one, but he described his maps in some detail in a book. Since current information wasn't available to any investigator in 1816, Brandes used observations that had been collected from across Europe more than thirty years before, but had never been mapped. He clearly understood the relationship between storms and low-pressure centers— they are the same thing—but he was also several decades ahead of his time, and his insights were lost for many years. Brandes was the first meteorologist to use isobars to indicate patterns of air pressure.

An isobar is simply a line on a map that connects areas of equal air pressure. For example, today's weather maps have lines connecting all locations at which the reported barometric pressure is 1008 millibars, 1012 millibars, 1016 millibars and so forth. (While the National Weather Service uses inches of mercury in its statements for the public, it uses the millibars, a metric measurement, on all of its maps.) There are no fixed values for "high" and "low" pressure areas. These designations are relative to one another. By common usage, however, any enclosed area on a synoptic map that confines barometric pressure readings lower than 1000 millibars is marked as a "low." Likewise, a "high" confines areas with pressures higher than 1000 millibars. If the low pressure is the center of a strong storm, there could be two, or three, or even more isobars squeezed tightly together around it, indicating sharp pressure differentials and therefore strong winds, because, as we've seen, wind speed increases as the change in pressure increases over short distances.

It was Le Verrier who brought the world up to speed four decades later. Today's weather maps are direct descendants of the maps he created to describe that Black Sea storm of 1854. A synoptic map is invaluable to the forecaster, because it not only locates storms at a glance but also gives a reliable indication of their strength. Le Verrier's "invention" was one of the key advances in weather and storm forecasting in the first half of the nineteenth century. After collating his 250 reports for the Black Sea storm into synoptic maps, Le Verrier reported within months that this data, *if* it had been received in timely fashion and accurately plotted on maps, would have made it possible to give one day's warning of the storm. *Timely fashion:* that's the key. For synoptic analysis to work, observers at dozens of locations—or hundreds, the more the better—must read their mutually calibrated instruments at fixed times, and they must be able to communicate their numbers to a central office without delays.

In short, real-time synoptic analysis required the telegraph, which had been invented several decades before Le Verrier made his maps. It is not much of an exaggeration to state that the telegraph would accomplish for the practical forecasting of storms what the work of Redfield and Reid and Espy had accomplished for our scientific understanding. Le Verrier had such prestige within the French scientific establishment that on February 16, 1855, Emperor Napoleon III ordered the establishment of a telegraphic storm-warning service. By the following year, the reporting network covered most of France, and by 1857 it covered most of Europe. Still, geography worked against forecasters in Europe, especially those trying to make predictions for the British Isles and western Europe, because the powerful storms on the Continent come off the Atlantic Ocean, where there was no reliable means of gathering information.

Hampered those forecasters were, but they weren't completely blind. In 1860, Christoph H. D. Buys-Ballot, the head of the Netherlands Meteorological Institute in Utrecht, used telegraph reports from stations around northwestern Europe to issue a warning for the Dutch coastline. History has noted this as Europe's first government-sanctioned storm warning. The same meteorologist also promulgated "Buys-Ballot's law," which says that if you stand with your back to the wind in the Northern Hemisphere, the center of the storm is to your left. This is simply a practical way of stating the fact that storms in the Northern Hemisphere have a counterclockwise circulation. In the northern quadrant of any storm, the wind is from the east. If you stand with your back to the east, the south—the center of the storm—is to your left. In the southern quadrant of the storm, the wind is from the west. If you stand with your back to the west, the north—the center of the storm—is to your left. Buys-Ballot's law works.

In England, the meteorological service that Robert FitzRoy had established began issuing daily forecasts and storm warnings for the British Isles. Even without data from over the Atlantic, his short-term warnings for storms whose effects could be ascertained from onshore locations worked well. But his two-day forecasts were less successful, and many of his meteorological colleagues argued that FitzRoy was using sailors' time-honored rules of thumb, not scientific principles. On April 11, 1862, the *Times of London*, which carried FitzRoy's forecasts, commented: "The public has not failed to notice, and, as we much fear, with some wicked amusement, that we now undertake every morning to prophesy the weather for the two days next to come. While disclaiming all credit for the occasional success, we must however demand to be held free of any responsibility for the too common failures which attend these prognostications. During the last week Nature seems to have taken special pleasure in confounding the conjectures of science."

The article made note of FitzRoy's admission that he needed more and better observations. Three years later, FitzRoy, who suffered from psychological problems that we today might label as manic-depressive, committed suicide. The following year a Committee of Inquiry looking into weather forecasting concluded: "We can find no evidence that any competent meteorologist believes the science to be at present in such a state as to enable an observer to indicate day by day the weather to be experienced for the next 48 hours throughout a wide margin of the earth's surface." The British stopped making forecasts. Many, especially in coastal communities, complained about no longer receiving them, but the government didn't try again for over a decade.

Meanwhile, Americans were also having their problems in the forecasting arena. In 1846, Joseph Henry, a leading American scientist, had become the first head of the new Smithsonian Institution, where he made meteorological studies the first major project. Henry's goal was science, not utilitarian forecasting, but science leads to forecasting, and forecasting is ultimately dependent on science, so Henry's network of voluntary weather observers mailing their data to the Smithsonian was a step in the right direction for both causes. By 1849 Henry had arranged with the newly organized telegraph companies to have some of the volunteers wire in their observations. Soon, a map of the United States displaying that day's reports of weather conditions from around the country was one of the major attractions at the Smithsonian. From time to time, the institution's researchers would hazard a forecast, but nothing on a regular basis. Even if they had developed the habit, it would have been curtailed by the Civil War, which ripped apart the Smithsonian's weather network as well as so many other American institutions.

Almost coincidentally with the end of that war in 1865, a series of powerful storms on the Great Lakes sank or damaged 1,164 ships, killing 321 people. The following year another set of storms on the lakes sank or damaged 1,914 vessels, killing 209 people. These disasters followed by a dozen years the Black Sea storm, which had helped spur Europeans into action on the forecasting front, and the same thing now happened on this side of the Atlantic. People were upset and complained bitterly, but it was three years after the last of the storms before Cleveland Abbe, the director of the Mitchell Astronomical Observatory in Cincinnati, Ohio, established a weather telegraphy service. In this endeavor he won the cooperation of the U.S. Army, the burgeoning telegraph companies, and the Smithsonian, which had not rebuilt its prewar network. Abbe's observatory began issuing weather reports on September 1, 1869, and the following month he began making daily forecasts for the Cincinnati area. Most of these were for twenty-four hours, but Abbe sometimes issued predictions for longer periods when he felt he had enough information.

On February 9, 1870, President Ulysses S. Grant directed the Secretary of War to take weather observations at posts across the United States and to give notice when storms threatened the Great Lakes and the Atlantic Coast. An advantage of having the army run the weather service was that military discipline should assure that the sergeants who made the official observations would do so more reliably than civilian volunteers. The U.S. Army Signal Corps set up the Division of Telegrams and Reports for the Benefit of Commerce and began making regular weather observations at 7:35 A.M., in Washington, D.C., on November 1, 1870. Finally, 350 years after Columbus had made the first New World storm prediction, this continent had an official weather service. One week later—and one decade after the Europeans—this nascent organization issued its very first storm warning, a bulletin dated November 8, 1870, that read: "High wind all day yesterday at Cheyenne and Omaha; a very high wind this morning at Omaha; barometer falling with high winds at Chicago and Milwaukee today; barometer falling and thermometer rising at Chicago, Detroit, Toledo, Cleveland, Buffalo and Rochester; high winds probable along the Lakes."

Now that the army was the official forecasting institution for the country, it hired Abbe from the Mitchell Astronomical Observatory, who began issuing twenty-four-hour "probabilities" for the eastern half of the United States. He used "probabilities" in the sense a forecaster might use the term "outlook" today, not in the sense of giving the odds of certain kinds of weather. A typical report from this period would first describe the general weather pattern, then it might end as this one from the mid-1870s did: "Probabilities; it is probable that the low pressure in Missouri will make itself felt decidedly tomorrow with northerly winds and clouds on the Lakes, and brisk southerly winds on the Gulf."

Pretty basic stuff. In the beginning, all forecasts based on tele-graph reports and synoptic maps were a matter of saying that a low-pressure area would continue moving as it had been moving. This obviously didn't allow for storms to change paths, as they do, or to strengthen or weaken, as they do. Still, it was a vast improvement over anything that had been available—for the eastern half of the country, that is. Maps from that era show isobars and centers of high and low pressure east of the Mississippi, but not in the West, where there were not yet enough weather stations to allow forecasters to plot pressure patterns. But most of the people lived in the East any-way, where this degree of analysis and forecast worked fairly well, because in the middle latitudes most storms do move in some fash-ion from west to east.

In 1872 the original federal law that had mandated forecasts only for the Great Lakes and East Coast was amended to require forecasts for the whole country. This was a noble intention, but the system did not work for most hurricanes, especially those that hit the southern United States, because there were no weather stations in the Atlantic Ocean or the Gulf of Mexico to collect data. Only after a hurricane crossed Florida and headed for the states along the Gulf Coast could forecasters give some warning. Realizing their limitations, the army began in 1873 to obtain reports from Havana and Santiago, Cuba, and from Kingston, Jamaica. These new stations might allow some warning for a hurricane that crossed Jamaica and then Cuba before hitting the Florida Keys or moving into the Gulf of Mexico. Fore-casters also became more skillful at locating storms off the East Coast, drawing maps with air-pressure readings and winds along the coast and extending the isobars over the ocean, in effect estimating those readings. Indeed, the official weather map for September 28, 1874, is the first to show a hurricane. It was offshore between Jacksonville, Florida, and Savannah, Georgia, and apparently hit the Carolina coast two days later with no reports of deaths or substantial damage from the sparsely populated region.

This forecast represented progress, but there's progress and then there's *progress*; the real forecasting advances in that era were made by Father Benito Vines in Cuba. The Jesuits had been expelled from Cuba as the movement for independence from Spain gained strength in the nineteenth century. Then they were invited back mid-century, and in 1870 Vines was made director of the 400-student Royal College of Belen in Havana. The order's long tradition of scientific education and research had made seismology something of a specialty, but Cuba's problem was hurricanes, not earthquakes. It and all of the other islands of the Caribbean and the eastern Atlantic Ocean had been periodically, tragically devastated by the great storms arriving almost unannounced on their shorelines. Within just a few years, Vines more or less single-handedly evened the playing field, and by the end of the century he and his fellow Jesuit Father Federico Faura, who was based in Manila, the Philippines, were the most proficient and best-known cyclone forecasters in the world. Considering that they didn't have radio reports from ships at sea, much less from airplanes or satellites, their contributions to the science of storms and to forecasting were extraordinary.

Father Vines was up-to-date on the latest theories, but he knew that the key to real progress in forecasting was empirical research. He started with the twelve years of detailed weather observations the college had collected before he arrived. To this database he added his own observations, compiled every hour on the hour from 4 A.M. to 10 P.M., seven days a week. He had no assistants for this work, but he did have a full complement of the equipment available at that time, including fine sextants, barometers, and anemometers. When a storm was near, Vines picked up the pace and collected his data twenty-four hours a day. The American Jesuit Father Walter M. Drum wrote of his brother decades later, "He studied the structure of the cyclone, the phenomena that preceded it, and the havoc left in its wake—in fact, he noted with ardor and painstaking care all meteorological signs and data which preceded, accompanied, and followed up the storm, and that, too, without neglecting the ordinary and toilsome routine work of the Observatory."

The grueling work paid dividends, when Vines predicted on September 11, 1875, that an intense hurricane would hit Cuba's southern coast two days later. When it did so, his reputation for accurate forecasts achieved immediate and wide circulation. This had never happened before—anywhere! Later that year he made another successful forecast. The following season a special edition of *La Voz de Cuba* announced, on October 19, "We have just received from Rv. Father Vines, the learned Director of the Meteorological Observatory of the Royal College of Belen, the following important communication that we hasten to make known to the public before the time of our evening edition. . . . We are very near to the vortex of a hurricane." Vines expected the wind to blow from the northeast, followed by "a calm that should not be trusted, and thereafter the wind would shift with sudden and terrific force to the southwest"—exactly what will happen as the eye of a hurricane passes directly over a location, moving east to west. Again, Vines's forecast was correct, and toasts were hoisted by the Royal Academy of Science in Havana.

In 1877 Vines expanded his operation with more reporting stations around Cuba and on other Caribbean islands. The Havana Chamber of Commerce and several private companies provided financial aid, the telegraph companies didn't charge for their services, and railroads and steamship companies offered the famous prognosticator free transportation along all their routes. The railroad even ran a special express if Father Vines needed immediate transportation, and sometimes he did, because he rarely if ever missed either firsthand observation of a storm or the earliest possible visit after the fact.

In September of that year Vines forecast that a hurricane still far over the Atlantic would strike Barbados soon. After it then did so, Vines predicted, on September 22, that the hurricane would miss Puerto Rico but would strike Santiago, Cuba, on the 24th. "Be on your guard," he advised. These successful forecasts were almost certainly more luck than skill, but they weren't *all* luck. After these correct forecasts, one newspaper in Puerto Rico wrote: "Thus Vines, whose voice has for us the authority of an oracle, calmed our souls by his timely warning. He well deserves the European reputation that he enjoys."

The idea floated decades before by William Redfield, that upper-air winds carry storms along with them through the atmosphere, somewhat in the way that a stream carries a vortex downstream, now enjoyed general consent by meteorologists, including Vines. But he was making his correct forecasts long before meteorologists had any means at all of measuring those wind speeds and their directions in the upper atmosphere. How was he able to do so? By dent of hard work and a genius for observation, it seems. Vines simply had the touch for tropical weather. He could feel the atmospheric forces at work—and he could see them as well.

For centuries, observation was all that most forecasters had to go on. The most basic such observation, well known by Christopher Columbus, was that huge swells rolling in on an otherwise calm sea portend a strong storm somewhere far out at sea. By Vines's era, it was known that a storm's winds create waves of all sizes, and the longer the wind blows, and the harder it blows, and the greater the distance over the water the wind blows (the "fetch"), the larger the waves. These waves move out in all directions from the center and begin sorting themselves into groups moving at the same speed and in the same direction. This action is incredibly complex, and only the fastest supercomputers can handle the simulations now used by oceanographers to study how these waves gradually smooth out and grow longer to form swells. These powerful swells can pound the beaches targeted by an approaching hurricane for many days. The surf resounds with a continuous roar that shouts a warning of lurking calamity. Even a supreme forecaster such as Father Vines, however, could not discern from the swells alone how far away a storm was, or in which direction it might be heading.

Besides, Vines's specialty was not waves but clouds. His forecasts relied to a large extent on detailed observations of winds at the surface and of clouds at different levels of the atmosphere, from which he was able to infer wind currents in the upper air. He was the first to do this, and it was a remarkable accomplishment. He correctly hypothesized that clouds—carried by the winds, naturally—converge *toward* the center of a hurricane at low altitude. At middle altitudes, the winds and clouds tend to circle *around* the storm. At high altitudes, the winds carry clouds *away from* the storm. Of course, reading the clouds is not as easy as it sounds. High clouds that seem to be radiating outward from a point in the distance might really be, because of perspective, just parallel rows of clouds that appear to be converging in the distance, like the rails of a railroad track. It takes the touch of an Old Master to paint clouds, and in the nineteenth century it took the touch of a Father Vines to read them. As his predictions proved, Vines worked out methods for making a good estimate of a storm's path, and he developed simple devices that observers could use to gain a clearer picture of a storm's location based on surface winds and the clouds they saw at various heights. These were a landlubber's rough equivalent of the storm cards Henry Piddington included with every copy of *The Sailor's Horn Book*.

Like maritime observers from time immemorial, Father Vines understood that "brick red" sunrise and sunset often indicated foul weather in the future. Like those old-time observers, he also knew that the puffy cumulus clouds that normally dot the skies around tropical islands disappear as a storm approaches, and, as we've just seen, that upper-air winds carry clouds away from the storm. What he did not and could not have known is that all three of these phenomena are the result of the same dynamic in the storm system. We now understand that air flowing out of the top of a hurricane — carrying clouds with it — descends to Earth in a ring. This descending air is warmed, which evaporates the puffy cumulus clouds. Satellite photographs of hurricanes and typhoons clearly show this "moat" of clear air around hurricanes and typhoons. This warming air also creates an "inversion," a layer of air that's warmer than the air below it — just the opposite of the state of affairs that's driving the storm itself, where warm air is rising from the surface. The inversion, which might be just a few hundred feet above the surface, traps the air at the surface and keeps it from rising along with dust and other particles, which otherwise would be carried aloft. These trapped particles create the vivid sunrises and sunsets that sailors have admired and worried about for ages.

Father Vines complemented all these close observations of winds, ocean swells, and clouds with historical data and developed a climatology that showed the paths that storms in different areas of the eastern Atlantic, the Caribbean, and the Gulf of Mexico were likely to follow at various times during the hurricane season. There are such patterns, and he was remarkably able to discern them through the fog of time. Across the Pacific, Father Faura used forecasting and research techniques similar to Vines's to record the same success with typhoons roaming the western Pacific. The two Jesuits were the best at what they did.

On the mainland United States, no one was even trying to compete. The army's weather service became the U.S. Weather Bureau within the Department of Agriculture, but the focus of the forecasts remained on the continental United States. Hurricanes were an afterthought. In defense of the Bureau's forecasters, we should point out that, unlike Father Vines, they faced numerous forecasting problems other than hurricanes, including thunderstorms that can bring hail and flash floods, tornadoes, heat waves, droughts, river floods, freezes, and blizzards. Any and all of these natural disasters are much more common in the United States than hurricanes. In most years, or even most decades, the fall, winter, and spring storms on the northeastern coast, which not only wash away beaches but also shut down big cities with snow, cause more disruption and economic loss than hurricanes. (One of the great storms of the last two centuries was an extratropical storm known as the "Ash Wednesday Storm." For sixty-five hours beginning March 6, 1962, this monster pounded the coast from North Carolina to New England with devastating, hurricane-like consequences.)

As the Weather Bureau's luck would also have it, no storm took the lives of a large number of people between 1870 and 1893, although a pair of storms that hit Texas a month apart in 1886 did play a considerable role in the *future* history of great storms. The first of those slammed into Indianola on Matagorda Bay on August 19 and 20, leaving the town "a universal wreck." It's sometimes said that Indianola was therefore empty when the second storm struck a month later, but this isn't quite true. A few people were there on September 22 and 23, when a tropical storm that was almost a hurricane dumped twenty-six inches of rain on Brownsville to the south and pushed waist-deep water from Matagorda Bay into Indianola. As it happened, Texas had been suffering from a serious drought. In Galveston, water was selling for ten cents a bucket, twice as much as beer. So this particular problem along the Texas coast was now alleviated, but the biggest impact of the two storms was indirect and fatally ironic. Prior to the hurricanes, Indianola had been the leading port in Texas, but the storms that year sent this business up the coast to Galveston, which now became a boomtown. Fourteen years later, it would be Galveston's turn to deal with a devastating hurricane.

By the 1890s the Weather Bureau had cable links to a few weather observatories around the Caribbean Sea, including Cuba, and in 1892 a cable connected Florida and Nassau on New Providence Island in the Bahamas, giving forecasters an outpost from which to keep an eye on hurricanes approaching from the southeast. The data was necessarily skimpy, but the system still worked reasonably well at times. It even worked to some extent in 1893. It just didn't work *effectively*, which was unfortunate, to put it mildly, because the six hurricanes that hit the United States that year killed more than 4,000 people. That season was the freakish equivalent on the mainland of the disastrous season that had crushed so many Caribbean islands in 1780, more than a century earlier.

In only two years since 1893 — 1916 and 1985 — have six hurricanes hit the U.S. mainland. Only one year, 1900, had a higher death toll. In fact, no subsequent decade, except for the one that includes 1900, had a hurricane death toll nearly as high as the single year of 1893.

After the first hurricane hit Florida, doing little damage, the year's second storm hit the New York City area on August 24 with winds perhaps as high as 90 miles per hour. "New Yorkers realized how the residents of a small Kansas town feel when a genuine tornado bursts upon them and smashes their houses into kindling wood," the *New York Times* reported. "Lives were lost and hundreds of thousands of dollars' worth of property was destroyed by the wind and the rain. It was a terrible night for shipping. Despite the warnings which the Weather Bureau had been sending out for several days, many craft were caught in the storm and driven ashore." The reporter then came up with this colorful figure of speech: "The cyclone gave the barometer a bad fright, and it crawled down its narrow tube until it was almost at the low record." The 29.23 inches of mercury reading, however, has turned out not to be all that low for New York City and definitely not that low for a hurricane.

More than a hundred magnificent trees in Central Park were uprooted. The beach at Coney Island was swept almost clean, and the ends of the two iron piers were ripped off. Most ominously, a sand spit off Rockaway Beach called Hog Island and the resort on it were all but destroyed. A hundred years later, when that storm of 1893 had been pretty much forgotten in New York City, Nicholas K. Coch, a professor at Queens College, led a field trip to study erosion of the beach at the Rockaways in Queens. The students found broken plates, beer mugs, bricks, and other old objects that they determined were most likely from that resort on Hog Island. Officials whose job is to worry about what a modern-day hurricane could do to the New York City metropolitan area, such as those of the Mayor's Office of Emergency Management, have used the disappearance of Hog Island in 1893 as a cautionary tale. And yet, fewer than twenty-five people lost their lives in that storm.

Two days later, on a Saturday, based on its telegraph reports from the Bahamas and elsewhere, the Weather Bureau issued a bulletin predicting that a hurricane that had passed north of Nassau the night before should hit the East Coast by Monday. Where would the storm hit? Somewhere south of New York, according to the Bureau. This forecast prompted harbor authorities from Boston to Norfolk, Virginia, to warn ship captains not to leave port for the Southeast—but with no real idea where the storm was likely to hit along the 1,000-mile coast, authorities didn't feel compelled to make full-scale preparations. They simply didn't think in those terms in those days. As it happened, the hurricane came ashore just north of Savannah, Georgia, on the night of August 27, pushing the Savannah River from twelve to fourteen feet above its normal tides, battering the city with high winds, and producing barometric pressure readings that put the storm in today's Category 3, with sustained winds between 111 and 130 miles per hour.

The eye of this storm apparently tracked directly over the city of Savannah. This meant that the dangerous semicircle took dead aim at the Sea Islands of Beaufort County, South Carolina, north of the city. Most of the residents of these islands were former slaves, or their children and grandchildren, who tended small farms or fished the ocean and the inlets and creeks that thread among the islands and marshes. Writing in the February 1894 issue of *Scribners Magazine*, Joel Chandler Harris described in the dramatic language of the day what that night must have been like on the Sea Islands: "The tangled thunders of chaos shook the foundation of things. The bellowing waters of the sea leapt up and mingled with the shrieking spirits of the air. Out of the seething depths disaster sprung and out of the roaring heavens calamity fell."

No one knows exactly how many people were killed that night or how many died over the next few weeks from injuries and disease on the wrecked islands, where salt water filled many wells and bodies drifted in the water or lay unburied on the ground. The best estimate was 2,000, perhaps 2,500. Another 20,000 to 30,000 were left destitute and homeless, their small farms and fishing boats destroyed. The storm surge of twelve to fifteen feet probably drowned most of the victims. Many were trapped in their small homes. We can picture the calamity of rising winds and waters, men, women, and their children clinging to rafters, climbing trees, only to be swept away in the end. The Sea Islands do have elevated spots, small ridges and hills high enough to keep those perched on top safe at least from the surge, if not from the winds and flying debris. So safety could have been only a few hundred yards away for many, but the storm hit in the middle of the night; the victims could not have known that the ocean was washing over their island until it rushed into their homes. Running for the high ground would have meant fleeing into darkness and chaos.

Could anything have been done beforehand? Most likely not. In the first place, the telegraph lines didn't reach from the city to the Sea Islands. Even if they had, and had delivered a warning, what could the residents have done? There were no emergency management centers in those days, no ready means of evacuation, no evacuation plans, no contingency planning of any sort. The *Savannah*

Morning News had carried a small front-page story about the Weather Bureau's prediction, but there was not a word about preparations.

When *Scribners*'s Harris visited the islands a few weeks later, he described the scene: "All around, and for miles and miles, farther than the eye can reach, as far as a shore bird can fly, the results of the storm lie scattered. Here a house has staggered upon its end, there a boat has been flung into the arms of a live oak, and yonder a phosphate dredge, weighing hundreds of tons, has been lifted from the water and turned completely over; here a magnificent grove of live oaks has been uprooted; there a broad-beamed [cargo boat] has been lifted across the marshes; and yonder hundreds of tons of marsh sedge have been spread over arable land."

Today, such devastation is addressed with immediate and sustained aid for rebuilding, and Harris made an appeal for help for the Sea Islands. Relief, he wrote, "means not a momentary ebullition of benevolence, but the actual means of subsistence for a period covering several months. The Negroes have lost not their possessions alone, but their growing crops. When the storm swooped down upon them they were just getting ready to market their cotton—the famous Sea Island cotton that enters into the manufacture of the finer grades of goods. But the wind whipped their cotton out of the bolls and off the stalks, the salt sea-water rose and ruined their potatoes, and wind and sea carried away their boats."

Help would be needed through the winter and until new crops could be planted and harvested the following year. This was obvious—or *is* obvious to us, more than a century later. There was no large-scale federal natural disaster relief at the time. That had to wait for the huge Mississippi River flood of 1927. Congress did from time to time appropriate minimal relief aid for specific disasters, including floods along the Mississippi and Ohio Rivers in 1884, but the Sea Islands were not deemed worthy of such federal assistance. South Carolina Governor Benjamin R. Tillman said the state couldn't afford to aid the victims, either. The governor asked Clara Barton, head of the American Red Cross, to help, but she was reluctant because the Red Cross had little money and fund-raising would be difficult, because the country was in a recession. But if the Red Cross

Red Cross workers hand out relief supplies after the 1893 Sea Islands, South Carolina, hurricane. Beaufort, South Carolina, is across the river in the background.

didn't take over the relief work, she knew the United States would wake up that winter to learn that famine was killing hundreds of people in South Carolina, so the organization did step in. However, instead of merely handing out food and other aid, the Red Cross required victims to earn food and other goods, such as clothing, by working on reconstruction projects, including rebuilding destroyed homes. Red Cross workers also began educating the victims on how to stay out of debt and how to use their own communities for self-help. "I had desired to do more than merely make a gift for distribution," Barton wrote. "I wished to plant a tree. I could have given them the peach, which they would eat, enjoy, and throw the pit away. But I wished them to plant the pit, and let it raise other fruit for them."

The fourth and fifth hurricanes of 1893 hit Louisiana. The first of these yielded no casualties, while the second left behind 2,000 bodies as it swept across the low islands of the coast south of New Orleans on October 2. No warning was issued for this storm. The *Monthly Weather Review* states that it formed quickly off the coast and hit the shore only hours later, but this is not correct. Later researchers used shipping reports and other records to determine that the storm had somehow escaped detection for five days as it followed a common path for Gulf of Mexico storms—forming in the western Caribbean, crossing Mexico's Yucatán Peninsula, then turning north across the Gulf. The hurricane was moving toward the Northeast when it raked the islands along the Louisiana coast before hitting the mainland in Mississippi. When it first came ashore, this storm was probably about the same strength as the South Carolina hurricane, but it quickly weakened. This didn't really matter, however, because as the edge of the storm's eye skimmed along the Louisiana islands, the counterclockwise winds on the east side of the eye blew from the south, literally driving the Gulf of Mexico across the islands into Barataria and Caminanda Bays in a wall of water up to fifteen feet high. Then, as the eye moved farther northeast, the northerly winds on its west side shoved the water from the bays back across the islands, carrying the bodies of many victims into the Gulf of Mexico. Perhaps 1,150 of the storm's estimated 2,000 victims lived in Cheneire Caminanda, the largest settlement on the Louisiana coast at that time. Even though the death toll and the nature of this terrain and damage was similar to the tragedy in South Carolina just five weeks earlier, recovery in Louisiana was quicker, because the economy there was based on fishing, not agriculture. Cheneire Caminanda was never rebuilt, but resettled survivors were ready to begin working as soon as their boats and tackle were replaced. Few people live along this exposed and vulnerable stretch of the Louisiana coast today.

The sixth hurricane in 1893 formed far out in the Atlantic Ocean on September 25, but it didn't reach the southeastern coast of the mainland United States until October 12. Then it skimmed up the coast, causing flooding from Cape Canaveral, Florida, north to Charleston, South Carolina, before turning out to sea. This was a powerful hurricane, as powerful as the one that struck the Sea Islands, but it killed only twenty to thirty people.

Six U.S. hurricanes total that year, with two more hitting eastern Canada after staying well off the U.S. coastline, and another hitting Nicaragua and Honduras. Still, the damage and the death toll brought no particular calls for increased federal investment in research or forecasting. That development had to wait until the Spanish-American War, which not only boosted the United States into a world power but also affected hurricane forecasting, in ways good and bad, even a little shameful. As war threatened in 1898, Willis L. Moore, the chief of the U.S. Weather Bureau, told his boss, Secretary of Agriculture James Wilson, that he feared a disaster if a hurricane struck an unwarned and ill-prepared U.S. fleet on the seas surrounding Cuba. He presented an ambitious plan for expanding the Bureau's Caribbean weather reporting system, and Wilson immediately took him to see President McKinley. The chief of the Bureau recalled that meeting years later:

> I can see him now . . . chin in hand and elbow on knee, studying the map I had spread before him. Suddenly he turned to the Secretary and said, "Wilson, I am more afraid of a West Indian hurricane than I am of the entire Spanish Navy." To me he said: "Get this service inaugurated at the earliest possible moment." When I told him I should need the authority of Congress, he directed me to report to Chairman Cannon of the Appropriations Committee, who would include the necessary authority in the bill that was then being held open for the purpose of giving to the President everything that he might need in the prosecution of war. . . . Thus was inaugurated as a war necessity the present West Indian weather service, which has been of such benefit to the shipping of our South Atlantic and Gulf waters, and to the commerce of the world in those regions.

That war, which was fought in part on behalf of Cubans seeking independence from Spain, in part on behalf of American business interests threatened by the guerrilla warfare on the island, and in part on behalf of "expansionists" in the American government, was brief and to the point. (Nevertheless, it made two indelible contributions to American lore: the sinking of the battleship *Maine* in Havana harbor on February 15, and the taking of San Juan Hill on July 1 by Theodore Roosevelt and his Rough Riders.) As it turned out, Moore's and McKinley's fears were almost beside the point, since the war was effectively over in less than three months (with Teddy's victory), before hurricane season got into full swing. The peace treaty with Spain gave the United States Puerto Rico and the Philippines as colonies, and de facto control over Cuba for the next few years.

This control over Cuba included the establishment of a branch office of the Weather Bureau in Havana, which could have been a wonderful chance to work with the Cuban meteorologists who had carried on the work of Father Benito Vines, who had died in 1893. The tradition of cooperation was already in place. The U.S. Army Signal Corps had printed an English translation of Vines's book, entitled *Practical Hints in regard to West Indian Hurricanes*, for the use of its forecasters, the Secretary of the Navy had sent an emissary from the navy's Division of Meteorology to consult with the great man, and the U.S. Hydrographic Office had printed Vines's laws on its marine charts. The May 1899 edition of the charts stated: "These important laws, established by the study and long experience of Father Vines, should be thoroughly understood by every navigator and utilized by shaping his course so as to avoid a hurricane."

At the end of the nineteenth century, instead of continuing the American cooperation with the Cubans, the U.S. Weather Bureau officials in Havana actually sabotaged the relationship, even trying to make sure the Cubans wouldn't be able to use the telegraph to transmit forecasts. The Weather Bureau, or at least its leaders, wanted to be the only source for forecasts for areas controlled by the United States, which now included Cuba. Did the Bureau chief, Willis Moore, and others hold the Cuban meteorologists and forecasters in disdain, or did they fear that the Cubans were better at the job? In the nearly quarter of a century since Father Vines had taken over meteorological studies in Cuba and completely recast theories and practices of forecasting—with demonstrably good, even startling, results—Americans had contributed very little. The great hurricane research tradition of Redfield and Reid had slipped into disuse. The only significant study was E. B. Garriot's *West Indies Hurricanes*, published in 1900, and this work broke no new ground. Mainly it just brought the data up-to-date with maps showing hurricane tracks from the previous twenty-five years. Its lessons on forecasting consisted of extensive quotations from Redfield and Vines.

At the turn of the century, Father Vines's work was still supreme, still the most useful for forecasters, and still the subject of disdain by the leaders of the U.S. Weather Bureau.

With today's knowledge of hurricanes and forecasting, we know it is highly likely that Vines missed many storms, either those that never struck or those that missed the forecast target. However, his work was remarkable for the time, and it seems that his successes were remembered and recorded, while his failures were less well-known. Neither the details of Vines's techniques nor his forecasting scoreboard were as important to the coming century as the notion that hurricanes *can* be forecast. Even if his successes were overblown by the standards of a later time, Vines's accomplishment late in the nineteenth century was similar to the accomplishments of William Redfield, William Reid, and Henry Piddington earlier in the century. They convinced those who followed that hurricanes could be understood, and Vines firmly planted the idea that an understanding of hurricanes could be used to save lives.

CHAPTER 3

EARLY 1900S

I N 1889, the good citizens of Galveston, Texas, complained to the U.S. Army Signal Corps that the soldier in charge of the local Weather Bureau office was lying down on the job. Galveston deserved better. Business had been good for a long time, and the two storms that had struck the coastline to the south three years earlier and destroyed the port of Indianola had sent a flood of a different sort into Galveston: even more business. By the end of the nineteenth century, this island town of 38,000 residents would be the wealthiest city in the state of Texas and the second-largest port on the Gulf of Mexico, second only to New Orleans. At the time, neither Houston nor Dallas were a match for the commercial clout of Galveston. More than 70 percent of the cotton exported from the United States was loaded on some of the 1,000 ships that called at these piers every year. The town even had the first telephone and electrical service in Texas. And then there was the climate, which attracted people from other parts of Texas and surrounding states to bathe in the warm, calm water of the Gulf of Mexico.

The inspector assigned to the investigation by the army found that the charges against the weather service were well-founded: the instruments were in poor condition, and the soldier in charge had absolutely refused to try to forecast the freezes that were rare—five a year, at most—but devastating for the profits of the sugarcane and vegetable growers. The army turned to one of its civilian employees, twenty-seven-year-old Isaac Monroe Cline, as the ideal candidate to make the office in such an important city a showcase for the weather service. Cline had joined the weather service in 1882 and had earned a medical degree at the University of Arkansas while serving as an assistant observer in Little Rock, but medicine never engaged his mind fully. He was more interested in the effects of weather on health, a field in which there had been much speculation since at least the time of the Greeks. Christopher Columbus had been far from the first sufferer to notice that aching joints often foretold storms. Cline would write in his autobiography, *Storms, Floods and Sunshine*, published many years later, "Medicine offered a field which could be tied in easily with my work in the weather service. A knowledge of both medicine and meteorology would enable me to make an intelligent study of the effects of weather changes and of climatic conditions on mankind in sickness and in health. Here was a field in which there had been little research. . . ." In addition to his weather duties, Cline taught medical climatology at the University of Texas Medical School in Galveston.

In 1894, four years after the U.S. Weather Bureau had become a civilian agency, Cline came in fifth in the Bureau's national forecasting contest—"only three-tenths of one percent behind the winner." The contest was part of the campaign by Mark W. Harrington, the Bureau's first civilian chief, to upgrade weather forecasting to a calling in the sciences. Cline and nine others won the chance to compete on the basis of their essays on "Improvement of Weather Forecasts"; the winners went to Washington, D.C., early in 1894, where their forecasts on the local weather were judged against what actually happened.

It's safe to say that Cline was something of the classic Victorian, a man with a great deal of confidence both in himself and in the scientific and technological advances of the day, including weather science. Like Father Vines in Cuba, he was among those practitioners who wanted to make weather forecasting a true science. In this ambition, however, forecasters still had a long way to go. Cline himself had a long way to go. On July 16, 1891, three days after a tropical storm had flooded parts of Galveston, he had written confidently in the *Galveston Daily News*:

The coast of Texas is, according to the general laws of the motions of the atmosphere, exempt from West India hurricanes, and the two which have reached it [in the last 20 years] followed an abnormal path which can only be attributed to causes known in meteorology as accidental. . . . The opinion held by some, which are unacquainted with the actual conditions of things, that Galveston will at some time be seriously damaged by some such disturbance, is simply an absurd delusion and can only have its origin in the imagination and not from reasoning. . . . It would be impossible for any cyclone to create a storm wave which could materially injure the city.

Nine years later he still believed this, but he was nevertheless disturbed when he got a call at 5 A.M. on the morning of September 8, 1900, from his brother, Joseph, who worked for him at the Galveston weather office, reporting that the tide had risen overnight and was now standing two feet deep in parts of the city. Isaac Cline immediately harnessed his horse to his two-wheel sulky and drove three blocks from his home on Avenue Q to the Gulf of Mexico to time the incoming swells and observe for himself the rising tide in the morning's first light. Now he was truly disturbed, because the huge waves and rising water were coming in *against* the wind, which was blowing briskly offshore. Cline understood that it would take a big storm to create swells that would keep their shape against the wind. What would happen if the wind turned with the water? Back at his office in the Levy Building in the center of Galveston, Cline telegraphed the Weather Bureau in Washington: "Unusually heavy swells from the southeast, intervals one to five minutes, overflowing low places south portion of the city three to four blocks from beach. Such high water with opposing winds never observed previously."

Returning to the beach several times, Isaac was concerned that the beachfront was attracting throngs of people to the water's edge to watch the leaden sea heave ashore. Children played in the water running through the streets; crowds gathered to watch the surf destroy the famous Galveston bathhouses. Apparently the townspeople believed that their weather forecaster had been correct when he'd written nine years earlier that their island was immune to a devastating hurricane. But was the intrepid forecaster now having second thoughts himself? Until the wires failed at 3:30 P.M. that

Saturday, the Cline brothers relayed to Washington, D.C., their weather and tide reports every two hours. Why Washington? Because at that time only the national headquarters could post hurricane warnings. The chief forecaster had already posted northwest storm warnings, and now, under Cline's urging, he changed them to northeast storm warnings. Northwesterly winds in Galveston do not presage a tropical disturbance. Such tropical winds would come from the northeast initially; Cline was upgrading the degree of danger. But there was still no hurricane warning.

The winds increased, blowing offshore until 4 P.M., reaching hurricane force at 5 P.M. By 8:30 P.M. the barometric pressure had fallen nearly an inch from the noon reading of 28.48 inches—the lowest pressure reading ever officially recorded in the United States at the time. The anemometer at the Galveston Weather Office blew away after registering 100 miles per hour. Decades later, National Hurricane Center researchers concluded that the pressure in the storm's center, which did not cross Galveston, was 27.49 inches of mercury, making it a Category 4 storm by today's standards, with winds higher than 131 miles per hour.

Immediately after the hurricane, Cline wrote in the *Monthly Weather Review* that the warnings and the worsening weather required him to "keep one man constantly at the telephone [at the Weather Bureau office] giving out information. Hundreds of people who could not reach us by telephone came to the Weather Bureau office seeking advice. I went down on Strand Street and advised some wholesale commission merchants who had perishable goods on their floors to place them 3 feet above the floor. . . . The Public was warned, over the telephone and verbally, that the wind would blow by the east to the south and that the worst was yet to come. People were advised to seek secure places for the night. As a result thousands of people who lived near the beach or in small houses moved their families into the center of the city and were thus saved." In his autobiography, Cline writes:

Early on the morning of September 8th, I harnessed my horse to a two wheeled cart, which I used for hunting, and drove along the beach from one end of the town to the other. I warned the people that great danger threatened them and advised some 6,000 persons, from the interior of the State, who were summering along the beach to go home immediately. I warned persons residing within three blocks of the beach to move to the higher portions of the city, that their houses would be undermined by the ebb and flow of the increasing storm tide and would be washed away. Summer visitors went home, and residents moved out in accordance with the advice give[n] them. Some 6,000 lives were saved by my advice and warnings.

An artist's rendering of what some victims of the 1900 Galveston hurricane endured.

However, research by Erik Larson, author of the 1999 book *Isaac's Storm*, found no account by any survivor who remembered seeing anyone, let alone the city's well-known Weather Bureau chief, shouting warnings of an impending hurricane. Larson argues that, until the very last minute, Cline did *not* have second thoughts about his assertion from nine years earlier and did not believe that any storm could do serious damage to Galveston. His final message, composed at 3:30 P.M. to the chief of the Weather Bureau in Washington, said, "Gulf rising, water covers streets of about half of the city." This was what Cline wrote in his *Monthly Weather Review* article, but in his autobiography, published forty-five years later, he says his message advised the chief "of the terrible situation, and stated that the city was fast going under water, that great loss of life must result, and stressed the need for relief."

By late afternoon, the Cline brothers returned to Isaac's home, which he had recently built and which was designed to withstand hurricane winds. In his autobiography he described the arrival of the storm surge:

> The water rose at a steady rate from 3 P.M. until about 7:30 P.M., when there was a sudden rise of about 4 feet in as many seconds. I was standing at my front door, which was partly open, watching the water which was flowing with great rapidity from east to west. The water at this time was about 8 inches deep in my residence and the sudden rise of 4 feet brought it above my waist before I could change my position. . . . The storm swells were pounding the other wreckage against our home. It held firm against these without trembling. But the street railway trestle was carried squarely against the side of the house. The breaking swells drove this wreckage (the trestle was held together by a quarter mile of track) against the house like a huge battering ram: the house creaked and was carried over into the surging waters and torn to pieces.

Isaac, his brother, and his three daughters escaped, but Isaac's wife, Cora, was killed.

The almost complete destruction of Galveston was described as vividly as anywhere by one Nellie Carey, in a letter reprinted in

The September 1900 hurricane reduced a large part of Galveston, Texas, to rubble.

Murat Halstead's book *Galveston, The Horrors of a Stricken City*, published almost immediately after the disaster:

> Have not had a minute to write and cannot collect my thoughts to tell you of the horrible disaster down here. Thousands of dead in the streets—the gulf and bay strewn with dead bodies. The whole island demolished. Not a drop of water—food scarce. . . . The dead are not being identified at all—they throw them on drays and take them to barges, where they are loaded like cord wood, and taken out to sea to be cast into the waves, now peaceful, which were so hungry for them in their anger. The bay is full of dead cattle and horses, together with human corpses, blistering in the hot sun. It will be impossible to remove the dead from the debris for weeks— the whole island is frightful.

Indeed, the dead were so numerous, with many of those dumped at sea returning on each tide, that officials decided to burn the corpses that lay within the mountains of wreckage of 3,600 smashed houses and businesses. The funeral pyres lighting the night sky could be seen from the mainland two months later. For years the estimated death toll for the Galveston Hurricane of 1900 was set at 6,000, the largest figure by far for a natural disaster in American history; later research has shown that it was considerably higher, probably 8,000, maybe more. Despite the incredible death toll, there was no great outcry from the press or in Congress about the failure of the Weather Bureau to provide sufficient warning. Isaac Cline's own story about saving maybe 6,000 people with his warnings delivered on the streets was accepted. Most of the reporters who entered the city during the following days wrote about the destruction, not about warnings delivered or not delivered, heard or not heard. Immediately after the storm, the politics of the situation must have been pretty clear to Cline: he did not want to blame the Weather Bureau's Washington office for not posting a hurricane warning, because that criticism might have hurt his career.

Galveston was not Indianola. It was too important. It could not be abandoned. Within days of the hurricane, local officials declared that the citizens of Galveston would rebuild their city. A quickly commissioned engineering study recommended that the entire city be elevated above the level of the 1900 surge to protect it from the ravages of future hurricanes. Every home, every church, every school, every sidewalk, every fence, every electric line, every *everything* would be raised to a level seventeen feet above mean low tide. More than 4,500 inhabited structures that still stood would be raised to the prescribed height. So would all trees and shrubs. In the end, it took eleven years to slurry more than eleven million cubic yards of sand under the elevated city.

The engineering study recommended that a massive concrete wall be constructed, three miles long, sixteen feet thick at the base, five feet at the top, buttressing the easternmost end of the island, protecting the raised city. Seawall construction began in 1902, with wood pilings to support the reinforced concrete pounded deep into the sand. By 1904, the initial wall was complete, but an extension nearly a mile long was immediately added to protect the city's north end. This bulwark against the sea faced its first test in 1909, before the job of pumping in sand to raise the city's structures had been finished. As the city held its breath, a powerful hurricane bore down on the island. That storm, with a central pressure of 28.00 inches of mercury, winds in the 135-mile-per-hour range, and a twelve-foot surge, killed 275 people, but none in the parts of Galveston behind the seawall, even though six feet of water washed into some parts of the city that hadn't yet been raised.

Even today, the memory of 1900 remains very much alive in Galveston, and the community is one of the nation's most progressive in dealing with evacuation issues. Galveston and the Florida Keys were the first areas to develop "last resort" refuge plans: after officials have evacuated as many people as possible before conditions become too dangerous for travel to the mainland, the only road out will be blocked, and all remaining men, women, and children will be directed to designated elevated buildings in the main part of town. This plan is updated periodically, and it will, in all likelihood, save many lives should the need arise, certainly compared to communities that essentially assume that everyone will get out and have no alternate plan for the many who may not be able to. Such plans are, in a way, a vindication of Joseph Cline. As the water rose around his brother's home on that fateful afternoon of September 8, 1900, Joseph urged his brother to take his family to the Weather Bureau office in the four-story, brick Levy Building downtown, which he felt would be a safer shelter. Proud of the house he had designed for just this purpose—to withstand a hurricane—Isaac disagreed, and by the time the danger to the house was apparent, it was probably too late to flee through the rising water and flying debris. But that downtown office building did survive.

Isaac Cline did not witness Galveston's impressive rebirth. After receiving a commendation from his chiefs in Washington, D.C., for his role in saving many Galvestonians, he was promoted to Chief of the Forecast Center for the Gulf States, with offices in New Orleans, and he and his three daughters moved to the Crescent City within a year of the Galveston disaster. The storm had destroyed the manuscript of a book on medical climatology that Cline was almost ready to publish. He did not rewrite it; in fact, he did no further research in the field at all. As he wrote in *Storms, Floods and Sunshine*, "The Galveston hurricane of September 1900 changed my objective. I gave up my studies of medical climatology and took up that of tropical cyclones."

After the tragedy in Galveston, the Weather Bureau considered giving the responsibility for posting hurricane warnings to local bureau offices, which were certainly in a better position to know what was happening "on the ground." However, the staffs in those offices generally had very little experience, training, or resources—such as data collection over large areas, and map plotters and analysts needed to forecast such events as hurricanes. Cline's own erroneous concepts about hurricanes and their possible effects on Galveston prior to 1900 probably also played a part in the Bureau's decision to make no change to the policy for posting hurricane warnings. The power remained in Washington, D.C. However, the storm did motivate Isaac Cline and some other meteorologists to concentrate on hurricanes to a much greater extent, and the postmortems were serious efforts to come to grips with the surprise with which the storm had struck the island. In his report on the storm in the *Monthly Weather Review*, Cline wrote, "The usual signs which herald the approach of hurricanes were not present in this case. The brick-dust sky was not in evidence in the smallest degree. This feature, which has been distinctly observed in other storms that have occurred in this section, was carefully watched for, both on the evening of the 7th and morning of the 8th."

He had seen cirrus clouds moving from the southeast on the morning of September 7, as would be expected before a hurricane, but by that afternoon a mixed bag of low clouds moved over the city from the northeast, continuing through the morning of the fateful 8th. Barometric pressure readings had given no clue until it was much too late. The barometer had fallen a little on the 7th, then risen slightly, then fallen slowly on the 8th until it began plunging around noon. In short, Cline concluded in the technical report, the only unusual signs were the heavy swells from the southeast and unusually high water, which had begun flooding parts of the city in the morning. Later researchers learned that the storm had reached hurricane strength just west of Key West, Florida, and had slowly gained power as it crossed the 800 miles of the Gulf of Mexico at the steady pace of around eight miles per hour. The trip took four days, a long time for the storm to whip up the big swells that alarmed Isaac Cline.

In that same issue of the *Monthly Weather Review*, E. B. Garriot, who was in charge of the Weather Bureau's national forecasting division, stated, "The devastation at Galveston was caused principally by a storm wave, which swept in from the Gulf in advance of the hurricane," adding that the shallow water off Galveston "renders it, in the presence of severe storms, peculiarly subject to inundation."

Of course, Isaac Cline had made exactly the opposite assertion nine years earlier, but Garriott had the advantage of hindsight. He was correct. Storm surge *was* the cause of the Galveston devastation, and Isaac Cline couldn't have been expected to understand the danger nine years before, because no one did. Garriott didn't really *understand* it, either; its consequences simply couldn't be missed. Today we know that the phenomenon of storm surge is quite complex, with a lot of if's, and's, and but's. To understand it, even in its simplest terms, we should begin with the basics, a single molecule of water.

If oceanographers could follow the movements of this one molecule as a wave rolls past in deep water, they would see it rise and move forward just a little as the water rises, then slip slightly down and backward as the wave passes. As the next wave comes along, the water molecule would follow roughly the same oval path, and so it would go, around and around, wave after wave. The molecule would *not* move forward with the waves. In short, ordinary waves in deep water, including swells, carry *energy*, not water. That's the accurate way of looking at them. But when a wave finally reaches shallower water—about half as deep as the wave's own height—the bottom of the wave begins to "feel" the seafloor below and is slowed down by the friction, while the top of the wave continues ahead. Now the marked molecule would surge forward as the wave grows taller and eventually breaks, sending a surge of water toward the shore. For ordinary waves, and even for large swells, the water that reaches the beach in the tops of the breaking waves sinks and flows back out to sea under the next incoming wave.

That's the basic picture, with incoming and outgoing water in balance; as a hurricane moves toward the shore, however, the wave process and associated "water transport" becomes much more complex. The simple explanation of this process is that the abnormally large waves generated by the winds of the hurricane bring to the shore abnormally large amounts of water in the tops of the breaking waves—too much water to be sent back into the sea beneath the following waves. Incoming and outgoing water are no longer in balance. In response to this crisis, strong currents are spontaneously created parallel to the shoreline or in narrow zones trying to run directly back out to sea (these currents are called "rip currents"), which try to transport the excessive water away from the targeted beachfront. But these currents will not be able to do the job for a major storm, and all the incoming water that can no longer go back into the ocean or be carried away along the beachfront, left or right, has only one way to go instead: up. The level of the sea literally rises along the coast over a distance of fifty miles or more. This action is called the "wave setup." The exact amount of rise depends on the forward speed of the hurricane and the depth of the water near shore.

If deep water is less than ten miles from the shore, the effect from wave setup can be significant, because it takes place over a short distance as the storm surge hits the shallower water. In the case of the Gulf of Mexico, where the water is shallow for long distances off the shore—fifty miles or more—the rise in sea level due to wave setup will be, at most, one to three feet, because the waves break well off-shore. The excess water in the tops of the waves is dissipated slowly over the long expanse of shallow water. Apparently this factor was the reason that Isaac Cline wrote so confidently in 1891 that "it would be impossible for any cyclone to create a storm [surge] wave which could materially injure" Galveston. (At the time he did not realize that what he called the "storm wave," or "storm tide," involved more than wave setup, that the real danger came from what we now call storm surge.) He believed that the shallowness of the Gulf water off-shore would protect the city, and this scientific understanding was correct—as far as it went. It just didn't go far enough. Cline did not understand—no one did—that the major contributor to storm surge in a strong hurricane is not wave setup. It is the converging winds in its right front quadrant.

In a storm, the wind not only creates the waves that eventually become the wave setup over shallow water, but it also creates and pushes ahead of the storm a mound of water on which these waves ride. This mound of water is the storm surge. In a Northern Hemisphere hurricane or typhoon, this mound of water is generally centered in the right side of the hurricane, for two reasons: the winds in the right rear quadrant (looking along the path of the hurricane toward shore) are pushing water toward the shore, and at the same time winds in the right front quadrant are spiraling into the center, pushing water toward the storm's center, where it converges near the inner edge of the eye wall. In addition, a storm also tends to pile up water with what we call the "soda-straw effect." Since the air pressure in the storm's center is lower than the pressure all around the storm, air is pushing down on the water away from the center with more force than the air in the center. This action is similar to what happens when we suck on a soda straw, radically decreasing the pressure inside the straw: the air pressure on the soda around the straw pushes the soda inside the straw upward. (It is also the same response measured by the column of mercury in a barometer, and is therefore sometimes called the "inverted barometer effect.") In a storm, the soda-straw effect is only a small part of the storm surge, pushing the water up about one foot for each one-inch difference in barometric pressure. In the strongest hurricanes, the rise in sea level caused by the low air pressure can be as much as three feet. In weaker hurricanes, it might be only six inches. But six inches of onrushing water is not inconsequential, because a single cubic foot of sea water weighs sixty-four pounds, an impressive battering ram.

So we have the storm surge pushing ahead of the hurricane over the sea hundreds of miles offshore. In this deep water, the force of gravity acts to pull the entire mound of water down, where it can flow away as underwater currents. As a storm and its surge move into shallow water, the underwater flow is stopped and the surge builds up. Therefore, it turns out that the shallow water offshore that protects a shoreline from the worst effects of one phenomenon of a hurricane, wave setup, actually creates a *higher* storm surge than deeper water—a phenomenon unknown at the time of the Galveston disaster. This ignorance assured that Cline's prediction that Galveston was safe from substantial storm surge would prove, sooner or later, to be disastrously misguided.

The fact that storm surge is much lower over deep water sounds like good news for shorefronts with deep-water beaches, but there's a catch. The waves riding on top of the lower surge will be higher themselves, because waves at the coast are normally about half of the water depth: the deeper the water, the higher the waves. This is why buildings right on a deep-water beach can be destroyed by wave action, while buildings just a short distance back escape any damage at all: the low surge—and the waves riding on top of it—never reached them at all. (The same phenomenon also accounts for the famous surfing off the north shore of Oahu, where the water is deep: winter storms over the Pacific Ocean a thousand miles to the north create large waves, which keep their height in the deep water all the way to the beach before crashing down as thirty-footers.)

The effect of wave setup, the soda-straw effect, and the onrushing storm surge is further complicated by the coastal configuration of bays, estuaries, nonuniform changes in water depth along the coast and seaward; by the topography of the land; and by the storm's forward speed, its size and strength, and the direction from which it's approaching the coast. Yet another factor is the regular astronomical tide, which can play a huge role, because the surge rides ashore on top of the tide. If a hurricane hits during low tide, its surge is going to cause less damage than if it the storm arrives during high tide. In Galveston, where the range between high and low tide is only about a foot and a half, the timing isn't as important as it is in, say, southern South Carolina, where the range is eight feet. The storm surge in Beaufort County in 1893 was elevated by the tide, which was about two and a half feet above mean tide.

At his new post in New Orleans, Isaac Cline began extensive studies on the now all-important subject of storm surge, including the detailed mapping of winds and storm surge from several hurricanes. These and many more charts and tables were included in his *Tropical Cyclones* (1926). It was the first truly extensive study of the nuts and bolts of hurricanes, including storm surge based on tide gauge records. Earlier investigations, beginning with William Redfield's and William Reid's eighty years before, were much more limited in

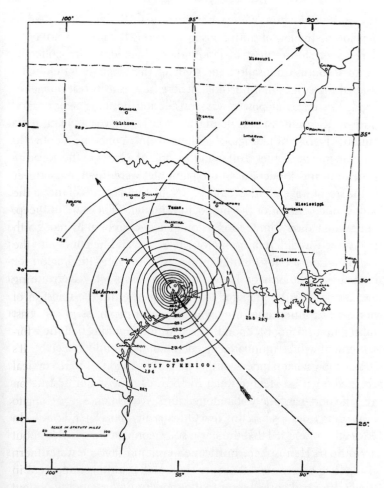

A diagram from Isaac Cline's *Tropical Cyclones* of the August 17, 1915,
hurricane that hit near Galveston. The lines are isobars, showing equal air
pressures. They are close together, an indication of the storm's low central air
pressure and high winds.

scope, by necessity of their much more limited data and understanding. Also, Redfield and Reid were mainly concerned with the effects
of storms at sea, because in their day that's where most of the deaths
were occurring. People hadn't started the migration to the ocean-
front that became a surge of humanity until after World War II.

Henry Piddington, who shares credit with Redfield and Reid for developing the law of storms, also was among the first to warn of the dangers of storm surge to landlubbers. In addition to collecting storm accounts from sailors and studying their logbooks, Piddington studied the surges that hit India, where he was a British official. In 1853, the imperial power was considering building a port about thirty miles southeast of Calcutta, as a way to relieve crowding at that famous facility. Piddington addressed his concerns about this scheme in a pamphlet written in the form of a letter to the governor-general of India. Sections of the pamphlet were titled "Description of the storm wave of the cyclones," "Nature and causes of the storm's wave," and "Extent of the inundation inland." The state of the science didn't allow him to form a complete picture, but he recognized that surge was different from ordinary waves, and he concluded that the proposed site for the new port was vulnerable. Piddington lobbied against the project. He wrote in the pamphlet, "Everyone and everything must be prepared to see a day when in the midst of the horrors of a hurricane, they will find a terrific mass of salt water rolling in, or rising up upon them, with such rapidity that the whole settlement will be inundated to a depth of five to fifteen feet."

We know what happens next. The port opened in 1864, a cyclone covered it with six feet of water in 1867, causing major destruction, and the port was finally abandoned three years later.

Writing from his base in New Orleans fifty years later, Isaac Cline correctly concluded that the storm surge comes ashore to the right of a Northern Hemisphere hurricane's eye, and that the water begins rising long before any other sure signs of the storm are apparent. By then Cline had come closer to the modern understanding of storm surge. In his 1926 book he wrote that the storm surge "results from the physical forces of the hurricane, driving the large waves forward and transferring the same in the same direction as the line of advance of the hurricane. In the open sea this storm tide is not so great. . . . The obstruction formed by the coast line acts as a barrier and the water gradually banks up." Cline urged coastal forecasters to monitor water levels as closely as they checked barometric pressure and winds. Cline believed that water rising above the expected astronomical tides would be not only the first positive sign of a major storm offshore but also a key predictor to its eventual landfall. Fifteen years after the Galveston disaster, in September 1915, he got the chance to test his ideas—before the actual publication of *Tropical Cyclones*, but after the research had been collected and the theories developed. The "hurricane listening posts" Cline had set up for the Weather Bureau on Swan Island, between Belize and Jamaica, and at Cape San Antonio, Cuba, radioed the first information about a hurricane taking powerful shape in the Caribbean Sea. This was a storm on a par with the Galveston storm, and it moved directly through the Yucatán Channel between Mexico and Cuba, into the Gulf of Mexico. Cline knew this, he wrote in his autobiography, because "it began sending its message . . . to the Gulf Coast in the form of long swells, which commenced building up a storm tide on the coast."

By the morning of September 27, water was a foot above its normal level along the Gulf Coast from Burrwood, Louisiana, to Galveston. By the following morning, it was 1.7 feet above normal at Burrwood, but back to normal at Galveston. Cline therefore concluded, "The rising storm tide at Burrwood indicated that the center of the cyclone was moving toward a point not far west of the mouth of the Mississippi River, and that all low lands along the east Louisiana, Mississippi and Alabama coasts would be flooded to dangerous depths extending well inland." By the early morning of September 29—the third day since the storm had entered the Gulf of Mexico—the water was 2.7 feet above normal at Burrwood and two feet higher than the normal tide at Fort Morgan, Alabama, about 110 miles northeast of Burrwood, and water was beginning to flood the Louisiana coastline. By eight o'clock that morning, Cline was convinced that the storm's center would move ashore over Barataria Bay, Louisiana, fifty miles south-southeast of New Orleans, on the west side of the Mississippi River Delta and north of Burrwood. Cline's office issued warnings by telegraph, telephone (the few that there were), and even by special messenger at the government's expense. Schools were advised to close, and police and fire departments were asked to warn people to stay off the streets "to avoid being killed or injured by wreckage which would be driven through the streets by high winds like missiles shot from a cannon."

As Cline predicted, the center of the hurricane shoved inland over Barataria Bay around 1 P.M. and moved northward to New Orleans, with the eye passing directly over Tulane University. A storm surge of ten to thirteen feet washed into Lake Pontchartrain, with the highest level recorded at the western end of the lake. To the east of the New Orleans area, a slightly smaller surge of nine to eleven feet submerged portions of the Mississippi coast. Pensacola, Florida, 175 miles east of the storm's landfall, recorded a surge of four feet. Meanwhile, the surge only twenty-five miles west of landfall, in Morgan City, Louisiana, was four-tenths of a foot *below* normal. These numbers were just as Cline had theorized they should be: nearly all of the storm surge was to the east of landfall. What surge there was to the west did not extend very far. (There probably had been some rise even in Morgan City while the hurricane was offshore, but the water went down as the wind shifted to the northeast as the center approached.)

The winds at Burrwood gusted to 106 miles per hour, and at New Orleans they reached 98. The lowest pressure measured was 28.01 inches of mercury on a ship in the New Orleans harbor. The town of Leeville on the coast suffered the same fate as had befallen Cheneire Caminanda in 1893: Leeville was wiped out, with only one of its 100 buildings left standing. The storm caused an estimated $13 million in damage, in 1915 dollars, with $5 million of this in New Orleans. On the other hand, the Cheneire Caminanda storm had claimed 2,000 lives, and this one almost a quarter of a century later, only 275 people, partially because the warnings in 1915 had been much more timely and widespread—and many who did lose their lives had not heeded the warnings to evacuate. The day after the storm, the New Orleans *Times-Picayune* commented accurately, "Never before, perhaps in the history of the Weather Bureau, have such general warnings been disseminated as were sent out by the local bureau."

In fact, those warnings would have come initially out of Washington, but they would have covered a broad area, as they usually did, and Cline probably influenced and perhaps amplified them with "local impact" statements, much as is done today. Cline was a hero, and it might seem that his theory of predicting the track of a hurricane based on the storm surge that precedes it would have been a great breakthrough for forecasters. However, the history of later storms has proved that it's not so easy. Not all hurricanes—not even the majority of hurricanes—are preceded for days in advance by rising coastal waters that establish a pattern clear enough to provide accurate advanced warning. In fact, we now have ample proof that surge measurements cannot be used to give precise landfall predictions even hours in advance, let alone days, for the simple reason that many storms veer left, veer right, weaken, strengthen, veer left again—all the while producing nothing but a confusing mess of storm surge readings. One storm that proved this point in spades was Hurricane Carla in 1961, which was so massive and powerful its outermost winds stretched across the Gulf of Mexico almost edge to edge. Carla wandered for days over open water hundreds of miles offshore, changing directions many times, triggering significant storm surges over a long stretch of the Gulf Coast. Eventually, the center stormed onshore in the Matagorda Bay area with tremendous force, causing tremendous damage from the middle through the upper Texas coast. This landfall was eventually predicted with good accuracy, but no thanks to the storm surge data from up and down the coast.

By contrast with Carla, the best, albeit incomplete, understanding of the track of the 1915 hurricane that struck New Orleans is that it held to a steady and straight course from the day it entered the Gulf of Mexico, pushing before it a straightforward, readable storm surge. By the time that Cline says he was convinced the hurricane was going to move onshore in southeastern Louisiana, the center of this powerful hurricane was only about ninety miles south of the coast, probably already lashing the coastline with near-hurricane-force winds and flooding low-lying areas. Thus the forecast was essentially a forecast of an event that had already begun, with peak effects to follow in about six hours. Because of the observations in southeastern Louisiana, some additional warning time was available for the Mississippi coast, which probably prompted the encomium in the *Times-Picayune*. Had the storm made landfall farther east, it is unlikely that any more warning time would have been available for Mississippi than had been the case for southeastern Louisiana.

Clearly, changes of sea level and abnormal swells along the coastline are tools that forecasters can and do use for forecasting, but they provide a rough measure, no more; the simplest data on air-pressure change along the coast is generally a much better indicator of potential landfall points, especially in the final countdown, twelve to twenty-four hours before landfall. While Cline turned out to be wrong about using surge to predict storm movement, he alone did the period's most important hurricane research and his *Tropical Cyclones* was the only scientific work about hurricanes, other than a few journal articles, until 1938 when Ivan Ray Tannehill of the Weather Bureau published *Hurricanes: Their Nature and History.* Today's hurricane forecasters are very much aware of Cline; his story is a cautionary tale of what can happen to a meteorologist who is overconfident about his understanding of storms and forecasting ability.

Isaac Cline's dream that careful monitoring of storm surge might prove to be the Holy Grail of hurricane forecasting didn't pan out, but an advance in technology in the early years of the twentieth century definitely did. First there had been the telegraph, roughly forty years earlier, and now there was the radio, an even more important invention because it did not rely on an infrastructure of cables. For the first time, radio allowed ships to join the network that provided real-time data to forecasters. The first such report was on August 26, 1909, when the SS *Cartago* got caught in a hurricane off Mexico's Yucatán Peninsula. Winds were estimated at 115 miles per hour. The storm weakened before hitting the coastline near Brownsville, Texas, two days later, but Brownsville knew the storm was coming. Ships also knew to avoid the southwestern corner of the Gulf of Mexico. Of course, as radio became widespread and more ships received more timely information from other ships and forecasters, they were able to avoid storms, so there were fewer ships to report storm information in the first place. Still, the radio was a net plus, and ships that weren't in a hurricane could supply information about suspicious swells and cloud patterns as well as report barometric pressures that forecasters could include on their synoptic maps. Radio also opened up the possibility of receiving timely reports from islands or land stations that telegraph or telephone wires didn't reach, including radio-equipped weather stations on Swan Island and on Cape San Antonio, at the western tip of Cuba, that Cline had set up. But there were inevitably a lot of large blank areas on the forecasters' synoptic maps, because information about conditions over the ocean was necessarily skimpy, even with reporting stations and ships equipped with the new radios. A case in point is the 1926 hurricane that smashed into Miami, Miami Beach, Fort Lauderdale, and Hollywood, Florida, with almost as much stealth as the 1900 Galveston Hurricane.

Richard Gray, chief of the Miami Weather Bureau office, first received word of this hurricane on September 14. It had formed east of the Lesser Antilles three days earlier and was now located northeast of St. Kitts in the Caribbean, headed west at about 14 miles per hour with winds up to 90 miles per hour. Coincidentally, a weak tropical storm had just turned away before hitting Florida. At that time storms were not named, and many residents of Florida assumed that subsequent reports from forecasters referred to the weak tropical storm. When people heard that a storm had turned away, they stopped worrying. Looking back, it's difficult for us today to see how those residents might have confused storms three days apart, but this may just reflect how much more "tuned in" we are today.

For three days there were no new reports about the hurricane, until September 17, when it wrecked Grand Turk Island southeast of the Bahamas. That evening, at 11:16 P.M., the Weather Bureau in Washington issued hurricane warnings for Florida. Even that warning was issued almost as an afterthought: the forecaster started to leave his office for the night but then returned and issued the warning around 11 P.M. Richard Gray received it on the Bureau's teletype line and immediately hoisted warning flags atop the Federal Building in Miami and then at the city docks, where the winds were already so strong he needed help. He also had the phone company dispatch the warning up the coast to Hollywood and Fort Lauderdale. But most people in southeastern Florida had already retired for the night and never learned of the warning.

At the same time, apparently unknown to the Weather Bureau, the hurricane had strengthened rapidly and dangerously, with winds now exceeding 130 miles per hour. Barometric pressure, which had been inching down all day Friday, plummeted near midnight. Sustained winds on the coast increased from 60 miles per hour at 2 A.M. to more than 100 three hours later. At 6:10 A.M., the wind abruptly slackened and for almost an hour blew at a leisurely pace from all points on the compass, and the morning sun began to shine on parts of the city—or so one report said, but it must have been an exaggeration, because the sun had risen only two minutes earlier. It could not have been exactly "sunny" as the eye passed over Miami.

The city was in the midst of an economic boom at the time; most people living there were new to Florida and had never experienced a hurricane. Believing that the storm had passed, hundreds of people poured into the streets to see the destruction. When Richard Gray saw this, he was terrified, because he knew that the pressure on his barometer had just bottomed out at 27.61 inches, a new U.S. record. Later investigations indicated that three prior storms had actually had lower pressures at landfall: the Galveston Hurricane of 1900; a hurricane that struck Grand Isle, Louisiana, in 1909; and one that roared across the Florida Keys and later southern Texas in 1919.

Richard Gray knew that this respite was just the eye of the storm passing over the central and southern sections of Miami—an eye that was later determined to be thirteen miles wide. He bolted out of the Federal Building screaming at the throng, "Seek cover! The storm's not over! It's not over!" Within minutes, the "second storm," as it was described in the newspapers, blasted the city even harder than the first half had. Gray said later that "many lives were lost during the second phase of the storm." Between 7:40 and 7:42 A.M., winds from the south and southeast were recorded by a well-exposed anemometer atop Allison Hospital, in North Miami Beach, at 138 miles per hour, establishing a new record for the United States. There might have been higher gusts later in Miami, but the anemometer blew away at 8:12 A.M. while measuring a steady 120 miles per hour. Nor was the hurricane finished. It proceeded across the Florida peninsula, where winds in Pensacola on the west coast were recorded at 116 miles per hour, the northeastern corner of the Gulf of Mexico, and then struck the Mississippi coast two evenings later, with winds still around 120 miles per hour.

Afterward, an American Red Cross report stated: "For the most part, though there were some notable exceptions, the large buildings of reinforced construction, the finer residences, and the more stur-dily built small buildings were not seriously damaged." Still, nearly 5,000 homes were splintered by the storm in Miami alone; most of the wooden part of the city was now gone. A 10.6-foot combination of storm surge and astronomical tide swept all of Miami Beach and spread more than a half mile inland. Fifteen miles to the north, every building in Hollywood, the brand-new city built just five years ear-lier, was damaged, if not wrecked. Tiny Moore Haven, a town of about 1,200 on the southwestern shore of Lake Okeechobee, was left with the biggest scars from the storm. After a dike used to control the level of the lake was breached by an eleven-foot rise in the water level, six feet of water surged into every home in Moore Haven. The damage was only a foretaste of the suffering another hurricane would bring to places all around Lake Okeechobee two years later.

The total death toll for that hurricane is listed as 243 people. The intensity of the storm and the immense wreckage left behind "the memory of a fearful night," Gray wrote in his official report. The twelve hours of destruction were often blamed, with some justifica-tion, for ending that particular Florida land boom. Streets and side-walks of towns abandoned before any houses were built dotted the Florida landscape four decades later. Thousands of displaced resi-dents accepted free passage north on the Florida East Coast Railway. In 1998, Roger A. Pielke, Jr., of the National Center for Atmospheric Research in Boulder, Colorado, and Christopher W. Landsea, of the National Oceanic and Atmospheric Administration's Hurricane Research Division in Miami, made an economic and meteorologi-cal study of hurricanes that have hit the United States since the 1920s and concluded that the 1926 Miami storm would cost $72 bil-lion if it struck today, taking into account increases in population and property values as well inflation. This is more than double the cost of Hurricane Andrew in 1992, by far the worst hurricane in United States history in terms of damage. Pielke and Landsea did not attempt to calculate the possible loss of life in their scenario.

As we might imagine, the story of the forecaster in Washington, D.C., who tossed off the hurricane warning as an afterthought gained wide circulation in Florida. As it had been after the Galve-ston storm of 1900, a quarter of a century earlier, focus was once again turned on the archaic system by which the Washington office issued all storm warnings. It also became widely known that *one fore-caster* handled everything in the office for a single day. All in all, residents of the hurricane-prone Gulf and East Coasts of the United States were beginning to get the feeling that their national Weather Bureau didn't take hurricanes seriously enough. A story that vividly illustrates this point was told by Gordon Dunn, who later became head of the National Hurricane Center. The story relates to a day in August 1933, but it was symptomatic of the situation that had been in effect for many years. Dunn was working at Weather Bureau head-quarters in Washington, plotting reports from weather stations. One evening he told the chief forecaster that the Cape Hatteras, North Carolina, station had reported what he thought was a significant fall in barometric pressure. The chief forecaster told Dunn to stick to drawing the map, and he, the forecaster, would do the forecasting. By the next morning the eye of a hurricane was over Norfolk, Virginia, with no warning at all from the Weather Bureau. During the day it traveled up the Chesapeake Bay to Washington, D.C., doing serious damage all of the way, all without warning.

Another incident helped persuade Congress to make changes. Before noon on a Sunday in August 1934, the Washington-based forecaster issued a hurricane warning for the upper Texas coast and then left the office. Since no new observations would be available to him until 7 P.M., he planned to return at that time to reevaluate the storm and issue new predictions. By that afternoon, the residents of Galveston saw no sign of a hurricane but were understandably skittish nevertheless. Finally the anxious chamber of commerce wired the Washington Weather Bureau demanding the latest information, and the conscientious individual who was plotting the map at the time wired back honestly but indiscreetly: "Forecaster on golf course—unable to contact." In his account of the incident, Dunn concluded, "In Galveston, the weather remained quiet, but temperatures in the chamber of commerce rose rapidly."

As it happened, the hurricane was a weak one and only sideswiped the Texas coast before turning back into the Gulf of Mexico to die, but that didn't dampen the increasingly strident demands for better work out of Washington. Finally, in 1935, Congress appropriated $80,000 to revamp the warning service. New hurricane forecast centers were set up in Jacksonville, Florida; New Orleans; Boston; and San Juan, Puerto Rico. These offices had the authority to issue warnings and also were instructed to issue bulletins on hurricanes four times a day, whether or not a warning was needed.

Grady Norton, who had worked for the Weather Bureau since 1915, was placed in charge of the Jacksonville office, the only truly complete hurricane center. The son of an Alabama farmer, Norton told a biographer that he hadn't been especially interested in hurricanes until one day in 1928 when he happened to arrive in West Palm Beach just as a mass funeral was being held for the victims of the September 16, 1928, hurricane that had pushed a mountainous pile of water out of Lake Okeechobee. This storm killed at least 1,836 people, most of whom drowned as the rising waters flooded their lakefront communities. Norton overheard a mourner comment that the victims would not have died if the Weather Bureau had given a timely warning. While the comment wasn't completely true—there had been some warning—Norton decided to devote his life to preventing such tragedies in the future. His assistant in the new Jacksonville office was Gordon Dunn, and the two of them covered all responsibilities, twenty-four hours a day, seven days a week.

Only a few months after Norton became the chief hurricane forecaster at the Jacksonville office, the strongest U.S. hurricane of the century hit the Florida Keys, on Labor Day, 1935. This disaster emphasized a fact of life that Norton and other forecasters would have to live with for years to come: lack of information. By that time, there were a number of reliable reporting stations scattered across Cuba, certainly—the Father Vines effect—and all around the Caribbean as well, but this treacherous storm didn't pass near any of them, and no ships made radio reports. Until the hurricane hit the Keys, the strongest winds that had been measured and reported were in the Bahamas, only 40 miles per hour.

The hurricane targeted Upper and Lower Matecumbe Keys, where three Civilian Conservation Corps (CCC) camps housed an estimated 695 World War I veterans who were building bridges for the Overseas Highway, which was to run alongside the Florida East Coast Railway all the way from the mainland to Key West. These veterans had been among the 15,000 "Bonus Marchers" who had set up camps in Washington, D.C., in the spring of 1932, at the beginning of the Depression, to demonstrate for the government bonus that had been promised veterans of World War I, which had concluded fourteen years earlier. On July 28, troops commanded by Gen. Douglas MacArthur, under orders from President Herbert Hoover, had violently driven the Bonus Marchers and their families from the capital. Smoke from the burning camps wafted across the city, and the widely condemned confrontation left a stain on the Hoover presidency and contributed to his defeat in the fall election. Determined not to make the same mistake when the marchers returned in 1933, the new president, Franklin Delano Roosevelt, welcomed them and provided accommodations at Fort Myer across the Potomac River. Their leaders met with Congress and secured an agreement with Roosevelt to transfer nearly 18,000 of the protesters to CCC camps in South Carolina and Florida.

As the 1935 Labor Day holiday weekend began, no one on the Keys had any reason to suspect anything abnormal in the offing. It was hot and humid, but that was a given in the Keys. On Sunday morning, 300 miles to the east over the southern Bahamas, a tropical storm was just growing into a hurricane—in a black hole between reporting stations on Nassau to the north and Cuba to the south. The Bureau had established a system of receiving four radio weather observations a day from ships during the hurricane season—routine data on air pressure and temperature as well as information on clouds, sea swell, water temperature—but if any ships encountered strong winds or anything else of note that day and the next, they failed to report them. On Monday, the Weather Bureau office in Jacksonville finally received enough data from some ships in the area, in addition to reports from Nassau and stations in Florida, to surmise that a storm was present, and announced that it was approaching the Keys from the south with possibly hurricane-force winds near the center—a weak storm.

Fortunately, the veterans working on the highway had received their monthly wage right before the holiday, and many were spending their money and enjoying the long weekend on the mainland. But at least 200 veterans, possibly many more, remained in the camps as the hurricane bore down. With the weather growing worse, Ray W. Sheldon, who was in charge of the three camps, arranged for the Florida East Coast Railway to send an eleven-car train to evacuate the men. But Sheldon miscalculated by more than three hours the time it would take to assemble the rescue train and get it all the way down to the southernmost camp on Lower Matecumbe Key. While waiting for the train, Sheldon and others had to abandon the crumbling station at Islamorada, near the northernmost of the camps, and seek shelter in a boxcar on a siding. In a congressional hearing the following year, he described how he ran to meet the doomed transport at 8:15 P.M., across rain-swept but otherwise dry ground. "As I reached the end of the boxcar," Sheldon continued, "the wind was sufficiently strong to blow me down. While I was crawling over to the locomotive, the [sea] water came over the rail. I am telling you this to show you how quickly it came up. As I got to the cab step and reached up for the handle, the water reached my waist."

The storm surge swept all cars but the locomotive and the tender from the track. Later, W. F. McDonald, of the Weather Bureau, wrote that the storm surge was so high across the Keys that the "track and cross ties of the railroad were in one stretch washed off a concrete viaduct 30 feet above ordinary water level." Waves no doubt aided in the destruction. Sheldon survived the night inside the locomotive, but the railroad itself, with more than forty miles of track washed out, was destroyed and never rebuilt.

J. E. Duane, a cooperative observer for the Weather Bureau in charge of a fishing camp on Long Key, wrote an account of his experience in the storm's center:

> About the middle of the lull, which lasted a timed 55 minutes, the sea began to lift up, it seemed, and rise very fast; this from the ocean side of the camp. I put my flashlight out on sea and could see walls of water which seemed many feet high. I had to race fast

to regain [the] entrance of [my] cottage, but water caught me waist deep, although I was only about 60 feet from [the] doorway of [the] cottage. Water lifted the cottage from its foundation and it floated.

Steady winds around the hurricane's core were estimated as high as 200 miles per hour—an extraordinarily tight, powerful storm. Engineering studies of the damage completed within weeks of the storm marked an area from Islamorada south to Lower Matecumbe Key—the zone on the dangerous semicircle side of the hurricane's eight-mile-wide eye—as likely having been raked by wind gusts well above 200 miles per hour. The total number of dead, including at least 160 CCC veterans, was estimated by the American Red Cross at 408. Shortly after the storm an article in the *Literary Digest* quoted Florida governor Dave Sholtz as decrying "great carelessness somewhere," but a hurried investigation ordered by FDR dismissed the tragedy as "an act of God." Ernest Hemingway saw it otherwise. The famous novelist, who knew the Keys well, wrote a controversial article for the *New Masses*, a radical weekly, titled "Who Murdered the Veterans?" In it Hemingway asked, "You're dead now, brother, but who left you there in the hurricane months on the Keys where a thousand men died before you in the hurricane months when they were building the road that's now washed out? Ignorance has never been accepted as an excuse for murder or for manslaughter."

Leaders of the Veterans of Foreign Wars and the American Legion joined the criticism and got a congressional investigation, which blamed Ray Sheldon and his superiors for botching the timely dispatch of the relief train, but the findings were effectively squashed and buried within the annals of the Veterans Administration. The veterans received their bonus in 1936, thanks to an act of God—the most powerful such act of God to strike the United States.

The main immediate factor behind the lack of early and accurate predictions of the Key West hurricane was a shortage of good data, and there was very little Grady Norton and his colleagues could do to rectify this situation anytime soon. Beyond the data problem, the larger theoretical problem for forecasters was understanding the role played by upper-air currents in the steering of, and interaction with, the great storms. Coming to grip with this issue would be the primary key to accurately forecasting the tracks of hurricanes and typhoons, possibly days in advance. William Redfield had implied as much almost a century earlier, when he suggested that his "whirlwinds" swept through the atmosphere like a little vortex, or like a chip of wood in a flowing stream. An understanding of the flowing stream of the atmosphere would lead to an understanding of any storm moving within it. The 1800s had passed with no progress, because there were no terms in which to even think about the problem. By the 1920s, however, meteorologists in the Weather Bureau were concentrating on the really big picture, and specifically on the role played in steering storms by large areas of high air pressure over the Atlantic Ocean and mainland North America.

In a 1924 issue of *Monthly Weather Review*, Weather Bureau meteorologist C. L. Mitchell had proposed that hurricanes tend to move north out of the tropics unless an area of high pressure blocks them—and it often does. Meteorologists of that era did recognize that during the summer and fall hurricane season, a large area of high air pressure called the "Bermuda High" (because it's often centered over Bermuda) dominates the western Atlantic Ocean. The location of this high, as well as other quasi-stationary highs around the globe, is determined by a complex interplay of other pressure systems and prevailing winds. The clockwise winds around this very large high-pressure area tend to steer the much smaller hurricane on the south side of the high to the west. As the storm reaches the southwestern side of the high pressure, the winds tend to steer it more to the north, and then finally back toward the northeast as the storm sweeps into the northern quadrant of the high. In effect, Atlantic storms coming west from the coast of Africa tend to make a big loop or circle around the dominating Bermuda High.

Sometimes the western edge of the high is over the eastern United States, sometimes it's offshore. If this edge is far off the East Coast, hurricanes are steered well east of the coast, perhaps as far east as Bermuda, as they make their northward journey. If this edge is far to the west, however, a hurricane may be steered westward through the Caribbean and then across Florida or the southeastern coast, or it might be pushed all the way into the Gulf of Mexico. Mitchell understood in rough terms this general picture of the importance of the Bermuda High. Of course, other weather systems moving across and along the edges of the mainland also affect hurricanes approaching the islands of the Caribbean and the United States, so the eventual track of any given storm is the result of a complex mix of steering forces at all levels within the troposphere, along with the actual structure of the storm itself and its interaction with the currents within which it is embedded. Forecasters of that era tried to factor in everything and make predictions for the following twelve to twenty-four hours, but it was dicey business, because they were stuck with incomplete measurements from the surface, few measurements at all from the upper atmosphere, and a still-limited understanding of how these systems interacted.

In the 1920s and '30s, it became immediately clear that the growth of aviation increased the need for upper-air data, and it was clear that such data would be helpful to all meteorologists, not just those making aviation forecasts. Earlier in the century the Weather Bureau had obtained a few upper-air measurements from recording instruments attached to huge kites, which flew as high as three or four miles. But these were expensive and hard to handle. Pilot balloons were the next advance, gathering information on cloud heights and upper-air winds. At first these balloons had no instruments; their value derived from the known rate at which they rose through the atmosphere. Today balloons are tracked by radar, but in those days observers tracked them with a stopwatch and a theodolite—a land surveyor's instrument that precisely measures horizontal and vertical angles—and came up with pretty good calculations of wind speeds and directions at various altitudes, as well as the height of the cloud base. Obviously, the balloons were grounded on days with a low cloud ceiling. Even on perfect days they didn't supply information for winds in the highest levels of the atmosphere, because that was too high for observers to see and follow. Soon the balloons were equipped with instruments and a radio transmitter to make a package called a radiosonde. For the first time, air temperature, humidity, and barometric pressure readings could be radioed down to receiving stations from higher altitudes. When the balloon burst, a small parachute floated the valuable instrument package to the ground, where it could often be retrieved.

A few airplanes also began recording some information, but such reconnaissance was expensive and sometimes dangerous. Real progress waited for the growth of Pan American Airways as the flagship airline for the United States in Latin America and across the Caribbean. It was a real boon to hurricane forecasters because Pan Am's stations made regular observations with pilot balloons, with all data forwarded to the Weather Bureau. By the beginning of World War II, grateful forecasters were receiving pilot balloon and other upper-air data from only six Weather Bureau or navy stations in Florida or around the Caribbean Sea, but from twenty-five or so Pan Am stations.

With the help of the new instruments, limited though they were, and the expanded network of reporting sites—mostly Pan Am stations—hurricane forecasters in the late 1930s began drawing maps of upper-air winds and using them for forecasts. Grady Norton was reputed to have made some remarkable forecasts of hurricane paths using these data. Probably the best-known among meteorologists was in October 1944, when he predicted, for internal purposes, that a hurricane then over the Caribbean Sea would hit Tampa Bay, Florida, at midnight forty-two hours later. And it did!

More often, hurricanes still managed to pull off some unpleasant surprises. The most notorious of these formed off the coast of Africa on September 10, 1938, gained strength as it crossed almost the entire Atlantic Ocean, became a hurricane on September 15, and topped out with winds estimated from ship reports at 160 miles per hour on September 19, when it was still east of the Bahamas. The storm had been inching just enough to the north as it crossed the Atlantic that it missed all of the islands of the Caribbean Sea, then a sharper turn to the north spared the Bahamas and the Outer Banks of North Carolina, which jut eastward into the ocean. This was good news for the islands and the southeastern coast, bad news for the Northeast. As the preceding description proves, Weather Bureau forecasters had kept in touch with the storm as it moved across the Atlantic, mostly with radio reports from ships, but as it rushed past the beaches of North Carolina and then the Middle Atlantic states on the morning of Wednesday, September 21, the forecasters at the Weather Bureau's Washington office couldn't keep up with it. The last observation arrived at the Bureau at 9 A.M., when the hurricane was 100 miles east of the Virginia–North Carolina border. After that, not a scrap of information was received. The five-column headline in the *New York Times* that morning read: "Britain, France Give Prague House to Submit on the Peril of Immediate German Attack; Czechs Are Declared Determined to Resist." On the following morning, the hurricane shared the front page with Europe's march toward World War II.

Moving twice as fast as normal for a higher-latitude hurricane, the eye reached the south shore of Long Island, New York, at 2:30 P.M., where a barograph (a barometer that keeps a continuous record of pressures) in Bellport recorded a central low pressure of 27.94 inches. A hurricane warning was issued at 3 P.M., but it was too late. Rapidly rising water and ferocious winds were already wrecking the beachfronts of Long Island, Rhode Island, southwestern Massachusetts, and Connecticut. Once inland, the 500-mile-wide storm brought fierce winds not experienced in New England since the hurricane of 1821, blowing down whole forests as far north as the White Mountains of New Hampshire and the Green Mountains of Vermont, leaving the land scoured and vulnerable to autumn wildfires. Seventeen inches of rain falling on ground that had already been soaked by rain for a week led to disastrous flooding, especially in the Connecticut River Valley.

By 9 P.M. the storm had roared across all of New England and passed into Canada — 300 miles in just six and a half hours. This forward speed of almost 50 miles per hour combined with winds of well over 100 miles per hour to yield truly extraordinary winds on the east side of the storm — the dangerous semicircle, of course. The observatory atop 600-foot Blue Hill southwest of Boston recorded a gust to 186 miles per hour. More than 600 people lost their lives. The price tag for the damage was $400 million, ranking it ahead of the 1926 Miami hurricane as the costliest in U.S. history at that time.

The following year the new chief of the Weather Bureau, Francis W. Reichelderfer, set out to improve hurricane warnings by increasing the number of land, sea, and upper-air observations. Reicheld-erfer instructed forecasters to issue hurricane advisories every six hours while a storm was at sea, and every hour if it approached any coastline. Reichelderfer also brought some of Europe's leading theo-retical meteorologists to the Weather Bureau. At the time, however, the Europeans were focused on middle latitude storms. The tropics were of little interest to them. In Cuba, Jose Carlos Millas was con-tinuing the tradition started by Father Vines in the previous century, but few of his journal articles were translated into English. In Sep-tember 1935 a typhoon caught several Japanese Navy ships conduct-ing an exercise east of Japan. The navy called off the exercise and all of the ships began collecting wind and wave observations. We can only imagine how such a flood of data might have spurred interest in hurricane science if it had been published in English in the 1930s. At the time, however, almost anything the Japanese Navy did was top secret, and the data weren't published until after World War II.

Grady Norton himself was a friendly man of the world, broadly educated, a student of the English language, and a master commu-nicator. This last trait was especially important for the nation's first chief hurricane forecaster and for all the others who have followed. As the era of mass communication took shape and forecasters were able to reach almost every citizen almost simultaneously, first over the radio, then on television, people had to trust the forecast and then respond. Norton set the standard, as described by Arva Moore Parks in her introduction to L. F. Reardon's *The Florida Hurricane and Disaster of 1926*. Parks had grown up in Miami, where Norton was known as "Mr. Hurricane." She writes,

> When I was a little girl, it seemed like hurricanes came every year, much like Christmas and my birthday. My father took them very seriously. As soon as he heard or read the word "hurricane," he set out the hurricane map and began tracking the storm. Everyone in my family knew that if "Mr. Hurricane" posted hurricane warnings, my father would metamorphose from a weatherman to a top ser-geant, galvanizing his wife and three children into a well-trained platoon of storm troopers.

Grady Norton (seated) considered to be the first Director of the National Hurricane Center. Norton specialized in hurricane forecasting from 1935 until his death during Hurricane Hazel in 1954.

Robert H. Simpson, a subsequent head of the Hurricane Center, wrote that Norton's greatest strength "was his ability to select precisely the right semantics and tone for his communications. . . . He was able to describe the hurricane, its location, and quality of threat to the complete reassurance of his constituents, and he did so as often as possible without indulging in explicit predictions of when and where—an omission rarely noticed. When the time for protective action came, however, he rang the bell loud and clear, and the public responded promptly."

Simpson was assigned to work with Norton because he had studied at the University of Chicago with some of the world's leading atmospheric scientists, and Reichelderfer wanted him to combine this solid background in meteorology with Norton's forecasting techniques and to publish details of the very latest methods. Simpson learned that Norton's basic model said that storms moved in the direction of the winds at the "top of the hurricane," and at a forward speed roughly 70 to 80 percent of the speed of those winds. But exactly how high were those highest winds, and what were they doing? For these answers, Simpson wrote later, Norton relied on "personal intuitive skill, which few of his associates could replicate objectively." Like Father Vines in Cuba, Norton just had the gift, the touch. The chief forecaster told his colleague: "Whenever I have a difficult challenge in deciding and planning where and when to issue hurricane warnings, I usually stroll out of the office onto the roof, put my foot on the parapet ledge, look out over the Everglades and say a little prayer. By the time I return to the office, the uncertainties are swept away and I know exactly what my decision will be."

CHAPTER 4

FLYING RECONNAISSANCE

M ETEOROLOGISTS HUNGRY for better information in the 1930s were dreaming about airborne reconnaissance. Like Henry Piddington, who had suggested sending ships into storms to study them almost a century before, they were frustrated by the restrictions imposed on their data gathering; even with radio reports from ships, hurricanes were sometimes difficult to locate. The value of upper-air data for all weather forecasting was well understood, but it was hard to get this information for storms. By the end of the '30s, balloons carried instruments aloft and radioed data back to Earth, but these balloons were shoved out of the way or shredded by storms. Airplanes had been used for routine data gathering, but bad weather grounded them. By 1940, with aircraft now much larger and stronger and with more powerful engines, forecasters began thinking aloud about the possibilities of sending pilots straight into hurricanes and typhoons. Unlike a ship, an airplane can cover an entire storm during a single flight. In 1941, in fact, the Weather Bureau sought governmental funding for this purpose. The Bureau of the Budget turned down the request and suggested that the forecasters solicit the army's or navy's support, but the approach of World War II and a shortage of military pilots spiked that notion.

Even if military pilots had been available as the war was breaking out, there would have been another problem: military pilots in those days were usually "contact" pilots, flying only in good, generally clear weather when they could stay in visual contact with the ground, using landmarks to find their way. They did not fly if they had to rely on their instruments for navigation. Today, pilots use the term "visual flight rules" (VFR) to describe such restrictions. More-over, navigating is almost the least of the problems when flying in clouds. A pilot who loses sight of the ground or doesn't have a clear horizon will quickly lose a sense of balance, a sense of up and down and which way the airplane is turning. To maintain control while fly-ing in clouds, the pilot has to rely on gyroscopic instruments—hence the term "instrument flying." One of the reasons the Army Air Corps did not emphasize instrument flying in the '30s was that budgets were tight in the Depression, and bad-weather and night flights requiring instruments were inherently riskier than contact flying. So even if they had been available to help the meteorologists, military pilots weren't really qualified to fly into storms, which definitely couldn't be accomplished without relying on instruments.

Help was on the way, however, in the form of a man named Joseph B. Duckworth, who earned his Army Air Corps pilot's wings and a reserve commission in 1928, but like most other reserve pilots had flown as a civilian, including ten years with Eastern Air Lines. While military fliers were restricted to contact work, commercial pilots navigated with radios that received signals from beacons on the ground. They developed techniques for flying in almost all weather and considered instrument flying almost routine. When Duckworth was called back to active military duty in 1940, he immediately understood that Air Corps pilots, trained only in contact flying, were not prepared for the coming war, which would not stop for bad weather. As director of training of the twin-engine flying school at Columbus, Mississippi, Duckworth worked out a new system to teach instrument flying, based on his airline experience. The acci-dent rate at the Mississippi base fell quickly, and Duckworth was soon charged with producing the Army Air Forces' first instrument-flying manual. He was also appointed commander of a new school at Bryan, Texas, which taught pilots to become instrument-flying instructors.

Duckworth was an authentic hero of World War II. The aviation writer Carroll V. Glines, who went through the instrument-instructor school in Texas when Duckworth was commanding offi-cer, says bluntly, "I think he saved thousands of lives by his encouragement and his training. He was responsible for a lot of people flying safely through a lot of weather." This contribution continued after the war as well, including during the Berlin Airlift in 1948 and '49, when Duckworth's students, and these students' students, "flew the Lift" day and night, through the clouds, fog, rain, and snow of a typical winter in northern Europe. Today, the air force presents its annual Col. Joseph B. Duckworth Instrument Award to "the unit or individual considered to have made the most significant contribution to the art or science of aerospace instrument flight in the preceding calendar year."

He was an unassuming man, not the Top Gun type at all. Glines remembers how Duckworth, now a colonel, would visit the flight line and chat with students and line personnel who maintained the airplanes. "He wore no rank on his flying suit and would sit casually with students waiting for their flights. At first, they were unaware of the identity of this slim, gray-haired, fatherly man who asked what they thought of the course and how it could be improved." Glines recalls one day when instruction had been called off because the weather was so bad you could barely see the runway *from* the runway. "I heard an airplane. It was Duckworth making a point. He was proving you could make instrument takeoffs even in that weather."

At breakfast on July 27, 1943, a group of British pilots with combat experience, students at the instrument-instructor school in Texas, overheard a conversation about the possibility of flying the base's AT-6 trainers to a base somewhere to the north, where they would be safe from an approaching hurricane. The AT-6, called the "Texan," was a single-engine, two-seat trainer less than thirty feet long, with a wingspan of forty-two feet. It was strong, built to survive ham-handed student pilots, and more than 15,000 were produced from 1941 through 1951. The British pilots had no idea what a hurricane was and began razzing Duckworth and the other Americans about how frail their trainers must be. Finally Duckworth had had enough of this teasing and bet the British pilots that he could fly an AT-6 into the hurricane and return. When the story is repeated among hurricane fliers even today, the bet is said to have been for highballs at the officers' club that night.

Duckworth asked Ralph O'Hair to go along as the navigator for this "experimental instrument flight." Because Duckworth didn't think that permission would be granted for the mission, he simply didn't ask. Unannounced, without fanfare of any kind, Duckworth and O'Hair became the first two men to fly into the heart of a hurricane—and they won their bet without any problem. Duckworth's mastery of instrument flying had prepared him, perhaps uniquely, for hurricane flying. This first-ever flight was, for him, simply one more in a series of flights in weather that had grounded less-qualified pilots. Returning to the base about two hours later, Duckworth and O'Hair matter-of-factly told the weather officer, First Lieutenant William Jones-Burdick, what they had done. Jones-Burdick promptly asked Duckworth to fly *him* into the hurricane.

On the first flight, neither Duckworth nor O'Hair made notes about the experience. On this second flight, both fliers did. Approaching the hurricane, which was now over land between Houston and Galveston, they encountered light-to-moderate turbulence, light-to-moderate static on their communication and navigation radios, and light-to-moderate rain. The references to the radio static probably helped justify this "experimental instrument flight." Then, for half an hour, very heavy rain and severe turbulence battered their little AT-6 before Duckworth broke into the storm's eye, and he and Jones-Burdick clearly saw the ground near Galveston Bay and the sun shining through the thin upper clouds. They circled around within the eye for fifteen minutes before heading west toward Houston, again running into moderate to severe turbulence and heavy rain. Their thermometer indicated that the eye of the storm at their altitude of about 7,000 feet was 73 degrees Fahrenheit, which was about 25 degrees warmer than the temperature at the same altitude outside the storm. Meteorological theory held that the eye of the storm should be warmer than the surrounding air at higher altitudes, but this was the first real measurement that confirmed the theory.

Word spread rapidly, because this flight was a dream come true for meteorologists. Francis W. Reichelderfer saw the great value of such observations and immediately wrote Duckworth and Jones-Burdick, asking about their observations and requesting permission to publish their reports. The Bureau chief was particularly interested in the large temperature difference recorded. In their response, Duckworth and Jones-Burdick verified their measurement, but it's now believed that the difference of 25 degrees must have been incorrect. It was too large; heavy rain had probably cooled the thermometer probe outside the AT-6 trainer. (One of the early challenges for airplane reconnaissance was developing instruments that would stay calibrated in storms and give accurate readings.) Duckworth and Jones-Burdick added, "It is to be regretted that the flight was not planned to satisfy a larger objective than our personal curiosity. We hope . . . that another opportunity may soon present itself for a more careful study."

Joseph Duckworth got his wish. Within a year, developments in both the Pacific theater, where the U.S. Navy was learning that typhoons could be as dangerous as the Japanese Navy, and along the Gulf and Atlantic Coasts, where hurricanes endangered navy ships and slowed civilian war production, motivated leaders to make airborne hurricane reconnaissance a standard weapon in the forecaster's arsenal. But the price paid for that motivation was high indeed.

On December 16, 1944, the U.S. Navy's Third Fleet, commanded by Admiral William F. "Bull" Halsey, headed east after supporting the U.S. invasion of the Philippines. The ships needed to refuel and take on supplies from cargo ships and tankers, and for this job of transferring supplies and fuel with the ships running alongside one another, they needed to be out of range of the Japanese airplanes based in the Philippines. So the rendezvous was scheduled for the middle of the ocean. But nothing worked out; every move that Halsey made over the next two days seemed to be the wrong one. Early on the morning of the 17th, Commander George F. Kosco, Halsey's meteorologist, advised the admiral of a "storm" well to the east and likely to turn north. Halsey therefore kept the fleet on its southeasterly course toward the proposed refueling area, safely out of harm's way, he believed. However, the forecast was wrong. The Third Fleet was steaming directly toward an intensifying typhoon. Over the following twenty-four hours, Halsey ordered several other course changes and new rendezvous points, only to end up sending many of his ships into the core of the typhoon, with sixty-foot waves and sustained winds estimated at higher than 145 miles per hour, with probable gusts to 185. It was not unusual for anemometers to blow out in the wind, but it was unknown for a barometer to bottom out. One of the barometers with the Third Fleet did. The best estimate for that typhoon was a pressure of 26.30 inches of mercury. It was a true monster.

C. Raymond Calhoun, commanding officer of the USS *Dewey*, a destroyer that survived the worst of the typhoon, describes the storm and its aftermath in his excellent account, *Typhoon: The Other Enemy*. By 11 A.M. on the 18th, the barometer on the *Dewey*'s bridge read 28.84 inches of mercury after dropping half an inch in the previous hour. "The wind's voice had become a wild howl," Calhoun

Radar image of the typhoon that hit Admiral Halsey's Third Fleet in December of 1944. Captured by a navy ship east of the Philippines, this was the second tropical storm ever to be observed on radar.

writes. "Above the din of the main gale were the higher-pitched sounds of the frequent and prolonged gusts. They were raging and overwhelming in their intensity. An octave or two higher were the screeching notes of our rigging and guy wires. It was hell's chorus, and we had to yell to each other at the top of our lungs to make ourselves heard above it."

Calhoun's worst fear was every mariner's worst fear, that his ship would roll past the point of no return and capsize, and he had a better than usual cause for concern with this ship: tests a few months before had shown that the *Dewey* and other destroyers of the Farragut class were not as stable as destroyers of other classes. Despite those results, radar antennas and other equipment had been added to high parts of the ship, making it even more likely to capsize. In theory, the *Dewey* could roll to a maximum of 72 degrees and remain upright. Before noon on the 18th, Calhoun writes, "we were going over consistently to 68 and 70 degrees. With each roll as I watched the inclinometer go farther and farther, I would dispatch a silent prayer, 'Dear God, please make her come back!' " Each time the destroyer rolled, the air intake on the deck that fed fresh air to the furnaces swallowed as much as 1,000 gallons of water and spit it into the fire rooms. Calhoun watched as the inclinometer on the bridge registered its highest number on the instrument, 75 degrees, which should have put the ship and its sailors into the sea. Yet the *Dewey* recovered.

By noon, the *Dewey*'s barometer was down to 28.10 inches of mercury, the waves were more than sixty feet high, and the winds were howling at a steady 115 miles per hour, with higher gusts. As the ship rolled, the officers and enlisted men on the bridge

had to grab a vertical stanchion, or some similar piece of the ship's structure and hang on for dear life. Many times I found myself hanging by my hands, with feet completely clear of the deck, in such a position that if I released my hold, I would drop straight down, through the starboard pilot house window into the sea. Several times I looked past my dangling feet, and saw the angry sea through the open window, directly below them.

By 6 P.M. that day, the *Dewey* emerged from the worst of the storm, and later that evening it joined other ships in searching for survivors from the vessels that had sunk. Eventually, ninety-eight men were found alive in the water. The Third Fleet's losses included three destroyers capsized and sunk, numerous other ships heavily damaged, and 146 planes on aircraft carriers destroyed when they broke loose and slid across decks, sometimes starting fires when their fuel tanks split. The storm killed 778 men, the largest U.S. Navy loss in a single day since November 24, 1943, when Japanese bombers had sunk the escort carrier *Lipscombe Bay*, killing 650 men.

In a long letter to the Pacific Fleet, Admiral Chester W. Nimitz, the theater commander in chief, commented: "It is possible that too much reliance is being placed on outside sources for warnings of dangerous weather, and on the ability of our splendid ships to come through anything that wind and wave can do. If this be so, there is need for a revival of the age-old habits of self-reliance and caution in regard to the hazard from storms." Nimitz concluded the letter: "There is no little red light which is going to flash on and inform commanding officers or higher commanders that from then on there is extreme danger from weather, and that measures for ships' safety must now take precedence over further efforts to keep up with the formation or to execute the assigned task."

The navy conducted a court of inquiry, of course, in which it was learned that an airplane had located the storm at nearly typhoon strength early on December 17, after "Bull" Halsey's meteorologist George Kosco had predicted that the storm should have diverted to the north. But weather messages had a low priority on the limited radio circuits available, and Kosco didn't receive the updated information for several hours.

Halsey: "I did not have timely warning. I'll put it another way. I had no warning."

Question from the court: "What seemed to be wrong with the weather service in this case?"

Halsey: "It was nonexistent!"

The court concluded that "the preponderance of responsibility for the [catastrophe] falls on Commander Third Fleet, Admiral William

F. Halsey. . . . In analyzing the mistakes, errors and faults . . . the court classifies them as errors in judgment under stress of war operations and not as offenses." The court made ten recommendations to help prevent any future such disaster. One of them stated that "weather ships should be stationed in the area to supplement the present weather system; and that at least two planes daily be designated as weather reconnaissance planes, to cover sectors where unusual weather was suspected."

Halsey made even stronger recommendations, which were probably the basis for his later statement that "we established a system so that such a thing couldn't happen again." Unfortunately, those sound recommendations were not implemented, and his own statement came back to haunt Halsey a few months later. It was May 1945, and the admiral, after a short time in Washington and at Pearl Harbor, had returned as commander of the Third Fleet, then operating near Okinawa. Despite the court of inquiry and the admiral's own recommendations months earlier, regular aircraft reconnaissance had *not* been started. Fleet commanders were sending out airplanes as they saw fit. Then, on June 2 and 3, navy forecasters decided that a typhoon was forming and should track near, if not directly over, Okinawa. George Kosco, still Halsey's fleet meteorologist, analyzed all of the reports and determined that the Third Fleet was not in immediate danger. He recommended against issuing a typhoon warning, but Halsey heeded the other forecasts, issued an "alert" anyway, and decided to get out of the way of the storm. He did not want to go west, where waters were shallow, maneuverability was limited, and Japanese kamikaze pilots could attack his ships, so he set the fleet's course generally eastward, expecting that the typhoon would therefore pass well to the west.

Also in the area was the *Ancon,* an amphibious operations command ship that had joined the Third Fleet after being fitted with the latest radar and other electronic equipment. The *Ancon* soon located the storm far south and *east* of its forecast position, heading on a track that would intercept the fleeing navy fleet. The *Ancon* changed its own course and disseminated the new location and storm track to all interested parties. But wartime practice dictated that all messages be coded, which meant they had to be decoded by those receiving them. This delay cost the Third Fleet five hours of warning—a critical loss of time. For the second time in seven months, a typhoon smashed into the Third Fleet on the open seas, with fifty- to sixty-foot seas, a central pressure of 28.30 inches, and sustained winds of about 115 miles per hour, with probable gusts to 150. Thirty-three ships were damaged, seventy-six planes destroyed, and six lives lost.

Halsey found himself squarely behind the eight ball this time. He immediately complained that early warning messages had been garbled, critical reports delayed by coding regulations, estimated typhoon conditions at bewildering variance, and predictions of the typhoon's course simply wrong. He repeated his recommendations for the creation of regular weather reconnaissance squadrons. Probably in response to Halsey's angry letter, the navy ordered seven bases from Eniwetok Atoll westward to each have three aircraft ready for weather reconnaissance flights as needed. Meanwhile, Admiral Nimitz was incensed by this second typhoon incident and convened a second court of inquiry into "Halsey's typhoons," as they were soon known throughout the navy. The court eventually recommended that Halsey be relieved of command, but this action was not taken. No disciplinary action was taken. In fact, after the furor subsided, President Truman even promoted Halsey to five-star rank, lauding his relentless pursuit of the enemy following the surprise attack on Pearl Harbor. "Bull" Halsey was a national hero, and "Halsey's typhoons" were forgiven if not forgotten.

Tropical storms were playing havoc with the war effort on the homefront as well. The very hurricane that Joseph Duckworth had used to demonstrate the reliability of his AT-6 trainer had seriously damaged the huge refinery of the Humble Oil and Refining Company at Baytown, Texas, where wind gusts of 132 miles per hour were recorded. The nation's leading supplier of aviation fuel suspended operations until repairs could be made. Production was also suspended at refineries in Texas City and Deer Park, Texas. The government censored news of this damage to the war machine and took immediate steps to assure better warnings in the future. In February 1944, the Joint Chiefs of Staff approved a plan for hurricane reconnaissance over the Atlantic Ocean, the Caribbean, and the Gulf of Mexico by Army Air Forces and navy aircraft with Grady Norton, chief of a joint military-civilian weather center in Miami, given the authority to order such flights. Early in that 1944 hurricane season several flights were made into tropical storms, and then on July 17 Captain Allan C. Wiggins piloted his aircraft into the eye of a hurricane between Bermuda and the southeastern U.S. coast. Since Duckworth had been flying without authorization a year earlier, Wiggins's flight was the first "authorized" flight into the eye of a hurricane.

On September 10 of that year, a navy plane flew from Puerto Rico into a storm 250 miles north of that island, the first of many navy and Army Air Forces flights into the storm now known as the "Great Atlantic Hurricane of 1944"—their work gave forecasters the most detailed real-time knowledge of a storm that had been compiled until that time. After it was first spotted north of Puerto Rico, the hurricane began a slow turn toward the north, which kept it off the mainland and all but its outer fringes also away from the Bahamas. But during the night beginning September 12, when it was centered about 300 miles east of Cape Canaveral, Florida, with winds well above 100 miles per hour, the storm sank the USS *Warrington*, a destroyer, with a loss of 247 men. Sixty-eight crewmen survived to be picked up by other ships. The hurricane continued turning slowly toward the north as it neared the Outer Banks of North Carolina, passing east of Cape Hatteras, where the weather office recorded winds of 90 miles per hour. In these seas the storm capsized two coast guard cutters: the *Jackson*, from which twenty of forty-four crewmen survived, and the *Bedloe*, from which only twelve of forty-eight crewmen survived. After clipping the Outer Banks, the hurricane's center stayed offshore until it finally made landfall over the eastern end of Long Island, New York, passed over Rhode Island—where it sank the coast guard's *Vineyard Sound* lightship, killing all seventeen aboard—and finally moved back out to sea north of Boston.

The Great Atlantic Hurricane of 1944 caused about $1 billion worth of damage (in adjusted dollars) and killed fifty people on land from North Carolina to New England, but these figures would have been much worse without the timely forecasts from the Weather Bureau, which were widely hailed as a breakthrough for hurricane forecasting. Much of the credit was given to the military planes that flew into the storm from the time it was first spotted until it struck Long Island five days later. *Time* magazine had its metaphor machine cranking at full speed when it reported that "hour after hour, radio stations from Delaware to Maine cried the alarm, like pygmies running ahead of a mad elephant. The people listened to the loudspeakers. Families were evacuated from coastal areas where people had been trapped in 1938." (That date referred to the hurricane that had hit Long Island and New England six years earlier, with virtually no warning, killing 600.)

The military was now convinced of the utility of reconnaissance flights to help its forecasters determine a storm's exact strength and location. The Weather Bureau shared that conviction and also knew the value of research flights to aid in the understanding of storms. In 1960 the military turned over responsibility for all research flights to a civilian Hurricane Research Program within the Weather Bureau. Military flights continued to collect data on specific storms for forecasters. The early civilian fleet had three planes: two piston-engine DC-6's leased from Trans Caribbean Airways and a B-57A, the air force jet bomber. In 1975 the two DC-6's were replaced by the two Lockheed WP-3D turboprops that still fly into hurricanes as part of the National Oceanic and Atmospheric Administration's (NOAA) Aircraft Operations Center, now located at MacDill Air Force Base in Tampa, Florida. All of those were and are strong aircraft, but the danger that cyclones pose for planes is not nearly as great as bystanders might imagine. (Henry Piddington's nineteenth-century proposal to send ships into storms to study them wasn't really a good idea because the last place you want to be during a tropical cyclone is on the turbulent water itself. He would have been astonished to find out that the best and safest place in a typhoon is in the turbulent *sky*.)

In the early days, neither scientists nor pilots knew very much about hurricane conditions at altitudes above the ocean. They had no idea how much turbulence to expect up there, how hard the rain would be, or whether wind speeds were higher or lower than on the surface. They soon learned that flow in cyclones is primarily *horizontal* to the surface, because the storms are so well-organized around a central core. Pilots think of their airplane as just part of the air, going with the flow. When the flow is horizontal, no matter what the velocity, the plane is in no real danger. Airliner pilots routinely fly in jet streams blowing 100 miles per hour or even higher when the stream is going where they want to go. They try to avoid the streams that are flowing toward them, but not because of any danger. The danger to aircraft is found in violent updrafts and downdrafts, and these are much more likely in powerful thunderstorms than in tropical cyclones, except in the large thunderstorms that make up a hurricane's eye wall, and from time to time in the generally weaker thunderstorms of a hurricane's rain bands. This is why the pilots and crews of hurricane hunters resolutely refuse to fly into Midwestern thunderstorms, when, from time to time, they take part in other kinds of weather research. Inside hurricanes, they use their onboard radar to avoid the areas of heaviest rain and the boundaries marking quick changes in rainfall intensity, where they are most likely to fly into intense updrafts and downdrafts.

In the early years, military pilots, especially navy pilots, flew into typhoons and hurricanes at very low altitudes that left little margin for error—only a few hundred feet above the ocean. Today's military and civilian crews don't fly that low, and it is amazing that the endeavors were as successful in the early days as they were. Still, hurricane flying was never a *reckless* enterprise, even in its infancy. The fliers were well schooled in the Joseph Duckworth tradition of flying into—and safely out of—all kinds of bad weather.

Occasionally, however, these reconnaissance flights can be rough—and scary. Bob Sheets (coauthor of this book) was on such a flight on the afternoon of October 16, 1968. Seventeen men were onboard a DC-6, flying from Miami International Airport into Hurricane Gladys over the Gulf of Mexico to investigate the theory that seeding the inner band of thunderstorms around the eye wall could reduce the strength of a hurricane. In order to make this determination, the crew would fly *along* rather than across these lines of clouds at an altitude just above the freezing level, about 19,000 feet above the ocean. This flight plan did entail more risk than the usual one, not only because the plane would be in the zone of maximum turbulence but also because it might encounter considerable icing.

Nothing drags a plane out of the sky faster than ice on the wings, which dramatically reduces the lifting force of the wings. But the flight down the eye wall was relatively smooth, with manageable ice buildup on the airplane's wings and fuselage. After three hours, everyone began to relax. Harlan Davis, the flight director, who acted as coordinator between the crew and the scientists, decided to descend and locate the exact center of the hurricane, measure its central pressure as well as the wind speed around the eye, and transmit the data back to the National Hurricane Center. Research flights routinely perform this basic reconnaissance service for the forecasters.

Most of the passengers had unhooked their seat belts and were checking equipment, unloading and reloading film canisters, and taking care of other routine tasks. Sheets, who was in charge of the flight's research, had returned to the primary scientific station, just behind the door to the cockpit, and had not fastened his seat belt. Harry Hawkins, deputy director of the National Hurricane Research Laboratory, was leaning over a work table about two-thirds of the way back in the cabin, talking with two reporters. Frank Noromoto, the camera technician, was in the back of the aircraft replacing film magazines in the side-looking cameras.

Without warning, the DC-6 bucked upward with enough force to pin everyone to his seat, if he were in a seat. Flattened onto the table, Hawkins locked his arms around it. The upward acceleration hesitated, and Sheets quickly fastened his seat belt. The airplane then accelerated upward again for a second or two before hitting a violent downdraft. All loose objects and many strapped-down objects as well—including heavy film magazines, oxygen bottles, and fire extinguishers—crashed against the top of the cabin. It was as if the aircraft had been turned upside down and shaken violently. In the back of the plane, Noromoto was thrown against the ceiling. The table was ripped from Hawkins's grasp; he crashed against the ceiling, bending a shelf with his shoulder and denting the top of the cabin with his head. The plane plunged almost 1,000 feet in four seconds.

With the first upward lurch, John McCann, the pilot, had simply locked his arms on to the armrests of his seat, firmly gripping the yoke. From this position, outwardly calm but churning inside, he simply rode with the action while trying to keep the aircraft level. When the plane bounced against the bottom of the severe downdraft, everything pinned against the ceiling crashed to the floor. Fortunately, because the top of the cabin was curved, all of the objects had been pushed to the highest point, so when they crashed to the floor, most fell in the aisle rather than on the people seated on each side. Film canisters, oxygen bottles, fire extinguishers, papers, pencils, briefcases, maps, rulers, notebooks, coffee cups, and spilled coffee littered the cabin. Hawkins got off with a severely sprained ankle, no broken bones. In the back of the plane, however, Noromoto wasn't so lucky. He landed on top of the tube used to drop packages of weather instruments from the airplane, severely injuring his back. To make matters worse, one of the film canisters smashed his face, breaking his nose, knocking teeth out, and, it was feared at the time, fracturing his jaw. Noromoto was bleeding profusely.

In the cockpit, McCann gently eased the aircraft out of its descent as the severe plunge ended. The radar systems were still working, and the crew used them to find a way out of the hurricane with as little turbulence as possible, since they didn't know whether the aircraft itself had suffered structural damage. All onboard were watching the wings to make sure they were still in place and weren't buckling. McCann radioed home base in Miami about their condition and was given a straight-in landing priority at Miami International. Fire engines and rescue equipment were waiting beside the runway as McCann brought the aircraft down on a smooth, gentle landing. A coast guard helicopter lifted Frank Noromoto to the emergency room for treatment. He eventually received a disability retirement because of the injuries in those terrifying few seconds. After X-ray inspection showed that the DC-6 hadn't suffered structural damage, it returned to hurricane flying.

That plane was fortunate to escape from the hazards of Hurricane Gladys, but almost all research and reconnaissance flights are successfully conducted without any kind of close encounter with tragedy. There have been, however, four fatal exceptions.

The first was on October 26, 1952. A WB-29—the weather reconnaissance version of the World War II B-29 "Superfortress" bomber—flying from the air force's 514th Very Long Range Weather Reconnaissance Squadron on Guam was lost while flying into Typhoon Wilma 350 miles east of Leyte in the Philippines. At the time, Wilma was a super typhoon with winds between 150 and 160 miles per hour; it hit the Philippines the next day with 130-mile-per-hour winds. The last radio message from the airplane said, "Eye very close. Radar burned out. Trying for low-level fix. Getting rough." The airplane's last reported position was about twenty-five miles from the forecast position of the eye, and certainly within the typhoon's strongest winds. Searches conducted for two weeks by U.S. Air Force and Philippine Navy ships found no trace of the missing airplane, not even an oil slick on the ocean. Crew members lost with the airplane were Sterling J. Harrell, the aircraft commander; Clifton R. Knickmeyer, pilot; William P. Burchell, navigator; Frank Pollack, also a navigator; Donald M. Baird, weather officer; Alton B. Brewton, flight engineer; Edward H. Fontaine, radio man; Tony J. Fasullo, also a radio man; Rodney E. Verrill, weather technician; and William Colgan, spotter. The air force's accident investigation report stated that Harrell "was a senior pilot with over 5,000 hours of flying time. Most of the squadron has the feeling that if any individual in the squadron were able to bring at least part of his crew safely through such an experience as this, Major Harrell is that man."

Robert Mann, a mechanic with the Very Long Range Weather Reconnaissance Squadron and the author of a history of the WB-29 storm flights, says, "I'm sure they hit the low-level cloud wall and the turbulence got them or the airplane came apart." For Mann and others in the Guam-based squadron, flying into typhoons was considered just another job. He and others who weren't regular flight crew members often volunteered to go on flights as spotters, especially on flights that would land elsewhere, because it was a way to get off their own island. A year before the tragedy with Typhoon Wilma, he had a seat on the airplane that flew into Typhoon Joan and then landed at the base on Kwajalein Island. The date was May 7, 1951. That crew didn't know that a series of atmospheric nuclear weapon tests code-named "Operation Greenhouse" had just been conducted on Eniwetok Atoll. "The typhoon turned out to be radioactive!" Mann exclaims. "We didn't know we were radioactive until we landed.

There was a guy in a silver suit with a Geiger counter. It started click-ing and they told us to take a long shower, that was all."

What did the spotter on these early reconnaissance flights do? "He was usually a ground crewman who sat there and made sure no one stole the number three engine," Mann jokes. "He watched for oil leaks, and they did leak." The huge piston engines that powered B-29's and other World War II–era airplanes were not as reliable as today's jet and turboprop engines and sometimes broke down in flight; sometimes they even caught fire.

The year after the Superfortress went down in Typhoon Wilma, General Thomas S. Moorman, head of the air force's Air Weather Service, ordered his pilots to maintain an altitude of at least 10,000 feet in all future typhoon and hurricane flights, but the navy contin-ued flying at low altitudes. Two years later, a navy P-2V-5F Neptune disappeared inside Hurricane Janet on the morning of September 26, 1955. The rapidly intensifying hurricane, with winds estimated at 160 miles per hour, was centered in the Caribbean Sea about 200 miles south of Jamaica and moving steadily west. At 8:30 A.M. EST, the airplane reported that it was about to penetrate the storm's main core at 700 feet above the ocean. No further report was ever received, and no wreckage was ever found. Grover B. Windham was the airplane commander. It was his first season as a hurricane pilot. The copilot, George W. Herlong, was in his second year in the squadron. The two navigators were Thomas Greaney and Thomas R. Morgan. The flight aerologist was William A. Buck, who had just qualified as a weather expert on hurricane flights. Joseph P. Wind-ham was in charge of maintenance on the aircraft and flew on its missions. The radio operator was Joseph F. Combs. Julius J. Mann provided onboard radio maintenance, and the navy photographer was Kenneth H. Klegg.

Two journalists were also on board: Alfred O. Tate, a reporter for the *Toronto Daily Star,* and his photographer, John D. Cronk. Both had served in World War II with the Canadian armed forces. The *Star* subsequently reported that the two men had been switched from another airplane only fifteen minutes before the fatal flight. The two Canadians were covering these hurricane flights because the previous year Hurricane Hazel, which had come ashore near Myrtle Beach, South Carolina, had remained an intense storm all the way north, crossing Lake Ontario into Canada, where its wind and floods killed sixty-nine people around Toronto. Suddenly, these cataclysms that had been so remote to Canadians now seemed important enough for the *Star* to dispatch two staffers to the Caribbean.

With no wreckage to study, the cause of the navy accident was never officially determined, but those who flew in the P-2V squadron had some theories. H. J. "Walt" Walter, who was a pilot in the squadron at the time, notes that the plane that went down in Hurricane Janet was an early model with a weaker wing design than later models. If the pilots had not been able to burn the fuel in the tanks on the ends of the wings, the extra weight at the wingtip could have caused one or both to break in severe turbulence. Or one of the two piston engines could have failed. While twin-engine airplanes can fly on one engine, that would have been nearly impossible only 700 feet above the ocean, maybe less, and in a strong hurricane. Later models of the P-2V had auxiliary jet engines in addition to the two piston engines. Walter suggests that if the plane had been the later model, maybe the pilots "could have lit off the jets and gotten out of there. But with one engine out close to the ocean, that would have been difficult."

Sometimes downdrafts pushed the navy pilots to within 250 feet of the unforgiving water. "At that altitude," Walter says, "you can't tell the water from the sky." One pilot would concentrate on using the flight instruments and the radar altimeter to keep the airplane level and at least 500 feet above the ocean. The other pilot would watch outside the airplane. "Sometimes we'd come back and the mechanics would empty seawater from the distributors on the engine." Fortunately, the engines kept running even with seawater blown into them.

The next fatal accident was back in the Pacific Ocean. On January 15, 1958, a WB-50—the weather reconnaissance version of the B-50 bomber—from the 54th Weather Reconnaissance Squadron based on Guam was lost at sea during a flight into Super Typhoon Ophe-

A WB-50 airplane used as a Hurricane Hunter in the Pacific and Atlantic from 1955 until the mid-1960s.

lia, southwest of Guam. During the briefing before taking off, the crew, headed by Albert Lauer, Jr., was told that the storm was "extremely hazardous." Reports from the last airplane to fly into the storm had reported "extreme turbulence." At one point an updraft in the eye wall of the typhoon had lifted that WB-50 from 10,000 to 17,000 feet within minutes. Severe clear-air turbulence was also reported within the eye. Given that ominous report, Lauer was told not to try to fly into the typhoon's eye, but to probe it by radar from the outer fringes. No problems were ever reported from the airplane. Everything was deemed normal—for a typhoon—before the radio lapsed into silence. An extensive air and sea search began ninety minutes after the airplane's last report, when a regular report was overdue. Again, no trace of the airplane or its crew was found. In addition to Albert Lauer, Jr., those aboard the WB-50 were Clyde W. Tefertiller, copilot; Courtland Beeler, III, navigator; Paul J. Buerkle, Jr., also a navigator; Delivan L. Gordon, electronics technician; Kenneth L. Tetzloff, flight engineer; Kenneth Houseman, radio operator; Randolph C. Watts, also a radio operator; and Bernard G. Tallgren, weather technician.

It was sixteen years before the next, and most recent, fatal hurricane flight, on October 12, 1974, when an air force WC-130 attached to the 54th Weather Reconnaissance Squadron on Guam went down in Typhoon Bess over the South China Sea. After taking off from Clark Air Force Base in the Philippines, planning to fly the entire mission at 10,000 feet, the airplane's crew reported no problems at any time. They had flown through the eye and were flying around the edge of the storm when they made their last radio report. Search airplanes picked up a signal from an automatic crash-position-indicator in the South China Sea about 470 miles northwest of Clark. The first planes on the scene after the weather cleared reported seeing what appeared to be seat cushions, insulation, and portable oxygen bottles floating in the ocean, but nothing else. Five days after the airplane disappeared, the air force declared all members of the crew lost at sea. They were Gary W. Cass, aircraft commander; Michael P. O'Brien, copilot; Timothy J. Hoffman, navigator; Edward R. Bushnell, weather officer; Kenneth G. Suhr, flight engineer; and Detlef W. Ringler, weather observer.

In the Pacific Basin, three flying accidents in typhoons have claimed twenty-five lives, none since 1974. In the Atlantic Basin, one accident in 1955 claimed eleven lives. This is a remarkably good record.

When the navy P-2V went down with eleven aboard in Hurricane Janet in September 1955, the navy was just beginning to switch its hurricane reconnaissance flights from that worthy plane to the even worthier WC-121 Lockheed Super Constellation. This three-tailed airplane with four huge piston engines represented the height of airline glamour in the 1950s and '60s, and it was only enhanced by the publicity surrounding the novel hurricane flights, especially along the Gulf and East Coasts. And soon enough—on August 23, 1964, to be exact—one of these airplanes got the opportunity to show the world that the "Super Connie" was as rugged as it was glamorous.

On that day, one of the Super Constellations with the code name "Snowcloud One" headed out from its base at Guantanamo, Cuba, bound for Hurricane Cleo, a small but intense storm centered about 100 miles south of the western end of Puerto Rico. With its wingtip fuel tanks fully loaded, Walter Reese, the commander, and his co-pilot, Don Edgren, headed for the storm at typical reconnaissance altitude for the navy at that time, 500 to 1,000 feet above the ocean.

As the plane drove into the hurricane's core, the crew reported the jolts of "washboard" turbulence that are normal in high winds at altitudes less than 1,500 feet. As the airplane entered the edge of the eye wall, Frank Morgan, the onboard meteorologist, reported that wind speeds had increased to 125 miles per hour. The washboard turbulence increased, blurring the cockpit instruments. Edgren, who was at the controls, struggled to keep the airplane level. He and his commander, Reese, tried making several turns to get out of the severe turbulence and into the storm's calm center. But they could not find the center, so Reese decided to leave the storm. His radar operator, Ron Walker, told him to head toward the southeast, which both theory and Walker's radar predicted should be the storm's "softest" area—the lightest rain and probably the smoothest ride. No sooner had Reese put the plane on the new heading when a heavy jolt knocked out the radar. Now the crew was blind in the strongest part of the hurricane, which was heaving their airplane up and down without respite.

Desmond Phelan, the third pilot on board, was watching the wings "flex hard" with the heavy fuel tanks at their tips. Unfortunately, the pilots had failed to burn off all the fuel in these wingtip tanks before flying into the storm, as standard practice called for. The wings of the Super Connie were designed to handle this wingtip load under reasonable flight conditions, but Cleo was a hurricane, not a cumulus cloud. Then Phelan was astonished to see the left wingtip tank yanked completely off by the winds, leaving the outer end of the wing torn apart and spewing fuel. The weight of the fuel in the other wingtip tank now threw the aircraft radically off balance, and it spontaneously banked sharply to the right. Edgren and Reese fought the controls, adding power to the right engines, trying to raise that wing, preparing to dump fuel to balance the load. Suddenly they felt a second jolt even stronger than the first one, followed by a wild plunge toward the sea. This turbulence ripped radios, toolboxes, and other gear from the straps that held them down. In the rear of the cabin, Morgan was torn from his seat belt and flung to the ceiling. Radar man John Lewis, his seat belt broken, found himself pinned to the ceiling. Technician Jim Kieffer, grabbing a table, had the end of his finger cut off as he was hurled to the ceiling. When the downdraft relented some seconds later, Kieffer was thrown violently to the floor and landed on meteorologist Norman Putrite, whose arm was broken.

Things looked bad, but now the crew caught an ironically good break when the *right* wingtip tank broke loose, helping to balance the airplane. The plane was still flying, but in questionable condition, just a few hundred feet above the ocean in the core of the hurricane, with the radar dead and with three crew members seriously injured. As the pilots contemplated ditching in the stormy water, the radio operator issued a distress call. Fortunately, the radio was still working: shore stations and other airplanes heard the Mayday message. Two U.S. Weather Bureau DC-6 research aircraft happened to be on their way to the hurricane from Curaçao in the Netherlands Antilles when they picked up the call, and they instantly asked Snowcloud One to turn on its transponder, a radio that sends out a signal used to enhance the image of an airplane on distant radars. The two DC-6's picked up the transponder signals and located the crippled navy plane on the south side of the hurricane, and they came up with a plan. One of them would fly into the storm at a low level to try to see the distressed plane, while the other plane would stay higher, monitoring the transponder signals from the navy aircraft and the Weather Bureau plane. A member of its crew would act as an air-traffic controller to make sure the two lower airplanes didn't collide.

The crews aboard the two low-altitude airplanes disagree about whether they ever actually saw each other. Either way, the Weather Bureau DC-6 finally caught up with the navy aircraft, which had lost its way and was now on the more dangerous north side of Cleo. The

Radar image from a Weather Bureau DC-6 aircraft recorded at 09:52 A.M. AST on August 23, 1964. Superimposed is the track of a navy WC-121 flight (Snowcloud) which suffered damage in the hurricane and the WB DC-6 that assisted the navy plane.

DC-6 crew used its own radar and information from their colleagues positioned overhead to search for the softest sectors of the storm and directed the navy plane out of immediate danger.

At the edge of the storm, a coast guard airplane took over the escort job and the two Weather Bureau airplanes returned to the hurricane to conduct their research. When the Super Connie finally touched down and rolled to a stop at Roosevelt Roads, Puerto Rico, a quick inspection found not only the ripped wingtips where the tanks had been attached but also wrinkles in the aircraft's skin (a sign that the airplane had been twisted), a crack in the covering over the lower radar antenna, and other telltale signs of serious structural stress. The damage was so extensive the navy decided to scrap the airplane, but the fact that the seriously disabled aircraft had made it home safely gave navy crews considerable confidence as they continued flying Super Constellations into hurricanes for another ten years.

That Super Connie had entered Cleo at an altitude less than

1,000 feet. Flying so low was not an act of mindless bravery. Flying low kept the airplane below the storm's clouds much of the time and allowed the technicians to measure surface winds, which are the ones that count in forecasting purposes, and to visually estimate the size of waves. One of the navy meteorological officers stationed on Guam who flew into many storms at low altitudes was Hugh Willoughby, whose first low-level trip into the eye of a storm was in 1970 aboard a Super Constellation destined for a rendezvous with Typhoon Olga. He well recalls those days when navy pilots skimmed the waves beneath typhoons and hurricanes: "The doctrine was to fly two-thirds of the way up from the sea to the cloud base. As we flew toward the eye, the cloud base would come down, but the pilots wouldn't fly below 600 feet. This means we often went into the eye wall with no visibility. Navy airplanes didn't fly into all typhoons or hurricanes. If the eye was less than ten miles across—a small eye is a sign of a powerful hurricane—the airplane would not fly into it, but would explore the storm with radar from around the edges."

Willoughby continues, "Occasionally we'd get caught in a down-draft and go from 800 to 300 feet. The pilots would first go to 'climb power' to arrest the descent. If they came within 500 feet of the ocean, they would use takeoff power. They couldn't use takeoff power for long, the engines wouldn't stand it. When they went to takeoff power, huge blue flames would come from the exhaust stacks. At night, it seemed like the blue fire from the engines illuminated the sea surface."

A danger of flying so low, especially in clouds, is that the airplane will fly too low and slam into the ocean. Pilots of an airplane inside clouds or even over the ocean on a dark night have to rely on the altimeter to stay at a safe altitude. Ordinary altimeters use atmospheric pressure to determine altitude, and in normal flying the instrument works well, because air pressure decreases at a regular rate as the plane climbs higher. The altimeter is really an aneroid barometer that's marked in feet of altitude rather than in inches of mercury, and it has a knob that the pilot adjusts in order to account for changes in atmospheric pressure at the Earth's surface. The catch is that the updated pressure reading has to come from weather stations. These stations are unavailable inside a hurricane or typhoon, so the unusually low air pressure throws off the altimeter, causing it to indicate that the airplane is higher than it really is, since low pressure is associated with a high altitude. (A change of one-tenth of an inch of mercury will throw off an altimeter by 100 feet.)

Understanding all this, engineers from the earliest days of hurricane flying equipped their planes with radar altimeters. A radar altimeter sends a radio beam directly down to the surface and measures the time elapsed before the reflected beam is picked up by the altimeter. In addition, radar altimeters give meteorologists a way to measure the sea-level air pressure in storms. They use the difference between the altitude as measured by an ordinary altimeter and the altitude as measured by the radar altimeter. The greater the difference between the two measurements, the lower the air pressure. In the old days, charts pinpointed the exact measurement. Today, the "D-value" is displayed on the terminals at the various work stations in the plane.

On the navy's Super Constellations that Willoughby flew in during the early 1970s, the radar altimeter had two indicators—a dial in the cockpit and a more accurate display on a radar screen called the "green worm," because it was displayed as a green line across the screen. One of the aerographer's mates monitored this screen and called out the altitude on the intercom system: "Green worm 1,500 feet, green worm 1,200 feet." Today, the radar altimeter is one of the many digital displays in front of the pilots, the flight meteorologist, and other researchers aboard the airplane. The NOAA WP-3's that fly into hurricanes have *two* radar altimeters, one for scientific purposes and one for the flight crew. The altimeter used for scientific purposes is displayed digitally at each research station and also on the monitor located in the pedestal between the two pilots. The altitude from the low-level altimeter is used by the pilots should the plane fly below a preset altitude.

On today's hurricane hunters, computers combine information from sensors aboard the airplane with data from a global positioning navigation system to calculate the speed and direction of the wind through which the airplane is flying. In the early 1970s, Willoughby and other flight meteorologists and navigators used much cruder devices to estimate wind speeds and directions. A basic tool was the

E6B Flight Computer—a misnomer now, because it was not a computer at all, but simply a circular slide rule. One side was used to calculate such important numbers as the distance the aircraft had traveled and the remaining fuel supply. The other side, marked with compass directions, was used to solve navigation problems, which can be difficult in a hurricane, when strong winds push the plane off any intended course. Today's pilots and navigators still learn how to use the E6B, and many still carry one to use as a backup should the onboard computers fail.

During typhoon penetrations, Willoughby used one hand to align the compass side of the E6B with the airplane's direction. He then aligned his other hand atop the E6B with the streaks of white the wind was making on the waves. (At night the pilots turned on the landing lights to enable him to see the surface.) He could then read the wind's direction from the E6B and estimate the wind's speed by its effects on the waves. With his estimates literally in hand, Willoughby conferred with the navigator over the intercom, who would use the wind data as he made navigation calculations on his own E6B. "All of this was pretty intense work," Willoughby says, in what sounds like an understatement.

The navy's version of the Super Connie usually carried a crew of twenty-two, including three pilots, two navigators, a meteorologist, a radar officer, two aerographers, two flight engineers, and, as Willoughby puts it, "a bunch of technicians. The equipment was so unreliable that the technicians were always busy." In no way was the Constellation ergonomically designed to make any of these men's jobs easier. As the flight meteorologist, Willoughby was hunched in a glass bubble on the side of the airplane behind the wing. If the airplane was bouncing around, he wrapped his legs around the seat. Hurricanes are warm and humid, and often the temperature inside the plane reached 100 degrees. Crew members wore standard navy flight suits made out of fire-resistant Nomex, which didn't absorb their sweat. At night, Willoughby recalls, "the cockpit was illuminated by red lights. The power assist for the controls wasn't strong. The flying was physically taxing for the pilots; both would be working the yokes while the flight engineer operated the throttles. Everyone had their flight suits rolled up to the elbows, the sinews of their forearms straining. It was like something Goya would have painted."

Hurricane flying wasn't reckless, but it wasn't easy, either. Nevertheless, the navy always had more volunteers for assignments to these reconnaissance squadrons than available billets. By the 1970s, however, armed forces leaders began to feel that storm reconnaissance was using money that should be used for more strictly "military" missions. In 1971, the navy phased out the "Typhoon Trackers" squadron stationed on Guam, but air force airplanes continued flying into Pacific typhoons. In the Atlantic Basin, the navy shut down its "Hurricane Hunters" squadron in 1975, but the National Hurricane Center still needed the critical data the navy had been supplying—especially with the burgeoning coastal populations in hurricane-prone areas—so the Air Force Reserve 815th Weather Reconnaissance Squadron stepped in to fill this breach in the Atlantic, and the regular air force was the only unit still flying into Pacific typhoons.

In 1987 the air force discontinued this typhoon reconnaissance and also proposed ending Atlantic flights by the reserve, stating that "meteorological satellite weather sensor technology made weather reconnaissance flights by aircraft obsolete." Neil Frank, who retired that year as director of the National Hurricane Center, his successor Bob Sheets, and many emergency management officials strongly disagreed. Forecasters do have techniques for estimating a hurricane's wind speeds by looking at satellite images, but those estimates are frequently incorrect, and clouds covering the storm often hide important features. Sometimes forecasters can't even locate the eye in satellite photographs. Frank and Sheets cited several cases in which estimates of hurricane strengths and positions based solely on satellite data contained such large errors that forecasts and warnings could have proved deadly and extremely costly.

Two examples used at the time were Hurricanes Harvey and Irene of 1981 in the North Atlantic, where on consecutive nights in each of these storms, the center was mislocated by satellite analysts by more than ninety miles, leading to twenty-four-hour forecast errors of 200 miles or more. In the case of Harvey, a French ship—which appeared to be responding to the hurricane on the basis of the National Hurricane Center forecasts, instead of being led away from the hurricane—was caught in its core. Fortunately, the ship survived its passage through the center, as indicated by some excellent observations transmitted to the National Hurricane Center. The ship crossed the storm, into the eye wall, the eye, and the eye wall on the other side. Fortunately, those transmissions were restricted to standard ship codes for winds and pressures; they didn't include any opinions from those on the ship about the quality of Hurricane Center forecasts.

Eight years later similar problems occurred in Tropical Storm (later Hurricane) Jerry in the Gulf of Mexico in 1989. Two consecutive reconnaissance aircraft missions had mechanical problems, leaving only satellite estimates of the strength and location of the northward-moving hurricane through the night of October 14. Estimated positions of the center of the hurricane varied by sixty miles or more during the night, leading to initial forecasts that it would come ashore over the central Louisiana coast, which prompted a hurricane watch. The center of the hurricane later struck near Galveston, Texas. These were not isolated cases, and it was routine to have intensity estimates in error by at least one category. Frank and Sheets pointed out that before satellite reconnaissance the air force and navy had burned a lot of fuel and crews had passed many boring hours looking in vain for any signs of a storm. When satellites took over this "early spotting" duty, planes were saved for specific reconnaissance jobs in specified targets. As a result, the military's airborne weather reconnaissance units were a fraction of the size they had been in presatellite days.

At the end of the 1987 debate, Congress directed the air force to continue providing the needed hurricane aircraft reconnaissance service for the Atlantic Basin and the central Pacific around Hawaii. However, budgetary constraints continued to feed the air force's desire to end its hurricane reconnaissance mission, and in 1991 the last active squadron was decommissioned, with the entire responsibility for operational hurricane reconnaissance being turned over to the air force reserve unit. Some meteorologists and air force officers wondered whether a reserve unit could provide the quick response needed for reconnaissance, but with the addition of some full-time air reserve technicians, this unit, based at Kessler Air Force Base in

Biloxi, Mississippi, has performed well. The air force reserve crews turned out to be much more experienced than the regular air force crews had been. Pilots and other personnel in regular air force units normally serve only three or four years before being transferred, while reservists are likely to stay in their units for many years, becoming more and more experienced in their specialties. No other nation flies airplanes into hurricanes (the former Soviet Union did conduct a few hurricane flights out of Cuba), but airplanes should be—and are—sent into every hurricane that threatens land anywhere in the Atlantic Ocean, the Caribbean, and the Gulf of Mexico, and into each of the rare storms that approach Hawaii or California.

There is simply no question that the information provided by the men and women who have been flying into hurricanes over the years has saved countless lives and reduced property losses by billions of dollars by helping to provide time for coastal residents to prepare for the onslaught. Moreover, the nation's military and civilian hurricane hunters have made possible a large share of the advances in our understanding of hurricanes since the 1940s. Today, a scientist who flies directly into a hurricane experiences and measures the storm's fury in ways that William Redfield in the early nineteenth century, Father Benito Vines late in the nineteenth century, and Isaac Cline early in the twentieth century could only have dreamed of. Even in the age of satellite reconnaissance and supercomputers, old-fashioned aerial reconnaissance remains invaluable and necessary.

CHAPTER 5

THE 1950S

Concerned about defending against German air attacks in the war that many saw coming, the Committee for the Scientific Survey of Air Defense, an arm of the British Air Ministry, asked Robert Watson Watt, a leading radio scientist, to look into various proposals for "death rays" that could destroy enemy airplanes or kill their crews. The year was 1934, so there would be plenty of time to work on the project, but Watt's calculations convincingly demonstrated that the proposals were flawed. It would *not* be physically possible to transmit enough radio energy to incapacitate an aircraft or its crew. That was the bad news, but there was good news as well. Watt calculated that an airplane—or any other object—could scatter, or reflect, enough radio energy to make it possible for a transmitting device to detect such a target. He recommended looking into "radio detection rather than radio destruction."

In a follow-up memo dated February 12, 1935, Watt suggested sending out the radio waves in very brief pulses. During the few microseconds between pulses, the waves from one pulse would travel at the speed of light, reflect off an airplane, and return to the antenna before the next pulse was sent out. Electronic circuits could immediately calculate the time elapsed against the speed of the radio wave—the speed of light—to calculate distance traveled. The next pulse of waves would return almost instantaneously with slightly updated information, as would the next pulse, and the next, and the next. Correlating the distance thus calculated with the compass heading and the angle of the antenna would determine the target's direction and altitude. For five years the British worked on Watt's idea in total secrecy before deciding in the fall of 1940 to share the work on this and other military technologies with the United States. To make use of this sudden infusion of scientific knowledge and technical know-how, the U.S. government set up the Radiation Laboratory at the Massachusetts Institute of Technology and also enlisted the help of the famous Bell Telephone Laboratories in New Jersey. In addition to Watt's work, many other scientific and technological advances since early in the century contributed to the effort, which the British had named Radio Direction Finding. Two U.S. Navy officers did better than that when they came up with Radio Detection and Ranging, which yielded a very nice acronym: RADAR.

Initially, of course, radar was designed to locate enemy weapons of war—aircraft and ships, specifically—and to aim weapons at them. Weather was just interference that added to the difficulties of spotting the target, because raindrops, snow, hail, sleet and even cloud drops also scatter some of the radio waves back to the antenna and distort or completely hide the images on the operator's screen. Researchers and radar operators quickly realized, however, that this interference could also help them "find" and, eventually, understand inclement weather of all sorts. Regarding tropical cyclones, specifically, observers had known for centuries that the strongest winds in storms are near the center and that the center itself is a relatively calm zone, but the new imaging technique soon taught meteorologists that hurricanes have an eye wall surrounding the calm eye. The airplane crews that began flying into hurricanes during the war learned to use their radar to locate with pinpoint accuracy both the eye and the eye wall. The successful effort that equipped World War II night-fighters with radar for spotting enemy airplanes gave hurricane hunters one of their most important tools: airborne radar that helps them avoid the worst turbulence. On land, the radar at the Lakehurst, New Jersey, Naval Air Station painted images of the Great Atlantic Hurricane of September 14, 1944, as the storm's eye passed sixty miles off the coast. A photograph of the radar screen clearly shows the hurricane's spiral bands. Because there had been no way of seeing a hurricane's structure on a large scale, no one had realized until this moment that a hurricane's rain-producing clouds were so well organized into spiral bands. It was a remarkable and ground-breaking moment for meteorologists and forecasters. In league with airplane reconnaissance, radar became one of the most important tools of weather forecasters and atmospheric scientists of every specialty.

And it was just in time, because hurricanes went on a rampage during the 1940s and '50s. In those two decades, twenty-one major hurricanes—with winds at least 110 miles per hour—and twenty-three lesser ones hit the U.S. mainland alone. Fourteen of these storms had also struck the Bahamas, one or more Caribbean islands, or the Yucatán Peninsula before hitting the United States, and twenty-two other hurricanes hit one of those areas but missed the United States. The public, who had heard about the advances in technology, expected better warnings to cope with all these storms. At first, however, the Weather Bureau used radar mainly to study thunderstorms and tornadoes, not hurricanes, because radar, just like human eyes, can't see over the horizon. An antenna mounted on even a high building generally can't detect a hurricane or anything else near the surface if it's more than about 150 miles away. Beyond that range, the line-of-sight radar is necessarily aimed too high in the sky to give a detailed picture of what's happening as near the surface as even the top part of a hurricane. The navy radar had beautifully pictured the Great Atlantic Hurricane of 1944, but the storm had been only sixty miles away. Until the middle of the 1950s, the Weather Bureau couldn't see any particular need for hurricane-spotting radar along the coast, because by the time the image showed up on the radar screen, the storm itself was already within a few hours of hitting land, and should already have been detected by reconnaissance aircraft, ships, or stations in the islands. In addition, the Bureau's network of coastal observing stations would be reporting data that forecasters could analyze to estimate the hurricane's possible movement and strength.

Early in 1955, however, the Weather Bureau installed a radar at Cape Hatteras, North Carolina. As it happened, all three of the hurricanes that hit the mainland that season—Connie, Diane, and Ione—passed within range of the new facility on their way to damaging landfalls in North Carolina. The fine details provided by the radar of the minute-by-minute movement, as well as the organization and intensity of the eye wall and rain bands and how they were changing with time, helped forecasters better estimate the precise track, speed, and intensity of these hurricanes. There was just no doubt about it. Forecasters were able to improve their last-minute alerts by providing more precise timing and locations for the strongest winds and rains and landfall. These last-hour adjustments were especially helpful for Hurricane Connie, which ducked and dodged this way and that as it approached the coast, and for Hurricane Ione, which abruptly turned out to sea after landfall, sparing the heavily populated mid–Atlantic Coast. Even Congress was impressed and soon appropriated funds for an extensive array of radar installations along both the Atlantic and the Gulf Coasts.

However, these radar units by themselves did not solve the basic problem, which was detection early enough to provide warnings ahead of time for the growing numbers of people in coastal areas. A line of radar installations shoulder-to-shoulder from Texas to Maine wouldn't discover a storm, even the tops of the clouds, lurking 150 miles away. For this longer range detection, the Bureau still relied on the valuable network of island stations and the increasing volume of ships in the seas of the Caribbean and around the mainland United States. Since the late 1940s, several hundred ships had been sending reports of weather observations every six hours, and more often when called for. The science of synoptic mapping developed a century earlier by Urbain Jean Joseph Le Verrier was now quite sophisticated. The dozens, if not hundreds, of reporting stations across the continental United States and near coastal areas allowed forecasters to pinpoint the most innocent-looking low-pressure area in those regions and follow it closely. Unfortunately, this density of reporting stations did not include the oceans, specifically the tropical oceans, outside of the shipping lanes. Storms could still go nearly undetected or change intensity between observations from ships. Routine synoptic aircraft reconnaissance flights helped fill the data void, thereby helping to reduce the number of "black holes."

The network of radiosonde stations that had been started in the 1930s was also expanded following the war, and improvements in design and materials allowed the balloons to lift their instrument packages to more than 60,000 feet. Radar or radio-direction-finding equipment (the equipment doesn't send out its own waves for reflection as radar does, but tracks the direction and angle of waves transmitted from the radiosonde) were now used to track the instruments at these unprecedented heights. It worked a lot better than a couple of people standing on the ground, one holding a stopwatch and the other looking into a theodolite, and provided forecasters with information on wind speeds and directions long after the balloon was out of sight of the ground. Within a few years, understanding of upper-air currents improved dramatically over the days not long before, when Grady Norton had used his skimpy knowledge of upper-air winds to make remarkably good predictions of storm tracks.

Nor did forecasters ignore the basics of their craft: swells and waves and clouds. They studied reports about these warning signs as closely as Father Benito Vines had in the late-nineteenth century; the new technology never replaced the old skills developed by the earliest forecasters.

One new technology didn't pan out at all. For a dozen years, beginning in 1944, the U.S. Navy attempted to detect hurricanes with a network of seismographs along the Atlantic Coast and in the Caribbean. A different network tried to detect typhoons over the Pacific. This effort was based on a belief that hurricanes or typhoons might affect certain kinds of "microseisms," mini-earthquakes that occur continuously around the globe and can be detected by sensitive seismographs. If this were the case, the navy's scientists could use the reports of microseisms of a minimum of three widely separated listening stations to pinpoint a storm by triangulation. The navy network did seem to locate a few storms before they had been found otherwise, but there were also many false alarms, and forecasters decided the information was of little help to them. The navy closed its network in 1956.

While few laypeople were aware of the great strides made in hurricane research in those postwar years, everyone who read or listened to a report about a hurricane or typhoon became aware of a different kind of innovation that grew out of World War II: the naming of storms. Until 1950, people talked about the "Great Galveston Hurricane" and the "Labor Day Hurricane." Forecasters simply referred to hurricanes by position, such as "the hurricane off the east coast of Florida." In Catholic parts of the Caribbean, hurricanes were often retroactively named for the saint's day on which they had struck. Puerto Rico, for instance, had two "San Felipe" hurricanes.

In the last years of the nineteenth century, the Australian Clement Wragge, the Queensland Government Meteorologist, named storms after women—and also after politicians with whom he disagreed. Australian meteorologists later discontinued this colorful if dubious practice—until forecasters begin naming Atlantic Basin hurricanes. *Storm*, a novel by George R. Stewart published in 1941, surely deserves some of the credit for the practice of giving women's names to storms in the Northern Hemisphere. The novel follows the career of a Pacific storm that eventually affects much of North America; a "Junior Meteorologist" plotting the storm on a weather map gives it the name "Maria" without telling his boss or his colleagues. "Not at any price would the Junior Meteorologist have revealed to the Chief that he was bestowing names—and girls' names at that—upon these great moving low-pressure areas. But he justified the sentimental vagary by explaining mentally that each storm was really an individual and that he could more easily say (to himself, of course) 'Antonia' than 'the low-pressure center which was yesterday in latitude one-five-five East, longitude forty-two North.' "

The reasons the Junior Meteorologist in *Storm* gave for naming storms make a lot of sense. Names avoid confusion. Since storms are moving all of the time, identifications by location constantly change. Looking back, one wonders why the idea of names didn't come along much sooner. *Storm* was read by many youth who were interested in weather, including many who became forecasters during World War II. Some of these military forecasters began informally using women's names to describe storms, especially those over the Pacific Ocean. This practice of naming typhoons later became formal for the military in the Pacific, but most countries around the Pacific didn't start naming storms until later.

The first official naming of storms in the Atlantic Basin began in

1950, using not women's names but names picked from the World War II–vintage "international phonetic alphabet," with each year's first storm named Able, then moving on to Baker, Charlie, Dog, Easy. These names were used from 1950 until 1952, when it was decided that confusion could arise because the phonetic alphabet was also used to spell out words over the radio. In 1953, the Hurricane Center switched to using only women's names. The same list of names was used in 1953 and 1954, but, perhaps because of the slight possibility that some people would associate the characteristics of last year's Hazel with this year's Hazel, forecasters decided to use six lists of names, which are repeated each six years. Six-year lists of only female names continued through 1978. The following year the policy was changed to include both men's and women's names, as it was for typhoons in the Pacific.

On May 5, 2000, when the Tokyo Typhoon Center of the Japanese Meteorological Agency assigned the name Damrey to the year's first typhoon, an entirely different way of naming Pacific storms began. Under the new system, devised by the World Meteorological Organization's Typhoon Committee, fourteen nations submitted a list of ten names each for a total of 140. The system brings a touch of poetry to this normally prosaic business. Selected names include animals, fish, flowers, astrological signs, as well as a few personal names and even an airport. Damrey is a Cambodian word for elephant. The second storm of 2000 was Longwang from China, which means, according to the Hong Kong Observatory's Web site, the Dragon King, the god of rain in Chinese mythology. North Korea contributed Kirogi, which is defined as "a wild goose, the flock of which comes in autumn to Korea and flies in early spring to the far North. Their appearance in Korea every year resembles what typhoons do." Hong Kong contributed Kai-Tak, the name of the old Hong Kong airport that closed in 1998. That name was used in 2000, and the next storm that year, a super typhoon, was called Jelawat, a name from Malaysia for a freshwater carp much sought after by gourmets.

Each Atlantic Basin list uses alternating male and female English, French, and Spanish names, all selected by the World Meteorological Organization's Western Hemisphere Hurricane Committee in

1981. The names of hurricanes that have major impacts are now retired, creating a rogues' gallery of the worst modern-day storms, and the committee selects names to replace those that are retired. To this day, hurricanes, typhoons, and tropical cyclones remain the only weather events or natural disasters that are given names upon conception.

The Atlantic Basin switch to women's names in 1953 came just in time for the hurricane assault on the United States in the mid-1950s. Especially hard hit was the Atlantic Coast north of Florida—1,200 miles of coastline that hadn't incurred a major storm since 1944. In fact, only three major hurricanes had hit that coastline since the turn of the century, while storms slammed into some part of Florida or the Gulf of Mexico coastline almost every year. The first indication that things were changing was Hurricane Barbara's fairly gentle swipe at North Carolina in 1953. This was shrugged off by residents as routine, but Carol the following season wasn't, after causing considerable damage along the Outer Banks and then smashing into Connecticut, Rhode Island, and Massachusetts. Eleven days later, Edna paid New England a visit, tracking to the east of Carol, crossing the coast in southeastern Massachusetts and Cape Cod. Winds gusted to 120 miles per hour on Martha's Vineyard. Damage was impressive up the coast to Maine, and twenty people lost their lives.

Hurricane Hazel was the monster of that season's trio. After gliding on a westerly course into the central Caribbean, this storm turned abruptly north and exploded into a 150-miles-per-hour hurricane while crossing the Bahamas before slamming into North Carolina on October 15. Accelerating as it came ashore, Hazel crossed the state, hurdled the Appalachian Mountains, and raced at 60 miles per hour into Ontario, Canada, all in twelve hours. Most hurricanes quickly lose strength and eventually dissipate once inland. Hazel maintained its violence by feeding off energy supplied by the clash between its own moist tropical warmth and an intense cold front to its west. In Toronto, gusts of 110 miles per hour were reported, and flash floods triggered by more than eight inches of rain killed seventy-eight people. It was Canada's worst natural disaster at the time. Total damage in the United States and Canada was $350 million. Including the nineteen people killed in the United States, Hazel's death toll was ninety-seven.

Then came 1955. In August, back-to-back hurricanes, Connie and Diane, created devastating flooding across southern New England—one of this century's biggest disasters. Each hurricane started her campaign in North Carolina. Connie then churned up the Chesapeake Bay, with its eye passing just east of Baltimore, Maryland, and on into Pennsylvania and up into Canada, dumping a foot of rain all the way. Diane was barely a hurricane as it came ashore five days later, but, like Connie, quickly dispensed more than a foot of rain on the mid-Atlantic and the Northeast, most of it falling within twenty-four hours as the dying center passed by. Disastrous floods in Pennsylvania, Massachusetts, Rhode Island, Connecticut, and southeastern New York earned Diane the distinction as "the first billion-dollar hurricane."

The unprecedented assault ended in September when Hurricane Ione wobbled across North Carolina then turned out to sea. By then, weather forecasters, civil defense officials, the press, weather mavens, and residents along the Eastern Seaboard were abuzz about what the 1956 hurricane season might yield. Were the six ladies of the previous two seasons—Carol, Edna, Hazel, Connie, Diane, and Ione—just a fluke, or had weather patterns shifted to target the East Coast with summer's worst? Some observers thought that the Earth's slow warming over the last few decades was responsible. As usual for the times, some blamed atmospheric testing of atomic and hydrogen bombs. These tests certainly were dangerous because of the radiation they spread, but no matter how big the bomb, the amount of energy added to the atmosphere was much smaller than that of the normal winds. Scientists have never found any proof that nuclear tests affected the atmosphere, except for the thunderstorm-size clouds created by the explosions and the radiation spread by the winds. In 1955, weather experts were sure that neither nuclear tests nor global climate change were responsible for all the hurricanes. They knew that the clockwise winds around the Bermuda High were centered farther north than normal, that these had steered the storms onto the Eastern Seaboard and funneled them up the coast two years in a row, and they viewed this as coincidence.

As it turned out, the following year was a relief. The only storm to hit the mainland that year was Flossie, which came ashore off the Gulf of Mexico between Pensacola and Panama City, Florida, as a weak hurricane whose rains were mostly a blessing, bringing drought relief across the Southeast from Florida to Virginia.

The hurricanes of 1954, all of which affected the populous mid-Atlantic and New England states, drew the attention of Congress, particularly Senator Theodore F. Green, a Democrat of Rhode Island, who criticized the Weather Bureau for not developing a comprehensive program for hurricane research. Francis W. Reichelderfer, the Bureau's chief, told the senator that he had included just such a proposal in his budget each of the three preceding years, but that the Eisenhower Administration had removed the item.

Robert H. Simpson was the man in charge of developing the plan that Reichelderfer described to Senator Green. Simpson had worked as a hurricane forecaster in New Orleans and Miami before becoming an executive assistant in the Bureau's headquarters. His experience with hurricanes went back to September 14, 1919, when a storm hit Corpus Christi, Texas, just as the Simpson family was sitting down to Sunday dinner. Simpson, who was then six, remembers how the family floated his grandmother out the back door in her cane wheelchair as the storm surge rolled in. He remembers watching with horror as his mother's arms grew tired carrying over her head the paper bag containing the fried chicken and donuts she had made for dinner. Her arms slipped lower and lower, until the bag was floating in the water.

It was Simpson who had organized the first purely research flight into a hurricane, in Panama in 1945. In 1951, when he was in charge of the Bureau's Honolulu office, he arranged a research mission into Typhoon Marge. When Simpson was based in Washington, he begged off from his office duties whenever he had the chance, loaded boxes of instruments onto reconnaissance flights

over the tropics, and piggybacked whatever research he could conduct as the rest of the crew focused on their duties. Simpson longed
for the resources to do the job right, to conduct organized research
into the inner workings of these great storms. He knew that the
Bureau and the military had the technology—including, of course,
radar. He knew that they had the corps of professionally trained
meteorologists, a new development just as important as any postwar
technology. During the war, the U.S. Armed Forces had trained
hundreds of young men, and a few women, as meteorologists, many
of them benefiting from accelerated meteorology classes taught by
the world's leading atmospheric scientists at some of the nation's
most prestigious universities. They then traveled to Europe, Asia, the
Arctic, and the tropics to observe and forecast the weather, and at the
conclusion of the war, many stayed in the field as forecasters or
researchers.

Now all the military and the Weather Bureau needed was the
will—Bob Simpson's will. The Eisenhower administration may have
turned down the research request that Simpson had persuaded the
Bureau's top managers to include in their budget proposal, but Senator Green was so impressed with what this enthusiastic mid-level
meteorologist had accomplished without any direct appropriation
that he vowed to hold congressional hearings on the hurricane
problem. He and the other senators from the states affected by the
1954 storms were eager to show their constituents that they were
doing something. Francis Reichelderfer and Harry Wexler, the
Weather Bureau's director of research, took Simpson to the hearing
as an "expert" to answer technical questions. As head of the Weather
Bureau, Reichelderfer was expected to toe the administration line
and not seek funding for a project the Bureau of the Budget had
rejected. Simpson was there as a technical expert, however, not as a
member of the administration. After the scheduled testimony, and
after Simpson had described some of his informally gathered and
unbudgeted research findings, a committee member asked, "What
do you think the Congress should do?"

Here was Simpson's opportunity, one that he knew he might never
get again. On the spot, he decided to summarize for this committee
the research plan the Bureau of the Budget had rejected.

Reichelderfer made himself look uncomfortable and Wexler looked embarrassed—as if this were all a surprise to them. (Eisenhower and his cabinet weren't the first to learn that lower-level officials have ways of getting what they want from Congress without directly confronting the boss.) Simpson's gamble paid off. Congress authorized the creation of the National Hurricane Research Project (NHRP). The following year, the Weather Bureau's budget jumped from $27.5 million to $57.5 million, with a significant portion of the increase going to the Hurricane Project.

The NHRP was arguably the single greatest step forward in improving our knowledge of hurricanes and our ability to forecast them accurately. It also provided funding that Simpson was able to use for other atmospheric-science research, including the permanent observatory atop Mauna Loa in Hawaii, with its important long-term record of atmospheric carbon dioxide, and for the National Severe Storms Project (later the National Severe Storms Laboratory in Norman, Oklahoma), studying severe thunderstorms and tornadoes. In addition to the Weather Bureau, the NHRP included the U.S. Air Force, Navy, and Army Corps of Engineers, as well as leading tropical meteorologists at various universities. A network of twenty-one weather-balloon stations was established in the West Indies, operated by the United States and seven other nations. The Air Force Air Weather Service assigned specially instrumented aircraft to the NHRP, including a WB-47 and two WB-50's, bombers adapted for weather research that carried the first airborne digital systems for recording meteorological data. During a hurricane, every attempt would be made to put all three aircraft into the storm simultaneously, each collecting data at a specific altitude between 1,000 and 40,000 feet. The funded plan called for intensive data collection beginning in May 1956 and continuing for thirty or so months. Researchers expected to finish their work with this data in four or five years.

One of the project's first challenges was designing meteorological instruments that would collect reliable measurements of wind speed and direction, temperature, humidity, and air pressure from an airplane flying at about 200 miles per hour inside a hurricane. Even such a straightforward measurement as the outside air's temperature turned out to be quite difficult, because the air hitting the airplane—and hitting the thermometer attached to the airplane—is compressed and therefore warmed. How much it's warmed depends on the plane's speed and the amount of water in the air. All of the measuring systems attached to the research planes were subject to similar distorting factors, and much work went into calibrating and recalibrating the systems to get the most accurate data possible. In 1955 all this computing and data recording were done with vacuum tubes and punch cards. William Gray, who flew on some NHRP flights as a University of Chicago graduate student in meteorology, recalls that era when he says, "This meant you would get off the airplane with these boxes of cards and they had to be processed. This would take weeks."

Scientists needed detailed information on the speed and direction of the winds in cyclones, but, once again, this was easier said than done. The first step in this calculation is to determine how the winds of the storm push the airplane, but these numbers aren't the answer because an airplane isn't a balloon that's merely drifting with the wind. It has its own speed and its own direction through the air, which have to be accounted for. The equation that gives an accurate answer has to account for the heading in which the plane is pointed, the direction it's actually going, the speed of the air flowing over the airplane, and the speed at which the airplane is actually moving over the Earth's surface. On a perfectly calm day, the heading of the plane is its course, and the airspeed is the ground speed. In any kind of wind, the *difference* between the heading of the plane and its actual course and the difference between airspeed and ground speed are both caused by the wind.

For hurricane researchers looking for definitive answers for the first time, the tricky factor in this equation was ground speed. Over land, navigators used ground-based navigation radios to follow a course. By timing exactly when they passed over particular stations, they could easily calculate ground speed. Once over the ocean and out of range of the navigation radios, however, life became harder. Navigators could only resort to "dead reckoning." That is, the navigator would estimate the wind's speed and direction, keep close track of the airplane's compass directions and times, and then use the E6B flight computer (really just a circular slide rule) to calculate the location. If the sky were reasonably clear, the navigator could use the position of the sun during the day—measured with a sextant—or of the stars at night to determine the airplane's location, and use this to check and correct positions determined by dead reckoning.

This term probably comes from the use of "dead" to mean "exact" or "absolute" in expressions such as "dead center." Some people believe it is a shortening of the word "deduced," because the navigator deduces the position. Whatever the case, dead reckoning could work quite well—Charles Lindbergh used it for his epochal New York to Paris solo flight in 1927—but it wasn't a good way to precisely measure the winds inside a hurricane, because it required estimating the winds that were supposedly being calculated.

The problem was solved by the new Doppler radar navigation systems first introduced after World War II. The technology was named after Christian Doppler, the Austrian scientist who had explained nearly a century earlier why a train whistle has a different pitch when the object is moving toward the observer than when it's moving away. With the oncoming whistle, the waves are "squeezed"; in effect, their frequency increases, and this yields a higher pitch. With the departing whistle, the waves are "stretched out," their frequency decreases, and this yields a lower pitch. Doppler's original analysis of what we now call the "Doppler shift" was fascinating but of little practical use until radar was invented. Then Doppler's work became invaluable. By measuring the frequency shift of the radio waves reflected from an object, the circuits in a Doppler radar can determine whether an object is moving toward or away from the radar antenna, and its speed *relative to the antenna*. That last phrase is the catch. The *absolute* speed can be measured only if the object happens to be moving directly toward or away from the antenna. A car speeding directly *across* the highway down which the highway patrol officer is pointing a Doppler radar gun would give a reading of zero, no matter how fast the car is moving.

To address this inherent limitation of the Doppler radar, the navigation system onboard the air force airplanes used for the National Hurricane Research Project broadcast radio waves at a 45-degree angle to both sides of the plane, front and rear—four directions in all. These four streams of radio waves bounced off the ocean, and the primitive computer of the day used the different Doppler shifts to determine both the airplane's ground speed and its "drift angle," the difference between the heading and the actual course. This data, in turn, could be used to calculate wind speeds and directions. "This was amazing," says William Gray. "They could go out and fly for ten or twelve hours and know exactly where they were. The Doppler allowed you to get winds over the ocean for the first time." These wind measurements combined with measurements of air pressure and the airplane's altitude to give researchers new insights into the relationships between air pressures and winds.

The NHRP's operating base was at Morrison Field in West Palm Beach, Florida. The first flight was conducted on one of the WB-50's flying into Hurricane Anna over the Gulf of Mexico in July 1956. Bob Simpson recalls, "The sensors and radar worked, but the IBM punch card system didn't, and we came back with only data hand recorded every few minutes from visual readouts. This was a much heralded flight, but the public never found out how chagrined we were about [the] loss of the ability to machine process data from this first flight." The second flight encountered more problems. "All systems were go, except that it turned out that data channels for longitude, time, and card count were garbled. Still not too bad—until the technician, stepping off the plane after the flight with four large boxes of punch cards, stumbled, dropped the cards, and the wind from the propeller of the one engine that had not been stopped distributed the cards over about a hundred yards of the tarmac. Florida State University students took more than a year to sort out the cards in proper sequence."

Despite the early snarls and mishaps, extensive data were obtained during flights into Hurricanes Carrie and Frieda in 1957 and Cleo, Daisy, and Fifi in '58. The multiple-level flights into Cleo, specifically, resulted in the classic scientific paper by Noel LaSuer and Harry Hawkins published in the *Monthly Weather Review* that revealed the first detailed picture of the vertical structure of the inner core of a strong hurricane. For the first time, the researchers actually measured the temperatures, pressures, and winds aloft through the core of the hurricane, showing the extreme warmth in the middle and upper levels of the atmosphere and how the wind speeds in the eye wall extended well up into the atmosphere. Although much was learned from the data collected during the three hurricane seasons the National Hurricane Research Project received funding, it soon became obvious that the original objectives could not be met under this constricted time frame. Researchers were finding wide variation in the basic structural elements from hurricane to hurricane, and wide variation in a particular hurricane from one day to the next. The storms were turning out to be much more complex than originally thought; the data raised as many or more questions than they answered. Researchers are *still* trying to answer some of these questions, especially those about how the storm and the environment interact to change a hurricane's intensity.

Within a span of one year in the mid-1950s, two giants of the hurricane community—perhaps the two men best known to the public at large—died. In September 1954, Grady Norton, the first director of the National Hurricane Center, was advised by his physician to cease and desist from his work. Norton suffered from migraine headaches and high blood pressure, but it was hurricane season. How could he stop working? The following month, Norton put in a twelve-hour day tracking and forecasting the latest of the storms of that year, Hurricane Hazel. The next morning, October 9, the sixty-year-old forecaster suffered a stroke at home and died later that day.

The following August, Isaac Cline, the most famous forecaster of an earlier era, died at the age of ninety-five. He had retired in 1935 after fifty-three years with the Weather Bureau, and opened "The Art House," in which he showcased his extensive collection of art and antiques in the French Quarter in New Orleans. He wrote in his autobiography: "Time has brought much of joy and much of sorrow, but the joy has greatly exceeded the sorrow. If I had my life to live over and could plan it, I would not change things in any way, for I am satisfied with my life as it has been. My objectives in life have been accomplished." Of his retirement from the Weather Bureau, he wrote that he had been "relegated to the shelf as too old to work."

Whether or not Cline himself had been too old to work, his ideas were. His technique of relying on the solo study of storms using weather and tide reports, and especially on the storm surge that precedes a hurricane, had been left behind by professional meteorologists. Even Grady Norton's famous intuition had proved more reliable. The new data and new understanding of hurricanes that forecasters developed following World War II were definitely more reliable. Yet still Cline focused on storm surge. Gilbert Clark, a Hurricane Center specialist at the time, was conducting research on storm surge when he met Cline in New Orleans in 1951. Clark reports, "He was [still] a nut on storm surge!" The elderly man recalled for Clark his wife's death from the surge in Galveston in 1900 and then said pointedly: "You've got to do better. You've got to get these hurricane surge forecasts better."

CHAPTER 6

THE 1960S

GORDON DUNN begun his meteorological career in 1924 as a messenger boy in the Weather Bureau office at Providence, Rhode Island. Later that year he was transferred to Tampa, Florida, as a junior observer, where he immediately had his first experiences with hurricanes—and with poor hurricane forecasting. As an assistant scoutmaster of a Boy Scout troop, he planned to take his charges camping on the last weekend in September. Before leaving town, he fulfilled one of his duties at the Weather Bureau, printing the handbills with the local forecast. The scouts helped with the printing chore and then distributed the handbills around the city, though there didn't seem to be a lot of reason to do so. The forecast called for fair weather. That night, after the fringe of a tropical storm hit the scouts' campsite with 40-mile-per-hour winds and at least six inches of rain, Dunn emerged from his dripping tent the next morning to find that the boys had fastened copies of "his" forecast to a number of trees.

Three decades later, in 1955, when Dunn took over as chief hurricane forecaster, the state of the forecasting art had considerably improved—a good thing, because he was immediately confronted with one of the busiest seasons on record. As we have seen, Connie, Diane, and Ione all hit the U.S. East Coast, and Janet sliced across the Caribbean Sea, where the U.S. Navy P-2V hurricane hunter was lost in the storm with its crew of nine and the two Canadian journalists. Two years later, in June 1957, the nation's deadliest hurricane since the 1938 New England storm hit Louisiana.

The first signs of this storm were detected the morning of June 24, when upper-air wind measurements found a weak disturbance over the Bay of Campeche in the southern Gulf of Mexico. Later that day, a shrimp boat radioed that it was encountering 45-mile-per-hour winds, and gusts above 60. The Weather Bureau's New Orleans's office issued its first bulletin at 10:30 P.M. that evening and requested the navy to send an airplane into the storm the next morning. The navy crew encountered winds higher than 74 miles per hour. At 7 A.M. June 25, this first hurricane of the season was promptly named Audrey, and the Weather Bureau office posted a hurricane watch for the Texas and Louisiana coasts. Audrey turned out to be a very healthy storm: the next morning, a navy reconnaissance flight recorded winds of 104 miles per hour as it flew into the eye. No other flights were made into the eye, but that night a navy airplane flying along the edge of the storm found that the rainfall had grown heavier. At 10 A.M. on that Wednesday, the New Orleans office posted a hurricane warning estimating tides five to eight feet above normal. At ten o'clock that night, the warning was changed: the tides would be nine feet higher than normal.

All in all, the warnings about Audrey were good, certainly much more timely and accurate than they had been for the New England storm of 1938. Yet Audrey still took at least 390 lives when it made landfall near the Texas-Louisiana border the morning of June 27. What went wrong? Several official and unofficial investigations mostly agreed that "there was a definite failure of the [New Orleans office] hurricane forecaster to get his message through to the people he was trying to warn and that the warnings failed to contain a compelling sense of urgency or emergency." That quote is from Gordon Dunn and Banner Miller's 1960 book, *Atlantic Hurricanes*. The warnings issued for Audrey had directed people to flee from "low or exposed places," but the residents of Cameron, Louisiana, where most of the deaths occurred, didn't think of their homes several miles from the Gulf of Mexico as "low or exposed." After all, they were seven to eight feet above sea level. Also, Dunn and Miller wrote, the warning had stated the time when the hurricane's center was expected to arrive, leading some people to think that they didn't have to worry until that hour. And then there was one final factor: almost all of the new residents of Cameron had evacuated, while longtime residents had stayed. Eight tropical storms and one weak hurricane had hit the area in the previous twenty years, but no major hurricane since 1917. Tragically, the long-time residents had grown to feel that hurricanes were not a threat to their community.

The experience with Audrey encouraged Dunn to begin holding hurricane preparedness conferences in coastal communities, bringing together representatives from the American Red Cross and local civil defense offices. Dunn began giving thirty to forty public lectures every year and continued these lectures after retiring from the Hurricane Center in 1967, almost up to his death in 1994. He also took his international responsibilities seriously, assisting other meteorological services in the region to improve their hurricane warning services. While the U.S. National Hurricane Center is also the World Meteorological Organization's Regional Specialized Meteorological Center for hurricanes all around the Caribbean Sea and

Cameron, Louisiana, in the aftermath of Hurricane Audrey, which struck the coast in 1957 and killed 390 people, mostly due to flooding.

the Gulf of Mexico, it does not have the authority to post warnings for other nations; only governments can do that. Since small Caribbean nations can't afford to establish hurricane centers staffed by full-time specialists, they usually rely on the advice of the U.S. Hurricane Center for watches and warnings. At times, an island's meteorological service has wanted to post a warning, but higher officials wouldn't allow it, or were slow to okay a warning. Language is also sometimes a problem, with meteorologists and other government officials speaking French, Spanish, and Dutch as well as English. Meteo France (that country's national weather service) issues watches and warnings for the French islands in the Caribbean (which are part of France, not overseas colonies), and there have been cases when a hurricane watch or warning was posted for the Dutch side of Saint Martin but not for the island's French side. We can only hope that no one has ever moved his boat from the Dutch to the French side of the tiny island, thinking it will be safe there.

Dunn's career had begun before airplanes were used for hurricane reconnaissance, and it continued well into the era of satellites. That's how rapidly the world was changing in the mid–twentieth century. In 1948 American scientists and engineers launched some of the German V-2 rockets captured at the end of World War II. One of the rockets sent aloft from the army's White Sands Proving Ground in New Mexico carried a camera that took photos of clouds over a wide area. Meteorologists were asked to study the photos, and they realized they could readily detect strong weather patterns. On the other hand, firing rockets straight up into the air would not be an efficient way to track any kind of weather, least of all cyclones that inhabit the oceans of the world. Still, that's where the technology stayed for nine years, until the Soviet Union launched *Sputnik 1*, the first artificial satellite, on October 4, 1957. No event during the history of the United States has ever acted as a stronger spur for scientific and technological research. Every field conceivably related to the space sciences was fully funded in the all-out effort to win the space race.

The first American weather satellite, *Tiros 1*, was launched in April 1960 and immediately showed the potential of space-based reconnaissance by photographing a tropical cyclone about 800 miles east of Brisbane, Australia—a storm that had eluded detection to that point. *Tiros 1* was a polar-orbiting satellite; that is, it orbited in the north-south direction, over the poles, as the Earth rotated under it to the east. At best, it could provide an overhead view of a specific location in the tropics only twice in twenty-four hours. From its altitude of 500 miles, *Tiros* could capture images only 3,600 miles wide in the tropics—a little over the width of North America. And the nighttime image was just about worthless, because the first cameras didn't have sufficient resolution. Sometimes meteorologists were in for a sunrise surprise as the sun began illuminating a storm's clouds. It was four years before this problem was solved with the first high-resolution nighttime images provided by the *NIMBUS-1*.

Much of what we take for granted today in satellite photography wasn't easy in the early days. The photographs weren't Kodak snapshots developed in a convenient laboratory. They were electronic analog images, and the early computers that converted the stream of signals into pictures were limited by the day's standards in capacity to handle the large quantities of data that make up a single picture. The finished product was something like that of the old-fashioned wire photo machines that made prints line by line, and they weren't nearly as good as the digital images that came later. Moreover, accurately positioning the images of a storm's swirl of clouds over a map proved to be quite difficult, particularly over the oceans, where few features—islands—were visible.

Tracking storms with polar-orbiting satellites was also difficult because a day's first picture of a hurricane could be from its east side while the next picture, twelve hours later, might be from the west side. In such a case, the location given for the storm's eye could be off by many miles. But at least forecasters did know about the disturbed weather, had a general idea where it was, and could then requisition a navy or air force plane to investigate. (Throughout the 1950s, these reconnaissance airplanes had flown regular tracks over areas of the oceans off the main shipping routes, collecting weather observations. Sometimes these had provided the first indication of a tropical storm, but the flights were expensive, and a lot of aviation gasoline and coffee were consumed as airplanes droned over empty

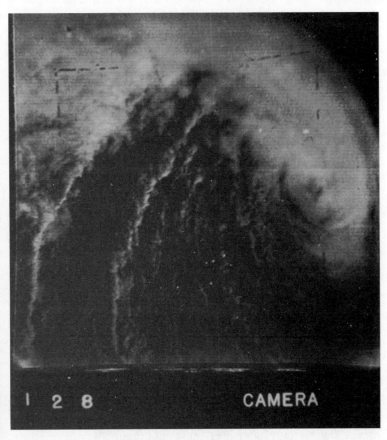

The first satellite photo of a tropical cyclone. TIROS 1 captured this image on April 9, 1960. The cyclone, which had not been previously detected, was about 800 miles east of Brisbane, Australia.

oceans with bored crews collecting fair-weather data. The satellites put an end to this.)

All of the early satellites were experimental. They were designed to test sensing, receiving, processing, and displaying capabilities. Worthwhile pictures were a bonus. The first *operational* meteorological satellites, *ESSA-1* and *ESSA-2*, were launched in 1966 by the new Environmental Science Services Administration. The two ESSA satellites used Automatic Picture Transmission (APT) cameras for the first time, and with these cameras our heavy reliance upon satellite data for tropical meteorological analyses truly began. Now, the data stream was continuously transmitted so that any ground receiving station within "sight" of the satellite as it passed over the station could automatically "lock" its receiving antenna on to the satellite, tracking it until it passed out of sight (over the horizon). The data was then automatically processed at each of these individual sites. A series of individual overlapping pictures was used to produce a "swath" image of the Earth below the path of the satellite.

For the first time, these images provided ironclad confirmation of the hypothesis that Gordon Dunn had first published in the late 1930s, that many Atlantic storms are born as "easterly waves" off the coast of Africa. The orbiting cameras showed that each year as many as 100 clusters of clouds move off the coast of West Africa and over the Atlantic Ocean, between latitudes 8 and 15 degrees north—the trade wind belt just north of the equator. The satellite images also led researchers to track the origins of these cloud clusters all the way back to East Africa.

Gordon Dunn had no way of knowing this part of the story, and even today atmospheric scientists don't completely agree on the specific origin of these cloud clusters, but they generally accept the idea that low-level and mid-level winds blowing from the east over the Ethiopian Highlands in East Africa create the initial disturbances. Mountains in these highlands soar to 14,000 feet. As the easterly breeze flows around and over these mountains, it forms vortices much like those that rocks stir up in white-water streams. The vortices then drift west with the upper-level winds across Sudan, Chad, and the Central African Republic, where hot, dry air from the Sahara Desert to the north mixes in, drying the air and causing the clouds to fade away. Farther west, however, humid monsoon winds from the Gulf of Guinea to the south inject moisture back into the vortices, allowing clouds to begin forming again. Sometimes these clouds grow into rain showers that bring welcome moisture to the semiarid regions south of the Sahara. When a vortex is strong enough and the air humid enough, the clouds coalesce into huge clusters that literally blossom within hours or a few days in the satellite images. This condensation of water vapor into clouds and showers releases latent heat, supplying energy to the system, helping to keep the vortex spinning.

As long as the cluster of clouds is over land, where the supply of humid air is limited, nothing much can happen. However, waters of the Atlantic Ocean off the African coast can offer—depending on the time of year—a rich supply of humid air. Very possibly the disturbance continues to drift west over the ocean after it crosses the coastline. Should it move over a ship or one of the Cape Verde Islands, a barometer would show a slight drop in air pressure, then a return to normal, and the surface winds would shift to the southeast for a while, and then back to the usual east-northeast flow—the trade winds. A line on a map showing this distinctive aberration of the winds would look like a kink, or wave; these mild disturbances are called "easterly" or "tropical" waves. This sequence, first articulated by Dunn, occurs during a one- to two-day period, followed by good weather for two, three, or four days, and then the process repeats itself as the next tropical wave passes by.

Tropical waves move over the eastern Atlantic beginning in April. The "official" hurricane season for the Atlantic Ocean is June 1 through November 30, but the season for these waves, specifically, to grow into storms is much briefer than that: August through October. Early- and late-season storms form in other ways, often in the Gulf of Mexico and western Caribbean. Before August and after October, the cooler ocean water off Africa slightly chills the air directly above it, creating a thin layer of air that's cooler than the air above it. A condition in which cool air is below warm air is called an inversion, because it reverses the usual pattern of air growing cooler with altitude. The inversion in question curtails rising air currents that could otherwise feed moisture to the clouds in the vortices. A wave moving over the ocean too early or too late in the season is starved for new moisture. The clouds dissipate.

As water temperatures off the African coast begin warming to their late-summer peak, dramatic changes occur. The now-warmer water heats the air above it, wiping out the inversion, allowing the warm, humid air to rise high into the sky. As tropical waves move off the west coast of Africa, their clouds no longer dissipate. With the infusion of the very humid air from below, the disturbance can grow. At the "kink," the winds blowing from the northeast and southeast converge at the ocean's surface. Such convergence pushes air up. As the air rises, it cools, and water vapor begins condensing into puffy clouds. Condensation releases the latent heat of the water vapor, warming the air around it, which causes it to rise even faster. Most of these waves travel across the Atlantic Ocean, Caribbean Sea, and Central America as mild disturbances that few observers other than meteorologists on the lookout for hurricanes ever notice. A tropical wave can bring a few more clouds than normal, and some will bring heavier and longer-lasting showers than usual in the tropics. A few will travel all the way across the Atlantic, cross Central America, and then, over the Pacific Ocean, to become the seeds for nearly all of the hurricanes that form in the waters of the eastern Pacific.

Of the total of a hundred or so waves created annually off the coast of Africa, only twenty to thirty move over the eastern Atlantic when conditions are ripe, from mid-August to mid-October, and then some of these waves become tropical depressions, the weakest kind of tropical cyclone. The term "depression" defines an area near the surface in which winds are flowing in a complete circle around a low pressure, but the winds have not yet reached the 39-mile-per-hour speed that, by definition, would make the system a tropical storm.

When Gordon Dunn retired as director of the Hurricane Center at the end of the 1967 hurricane season, Robert H. Simpson succeeded him and served through 1973. Without question, Simpson's "most critical and hair-raising experience," as he puts it, was Hurricane Camille in 1969. This storm formed over the western Caribbean south of Cuba on Thursday, August 14, moved north over western Cuba, and then motored into the warm Gulf of Mexico on Friday. Camille was taking dead aim at the northern Gulf Coast, and one of Simpson's most important forecasting tools—reliable airplanes that could bore into the storm's center and discover just how strong it was—were not available. Why? The navy, which was responsible for reconnaissance flights over the Gulf of Mexico, had ordered most of its airplanes to Puerto Rico to fly into another storm, Hurricane Debbie, on behalf of Project Stormfury, the government's effort to see if cloud-seeding methods could weaken hurricanes. Simpson picks up the story: "The navy had two old, decrepit planes left in Jacksonville. One got [to Camille] and said the storm was too strong to penetrate and came back. The other never got off the ground." But even if all of the navy's Super Constellations had been available, Simpson might not have gotten the eye measurements he so desperately wanted, because by 1969 navy pilots were reluctant to penetrate extremely strong storms in the aging Connies. Simpson did have satellite pictures, but in 1969 they were primitive compared with what would come later. Still, they were all Simpson and his staff had to go on. "There I was, trying to make up my mind on how to put up the warnings for this thing." Even without all of the information he would like, Simpson put up a hurricane watch Saturday morning, August 16, for the coast from Biloxi, Mississippi, east to St. Mark's, Florida. "The people in Washington who were analyzing the satellite images were sure the storm was losing intensity. I was sure the storm was getting stronger. I was convinced it was becoming close to a *record* storm just from the way the eye structure was changing. We could see the structure [in satellite photos], but not what the central pressure was, or what the strongest winds were."

That weekend, Camille shared the headlines and television news shows with the "Woodstock Music and Art Fair" in New York's Hudson Valley. However, Simpson was so focused at the Hurricane Center he never heard about the famous counterculture get-together until Camille had come and gone. He needed airplanes, desperately. "So I had to get on the horn with the commander of the Air Weather Service, which was at Scott Air Force Base, Illinois, and told him what was at stake, not only for the military, but for millions of people along the coastline. He said, 'I think I can help you, but it's going to take eight hours before I can get something to you.'" That evening—August 16—an air force C-130 found a central pressure in Camille of 26.72 inches of mercury, which was only slightly higher than the record 26.35 inches of mercury recorded in the 1935 Florida Keys Labor Day hurricane. "This shook everybody up. I rang the bell pretty loud." Camille's sustained winds were blowing at about 160 miles per hour. At 5 A.M. the following morning, Sunday, Simpson posted a hurricane warning that included the Mississippi coastline. Wade Guice, the civil defense director for Harrison County, Mississippi, later said: "If I had to pick a day for a storm, I would pick Sunday, and I would pick the warning time of Sunday morning because everybody is at home. Sunday is an ideal time to have an evacuation."

As it happened, a few researchers, especially Chester Jelesnianski at the Weather Bureau's Techniques Development Laboratory in Washington, D.C., had been working in the 1960s to develop computer models to forecast the height of the storm surge that precedes a hurricane approaching a coastline. This research was *not* an attempt to follow Isaac Cline's dream of using storm surge numbers to predict the path of a storm, but to more accurately predict how high that surge would be. By early 1969 Jelesnianski had completed the first storm surge model, called SPLASH (Special Program to List Amplitudes of Surges from Hurricanes). Storm surge is so complex that it is impossible to forecast, except in the most general way, without the aid of computers. Jelesnianski's model used such factors as the topography of the ocean bottom offshore, the direction from which the hurricane was approaching, the wind speeds, how far from the center winds of different speeds extended, and the amount of time the wind had been blowing across the ocean. As Camille charged north across the Gulf of Mexico, Jelesnianski ran the SPLASH model and calculated that the hurricane could push more than twenty feet of storm surge ashore.

Most of the forecasters thought twenty feet was ridiculous, but Simpson didn't. He took the prediction seriously. At that time, forecasters weren't authorized to get specific with wind speeds and surge numbers. They were supposed to stick to such statements as "strong winds and dangerously high water are expected," but Simpson set a precedent by saying in the forecast for Camille that the storm surge could be fifteen feet or more.

On Sunday afternoon, August 17, an air force C-130 piloted by Marvin A. Little penetrated Camille's eye and measured a pressure of 26.62 inches of mercury. "Just as we were nearing the [eye] wall cloud we suddenly broke into a clear area and could see the sea surface below," the copilot, Robert Lee Clark, wrote in 1982. "What a sight! Although everyone on the crew was experienced except me, no one had seen the wind whip the sea like that before. . . . Instead of the green and white splotches normally found in a storm, the sea surface was in deep furrows running along the wind direction. . . . The velocity was beyond the descriptions used in our training and far beyond anything we had ever seen." Those descriptions used in training accounted for winds up to 150 miles per hour. After describing what they saw over the radio to the National Hurricane Center, the crew and the forecasters decided to estimate the winds inside Camille at 190 miles per hour. Soon after leaving the eye, a generator on one of the C-130's engines failed. Clark brought his plane back safely to Ellington Air Force Base near Houston on three engines; no other flights were made into Camille. The National Hurricane Center advisory issued at 9 P.M. Sunday evening stated that a surge of fifteen to twenty feet was possible along the Mississippi coast from Gulfport to Pascagoula, and that Camille's winds were estimated at 190 miles per hour. This warning and the airplane's report of the actual conditions spurred efforts to evacuate even more people along the threatened coast.

Camille's center moved across the beach about 10:30 P.M. Sunday near Clermont Harbor, Waveland, and Bay St. Louis, Mississippi. The estimated surge of twenty feet that had been dismissed by some forecasters was actually on the low side. An incredible 22.6 feet of extra water surged over and through Pass Christian, Mississippi. The "official" death toll is 144, but later investigations showed that 172 people lost their lives along the Gulf Coast in the hurricane. As has often been the case, the exact number will never be known.

Looking back on how the Hurricane Center had handled Camille, Simpson says he failed in one regard. "I wasn't able to communicate with people like the Office of Emergency Planning [now the Federal Emergency Management Agency], the American Red Cross, the Salvation Army, and all the state agencies that were preparing for the storm. I couldn't get a handle on the storm to answer their question, 'What kind of resources must we put in this particular area to do our job?' I didn't know their job that well, and I couldn't equate it to the central pressure of the storm, which I could tell them about. I needed something to give them a handle on it, so they would know what resources they needed to deal with a storm."

Trinity Episcopal Church, built in 1849 one block from the Gulf Coast in Pass Christian, Mississippi, prior to the passage of Hurricane Camille in 1969.

Trinity Episcopal Church after the passage of Hurricane Camille illustrating the power of the winds and storm surge, which with wave action exceeded 25 feet in the area.

As it was, officials were able to evacuate an estimated 81,000 of the 150,000 residents in the evacuation zone, a major accomplishment. As Camille moved inland across Mississippi, Tennessee, and central Kentucky, it weakened to a tropical depression with winds less than 39 miles per hour, but it was still a very wet storm. In Virginia, it combined with another weather system to produce twelve to thirty-one inches of rain on the east slopes of the Blue Ridge Mountains. The resulting floods and landslides killed another 112 people in Virginia and West Virginia. It destroyed 5,500 homes and severely damaged 12,500 more. Some 700 businesses were destroyed or damaged. "By any yardstick," Simpson said later, "Camille was the greatest storm of any kind ever to have affected the mainland of the United States." Although slightly weaker than the 1935 Florida Keys Labor Day hurricane, Camille was a much larger storm that affected not only more square miles but also an area that is much more populated than the Keys of the 1930s.

In 1971 Herbert S. Saffir, an engineer and expert on wind damage who had helped write the building code for Dade County, Florida, prepared a report for the United Nations on low-cost construction that could withstand high winds. As part of the report, Saffir created a table of the damage expected from various ranges of wind speeds. The following year, Bob Simpson correlated Saffir's wind damage rankings with the potential for storm surge flooding to create the Saffir-Simpson Hurricane Potential Damage Scale, with ratings from one to five. The "wind" component of the scale applies for any locale and any hurricane, because the potential wind damage is essentially the same for a given structure of comparable construction no matter where it's located, or from what direction the hurricane is approaching. The storm surge component can vary widely for a given category of storm, as variations in a hurricane's size and the direction and the speed of its approach create important differences in the height of the storm surge and the areas it affects.

The National Hurricane Center first began using the Saffir-Simpson Scale in 1972 for communications with disaster officials and started including it in public advisories in 1975. After adopting the scale, the Hurricane Center went into the historical records and assigned a category number to every hurricane since 1886. Under the Saffir-Simpson Scale, the unnamed 1935 Florida Keys hurricane and Camille are the only Category 5 storms to have hit the United States. The Great Galveston Hurricane of 1900 was a Category 4 storm.

All in all, Bob Simpson undoubtedly has had more impact on hurricane research and forecasting than any other single person. He realized the need for concentrated hurricane research, he had the skill to help sell the specific idea of a National Hurricane Research Program, and he had the ability to organize and lead the program. It continues today as the NOAA's Hurricane Research Division in Miami, the world's leading tropical cyclone research institute. As director of the National Hurricane Center, Simpson incorporated all the available science and technology into a single coordinated attack on research and forecasting problems.

CHAPTER 7

CONTROLLING STORMS

SINCE THE BEGINNING of human history, wizards and shamans of all sorts have been promising to end droughts or turn away storms. In agrarian America, hundreds of "rainmakers" traveled the Great Plains in the nineteenth and early-twentieth centuries, harvesting payments from drought-stricken farmers in desperate need of rainfall. From time to time, hurricane forecasters still hear from latter-day rainmakers who believe they can do better than merely deliver rain. They promise to deliver us from tropical storms. During one major hurricane in the late 1980s, Bob Sheets, director of the National Hurricane Center at the time, received an urgent telegram from a French engineering firm offering to destroy the storm if the U.S. government would pay a substantial amount of money and then fly the company's engineers and equipment into the storm. Of course, no details could be given about the methods to be used, the telegram stated, since that was proprietary information. Also, the money had to be paid in advance. Others have sweetened the terms of the deal by offering money-back guarantees. This is similar to some of the rainmakers who took advantage of desperate farmers by guaranteeing, "If you don't get rain, you don't pay." If rain happens to fall naturally, the money changes hands. With a hurricane, if the storm were to weaken or turn away from the coast naturally, as hurricanes often do, the payment would be made. Reputable scientists simply don't fall for that kind of logic.

Some proposals are just ridiculous, such as the individual who said, "Take me out to the hurricane in an airplane and let me say the magic words that my grandmother taught me on Christmas Eve and

I will divert or destroy it." Then there was the fellow who suggested having a fleet of propeller-driven aircraft—all such aircraft owned by all the nations and corporations of the world, apparently—fly in a clockwise direction through a hurricane in order to blow against the counterclockwise winds and thereby "unwind" the storm. Not only was this idea inherently silly, but this mad scientist had the airplanes flying the wrong way if the goal was to unwind a storm. Other ideas, such as installing giant windmills along the coast to blow the storm back out to sea, are also based on misconceptions. Even if giant windmills could create a wind powerful enough to be felt miles away, the blast wouldn't help. Hurricanes are steered by winds from the ocean surface to above 40,000 feet, and these winds are con-trolled by the location and strength of huge areas of high and low pressure. No atmospheric scientist has ever been able to conceive of a way to influence these enormous features of the atmosphere and the winds they control. Even if we could influence these pressure systems for purposes of steering a hurricane, what unintended conse-quences would also flow from the manipulation? It would be the height of human folly and hubris to even think in such terms, but neither these considerations nor scientific fact has stopped some people from claiming that they could do it.

By far the most frequent suggestion since the 1940s has been to drop several hydrogen bombs in the center of a hurricane and blow it up. But the amount of energy released by a few hydrogen bombs is minuscule when measured against the energy generated by the aver-age hurricane. Several years ago, a hurricane researcher calculated that the latent heat energy released in a hurricane in just one day can be the equivalent of 400 twenty-megaton hydrogen bombs. Putting this power in other terms: if it could be converted into electricity with 100 percent efficiency, it would supply the electrical needs of the United States for six months. So a few bombs aren't going to stop a hurricane. In fact, since heat is what powers hurricanes, the nuclear explosions could actually add to the storm's total energy. And there's also the little matter of the radioactive fallout, which the storm would disperse over a wide area of the globe. Truly, this is one of those ideas whose time will never come.

The record of the swindlers, the wizards, and the well-meaning but misguided dreamers rightfully have created a great deal of skepticism toward anyone claiming the talent to control the weather. On the other hand, by the end of World War II, U.S. scientists and engineers had utilized the properties of radio waves to see enemy ships and planes in the dark, and harnessed the power of the invisible atom in unbelievable ways. The postwar public was introduced to new marvels of technology almost daily, and suddenly the idea of controlling the weather, maybe even influencing the hurricanes that were visiting the East Coast with what seemed like increasing regularity, now seemed plausible. Science and technology, mind you, not magical incantations. Even a few leading researchers at top institutions were becoming optimistic that possibly, just possibly, we could control other forces of nature as we had controlled the atom, at least to some degree.

One of these optimists was Vincent Schaefer, a meteorologist working at the General Electric Laboratory in Schenectady, New York—a premier research facility directed by Irving Langmuir, winner of the 1932 Nobel Prize in chemistry. During World War II, Schaefer had conducted research in supercooled water droplets—that is, water droplets that have formed from condensed vapor but have not frozen, even though the air temperature is below freezing. In a cloud, conditions needed to form supercooled drops often exist, particularly where there are strong upward currents carrying large quantities of water droplets above the freezing level. Schaefer's, and the government's, real concern was aircraft icing, an extremely dangerous phenomenon caused when some source of water—a supercooled cloud, drizzle, or raindrops—instantaneously freezes when it hits the surface of an aircraft, which can change the delicate shape of the wings, reducing its ability to maintain altitude. Continuing his research after the war, Schaefer discovered that finely ground dry ice (frozen carbon dioxide) can induce supercooled cloud droplets to turn into snow crystals. He apparently started a little snowfall over Pittsfield, Massachusetts, on November 13, 1946, by dropping dry ice from an airplane into a cloud.

There is no doubt about the basic science of "cloud seeding." Until the temperature drops to around minus 40 degrees, a drop of water requires some kind of a freezing nucleus in order to trigger the freezing process. The nucleus can be an ice crystal, a tiny bit of clay, or vegetation—almost any particle roughly the size and shape of an ice crystal. If a cloud has enough supercooled water, "seeding" those clouds with dry ice will encourage precipitation. As it turned out, one day after Schaefer's first cloud-seeding flight, his General Electric colleague Bernard Vonnegut, a physical chemist (and older brother of the novelist Kurt Vonnegut), discovered that silver iodide could also turn supercooled water drops into ice. In fact, silver iodide crystals work better than dry ice—better even than dust particles. When the crystals are spread into a cloud of supercooled water droplets, many of the droplets will freeze around them, and these artificially created ice crystals act just like naturally formed ice crystals. They splinter and form many more nuclei, which in turn splinter and form still more. In the early stages of this process, the drops of water or the ice crystals that make up the cloud are held aloft by rising air. As the water drops or ice crystals grow, they each eventually become too heavy to be held up by the slowly rising air in the cloud, and begin falling. If both water droplets and ice crystals are together in a cloud, the ice crystals will grow at the expense of the water drops. If those particles become large enough and it's cold enough, they fall to the ground as snow; if it's warmer, they melt on the way down to fall as rain. Either way, the cloud seeding has worked as predicted.

Schaefer's and Vonnegut's 1946 experiments in seeding led directly to Project Cirrus, which was funded by various government agencies and headed by Irving Langmuir, an enthusiastic advocate of efforts to exercise control over the weather. Project Cirrus used military airplanes to conduct cloud-seeding experiments in different parts of the United States from February 1947 through September 1952, including seeding a hurricane off the southeast coast on October 13, 1947. On that noteworthy occasion, a B-17 bomber dropped a total of 180 pounds of dry ice into clouds on the edge of the storm off the coast of South Carolina, while another B-17 took photos and a B-29 acted as the "control" airplane. The experimenters had to use dry ice instead of silver iodide, because the necessarily fine particles of silver iodide could be created only by making a smoke of the vaporized compound, and the first silver iodide generator, which Vonnegut invented, wasn't available until the following year.

When the seeding of this hurricane began, it had apparently started to turn toward the northeast, away from the U.S. coast, but around the time of the seeding, it turned abruptly westward, eventually moving ashore near Savannah, Georgia, where it did considerable damage. The Associated Press reported: "Converted bombers of Operation Cirrus radioed 'mission completed' today and headed homeward to MacDill Field after the first attempt of science to attack hurricanes with dry ice." The story also said, "Those engaged in the test were tight-lipped, but it was understood that the project carried a high degree of responsibility because of the possibility of criticism in the event storm damage occurred after the experiments."

The AP story hit the mark. Some people blamed the cloud seeding for the storm's turn toward the west. The November 10 issue of *Time* magazine said, "In Savannah last week, Southern blood bubbled toward the boiling point. A Miami weatherman had hinted that last month's disastrous hurricane might have been not an act of God, but just a low Yankee trick." *Time* went on to say that Grady Norton, the Weather Bureau's chief hurricane forecaster, had stated in a letter to a Savannah official that the seeding might have caused the hurricane to turn. The magazine then continued, "In Washington, army and navy officials remained mum. But Dr. Francis Reichelderfer, chief of the U.S. Weather Bureau, took a stormy view of the Miami suggestion. Said he: 'The Weather Bureau has no evidence which would indicate that artificial factors had anything to do with the development of the hurricane. There have been other hurricanes which behaved just as erratically.' " Reichelderfer then pointed to a hurricane in 1906 that had behaved similarly as this one in 1947, and, he told *Time*, " 'that was long before we ever heard of dry ice.' "

Later analyses clearly showed that the westward turn in the 1947 hurricane had actually taken place before the seeding, in response to winds around a large high-pressure area centered over the East Coast. This was not the famous Bermuda High, which was centered over the ocean, but a different system centered inland whose clockwise winds on its east side turned the storm back to the west. This was not a typical path for hurricanes, but, as Reichelderfer pointed out, it had happened before. In addition, and more fundamentally, further research demonstrated that the only probable effect from that kind of seeding of a small area of clouds on the edge of the hurricane would be on the immediate clouds seeded, at best, with no discernible impact on the hurricane itself.

By later standards, this first attempt to seed the clouds of a hurricane was, all in all, unbelievably casual, with no clear goals and with hardly any knowledge whether hurricanes even contain much supercooled water or, if they do, what part of the storm it might be in. The Project Cirrus scientists had no theory of how seeding should affect a hurricane. To future scientists, those involved seemed to be almost like high school kids playing with a chemistry set in the basement: "Let's mix these chemicals and see what happens." A history of Project Cirrus that General Electric published in 1952 says that the researchers "hoped that the experience thus gained would permit the planning of further operations in the future, with the hope of possibly steering or in other ways modifying tropical hurricanes." Soon after the experiment, Langmuir wrote: "The main thing that we learned from this flight is that we need to know enormously more than we do at present about hurricanes. . . . I think that, with increased knowledge, we should be able to abolish the evil effects of these hurricanes."

Such optimism continued from the late 1940s into the 1960s, as Langmuir and others made claims about the prospects of "weather control" that went far beyond the accomplishments of cloud seeding. Newspaper and magazine writers enjoyed writing about these speculations, a fondness reflected in the *Readers' Guide to Periodical Literature*, which had a section for articles about weather control from 1947 until 1973. Overblown claims led some scientists to see the cloud seeders as nothing more than contemporary versions of the nineteenth-century rainmakers, and this bias tarnished the image of those researchers who were conducting well-thought-out experiments in what came to be called "weather modification."

In the area of hurricane research, specifically, serious attention was given to ways of weakening the storms by disrupting the heat pump that drives them. Since hurricanes draw their power from water vapor that has evaporated from the warm ocean waters of the tropics, many suggestions were put forward for reducing evaporation. Most involved cooling the tropical ocean in some way. Cooler water would yield less evaporation and therefore throttle the supply of water vapor: the idea is correct, but the implementation turns out to be essentially impossible. At one time or another enthusiasts have suggested that large amounts of dry ice would do the job, or maybe giant icebergs towed to tropical waters from the Arctic or the Antarctic. But again, all the dry ice in the world, and most of the icebergs as well, would soon be absorbed and forgotten by just a small portion of the ocean from which even a modest hurricane draws its incredible energy. Even if such methods could work, the shipping and handling costs would be astronomical.

Another idea was to use Ocean Thermal Energy Conversion (OTEC) systems, which work in areas with warm ocean water at the surface and water at least 36 degrees Fahrenheit colder within about 3,000 feet of the surface; such conditions are common in the tropics and parts of the subtropics. These systems use the warm water to evaporate a "working fluid," such as ammonia in sealed pipes, which boils at about 78 degrees. The working fluid boils into expanding vapor, which drives a turbine attached to a generator to produce electricity. Deeper cold is used to condense the vapor back into liquid, and the cycle continues. During the oil shortages of the 1970s, when the federal government was funding research on various kinds of alternative energy sources, suggestions were made that OTEC systems could be installed along the Gulf Coast to produce inexpensive power. The systems could be of the type that pumped cold water to the surface to cool the working fluid, which would have the side benefit of cooling the ocean's surface water in places. But there are several enormous problems, including the cost of building the systems, maintenance in the harsh ocean environment (including saltwater corrosion, a problem that also stands in the way of harnessing the tides for energy), and damage from storms. Moreover, even the largest systems would affect only a minuscule portion of the Gulf of Mexico, since the cooler water pumped to the surface would be quickly dispersed and replaced by warmer water. Even if the water along the coast were cool, a hurricane that gains strength far out in the Gulf and moves quickly inland would be weakened little by the cool water right along the shore.

No, deep pumping of cooler water wouldn't work, but another way to reduce the amount of ocean water that evaporates to feed hurricanes might be to spread monomolecular films over the surface of the sea. Such films are used on some freshwater reservoirs to reduce loss of water through evaporation, and they do have an advantage over other materials that might be spread to reduce evaporation—they are harmless to the environment, at least on the relatively small bodies of water on which they're used. We could wonder what the potential environmental effects would be if such films could be spread over an area of the ocean large enough to block enough evaporation to actually weaken a hurricane, but the question is made moot by one obviously insurmountable problem: winds above 30 or 40 miles per hour break up the films.

With any and all of the methods that were proposed to lower evaporation, one barrier is greater than all others: a hurricane's immense size. In addition, hurricanes move and would quickly pass over any treated area and would replenish their strength in virgin water. Even in their formative stages, tropical cyclones cover tens of thousands of square miles and suck energy from thousands of square miles of ocean surface. And if we could, in theory, somehow implement one of the proposed ideas, the cost would be prohibitive.

In the end, almost all researchers and thinkers concluded that attempts to cut off the supply of warm, humid air that flows into a hurricane's lower levels are just not feasible, for a host of reasons. But what about taking a look at the all-important top of the storm? Scientists refer to a hurricane as a "heat engine" because its power ultimately depends on the differences in temperature between the warm ocean under the storm and the cold air aloft—specifically, at the boundary between the troposphere (the lower layer of the atmosphere) and the stratosphere. In the tropics this boundary is around 55,000 feet. Powerful storms also need some mechanism or dynamic at the very top that can serve as an "exhaust system." That is, if the air spiraling into the developing system at low levels does not flow freely out at some upper level, the low-pressure area below would soon fill with air, increasing the pressure, and the system would die. Frequently, the exhaust system is an existing upper-level anticyclone that moves over a developing tropical storm. Such an upper-level anticyclone is an area in which the air pressure at a particular altitude, say 40,000 feet, is higher than the pressure of the surrounding air at the same altitude. Air spiraling out of the anticyclone, opposite to the flow of the cyclone below, carries away the air that's rising in the storm. It serves as a super-flue, and it stokes the fires below like nothing else.

Researchers wondered whether it would be possible to warm up the top of the storm, and in this way diminish the temperature differential that helps drive the storm and perhaps slow down the exhaust system. In the early 1960s, scientists looked at one idea for doing just this, involving an innovative methodology and technology developed at Johns Hopkins University. The plan called for producing enormous numbers of very small plastic bubbles only a few microns across that would be impregnated with materials that absorb infrared radiation. Aircraft would spread the tiny bubbles in the top of the hurricane, where the bubbles would absorb the infrared radiation and thereby warm the air around them. Theoretically, this artificial, small-scale greenhouse effect at the top of the storm would reduce the temperature difference with the bottom of the storm, which should weaken the whole system. However, the infrared-absorbing bubbles never got beyond the idea stage because there are good reasons to think that they would not stay where they were spread, but would be dispersed fairly quickly by the storm's outflow.

The scientists thinking about the bubbles were working under the auspices of Project Stormfury, an adjunct of the work of the National Hurricane Research Project and the government's major hurricane-modification study between 1961 and 1983. The goals for the modification project were modest: "to investigate possible thermodynamic imbalances which may permit modification of the structure and movement of hurricanes." Bob Simpson had begun thinking about the prospects of seeding the top of the hurricane years before, shortly after the war when he flew into a hurricane off Bermuda on an air force WB-29. Simpson was trying to investigate the upper-level currents in the hurricane and had expected the storm's top to be about 30,000 feet. But even after climbing to nearly

40,000 feet, essentially as high as the B-29 could fly, he found that
the cirrostratus clouds were still sloped sharply upward. As the airplane turned toward the center of the storm, Simpson reported,
"Through this fog in which we were traveling at 250 miles an hour
there loomed from time to time ghost-like structures rising like huge
white marble monuments. . . . Actually, these were shafts of supercooled water which rose vertically and passed out of sight overhead. . . . Each time we passed through one of these shafts, the
leading edge of the wing accumulated an amazing extra coating of
rime ice. . . . We were so close to the center of the storm by the time
the icing was discovered that the shafts were too numerous to avoid."

Simpson correctly concluded from the icing phenomenon that
hurricanes contain large amounts of supercooled water at high altitudes—good targets for some kind of seeding that might generate
heat. A dozen years later, as he began formulating plans for Project
Stormfury in 1960, Simpson received something like confirmation
for his earlier observations from Herbert Riehl, one of the world's
leading tropical meteorologists. Riehl told Simpson about a flight he
had made in a navy jet through the top of Hurricane Donna, where
he found that the outflow at the top of the hurricane emanated from
the huge towers of cumulus clouds in the hurricane's right front
quadrant. Riehl believed that these towers were the sole source of
mass outflow to a colder environment, and he felt that air rising in
the other parts of the storm was sinking and disappearing within the
area encompassed by the rain bands. In short, Simpson concluded
that the supercooled cloud droplets he had seen might be concentrated in just one part of most large hurricanes. If that were correct,
seeding this single area might make things happen.

While he was working on the Stormfury proposal, Simpson also
recalled a conversation he'd had some years earlier with Evguenij K.
Fedorov, the head of the Soviet Union's Hydrometeorological Service in Moscow. When Simpson had asked Fedorov whether he had
a good physical basis for the hail-prevention seeding experiment the
Russians were conducting, Fedorov answered, "I can tell you one
thing. We're learning a great deal about severe storms that produce
hail, why some severe storms don't produce hail. I think it's worth

any cost we have just from the prediction point of view rather than whether or not we ever learn to prevent it."

Even if seeding the tops of storms didn't turn out to be a good way to "control" them, Simpson believed that seeding could prove to be valuable in learning about their basic structure. "No matter what we do, we can't lose," he decided. "Punching or stimulating some aspect of this big thing, the hurricane, might tell us a great deal about the energetics of it, which might help us in the forecasting of it." The idea for seeding storms had come a long way from the earliest work of Vincent Schaefer and Bernard Vonnegut. Simpson and his Project Stormfury colleagues hypothesized that spreading silver iodide into a hurricane's huge tower would cause the supercooled water in the tower to freeze, which releases heat. This heat in turn could cause the eye wall to die and reform a greater distance from the center, which would weaken the hurricane's winds.

Herbert Riehl and Joanne Malkus, a leading tropical meteorologist and a pioneer in computer modeling of clouds, were consultants to the National Hurricane Research Project. Malkus acknowledges that she became involved in Project Stormfury as "an antagonist rather than a protagonist. I thought that this was a rather speculative idea, and I expressed rather strong doubts in view of the huge amounts of energy that the hurricane released." Still, she thought the modification research "was a long shot worth trying" because of the damage hurricanes cause. Maybe the researchers could find the cyclone's "Achilles' heel," she wrote, "some internal instability that can be triggered in such a way as to set off a predictable chain of events leading to a reduction in the storm's intensity."

Malkus and Bob Simpson were married in 1965, and she headed Project Stormfury in 1965 and 1966. In various articles and reports, the Simpsons hypothesized that seeding could reduce hurricane wind speed by 10 to 15 percent. Perhaps this doesn't sound like much—or enough—but since the force exerted by wind is proportional to the square of the speed (a wind of 100 miles per hour exerts four times the force of a 50-mile-per-hour wind), small changes can have dramatic effects. The reduction in the wind speed that the Simpsons hoped for would result in a 20 to 30 percent reduction in the force of the wind, with a similar reduction in damage, at the very least. One study of hurricane damage in the United States concluded that the cost of wind damage, specifically, goes up at an even higher rate than the force of the wind. According to this study, a reduction of wind speed from 100 to 90 miles per hour could cut total damage by 65 percent. A similar study in Australia concluded that a 10 percent reduction of average wind speed would cut average annual damage in half.

Given these numbers, the 10 percent reduction in wind speed no longer sounds insignificant. It sounds almost utopian instead, but the math does work. Even using the very conservative direct relationship between wind speed and force as a damage relationship, a 10 percent reduction in the wind speeds of Hurricane Andrew over south Florida in 1992 could have resulted in damage reductions of as much as 20 percent—or $6 billion. Even more property and money could be saved if a particular reduction in wind speed coincided with some threshold value for building failures. For instance, if roofs begin lifting off at 120 miles per hour, but stay in place at 110 miles per hour, then damage reduction from that particular 10-mile-per-hour reduction in wind speed could be huge.

The Stormfury hypothesis about using cloud seeding to weaken a hurricane was first tested by Weather Bureau and navy scientists and aircraft crews on September 16, 1961, when a navy airplane working with Weather Bureau airplanes spread silver iodide in the eye wall of Hurricane Esther, about 400 miles north of Puerto Rico. One reason Esther was picked was that it was far enough out at sea that if it did make a sudden turn after the seeding, it wouldn't hit land in the next few days. Those involved didn't want a repeat of the flap that followed the 1947 Project Cirrus seeding experiment. When seeded, the strengthening Hurricane Esther immediately stopped growing stronger and even showed signs of weakening. The following day the aircraft returned to seed, but the seeding canisters fell outside the eye wall, and the storm showed no changes. Over the next five days the northwestward-moving hurricane turned toward the north, remaining off the East Coast, which was very good news for the researchers.

The results of the experiment were encouraging, and Project Stormfury was formally established for the following hurricane season. The scientists were much more prepared to conduct meaningful research than the Project Cirrus scientists had been fifteen years earlier. They collected detailed measurements from the inner cores of half a dozen hurricanes and published almost sixty reports. Computer models of individual clouds, developed by Joanne Simpson and others, allowed researchers to simulate the effects of seeding, giving them a much better idea of what might work. Also, Pierre St. Amand of the navy's Weapons Laboratory at China Lake, California, had developed a silver iodide generator that could be dropped like a bomb, an improvement over the old canisters as a way to spread the silver iodide crystals.

When Hurricane Beulah showed up about 400 miles north of Puerto Rico on August 23, 1963, Project Stormfury was ready with ten airplanes. Two navy A-3 Skywarriors dropped several of the new generator bombs as they flew across the eye wall. The idea was that the hurricane's winds would carry this dense sheet of silver iodide crystals all the way around the eye. Two Weather Bureau DC-6's and a WB-57 measured the storm's core for a five-hour period, from two and a half hours before seeding until two and a half hours afterward, at altitudes of 7,000, 18,000, and 40,000 feet. A B-26 studied clouds and rain bands, a navy Super Constellation dropped instruments on parachutes into the eye wall, and two high-flying airplanes photographed changes in the storm's clouds. A second navy Super Constellation coordinated the whole show, which went off without a hitch—except for the fact that the seeding failed to produce any results as measured by the instruments aboard the ten aircraft. The problem? The silver iodide had missed the highest clouds around the center of the storm. But this misfire might not have been the only problem; the team knew that the storm at that stage wasn't a good seeding candidate anyway, with highest winds of only 90 miles per hour and without a clearly outlined eye. They were hoping for radically "better" conditions in a day or two, for purposes of comparison. The following day they got those conditions: Beulah now had a well-formed eye and maximum winds of up to 115 miles per hour. The bombardiers aboard the Skywarriors hit the target perfectly with their silver iodide bombs, and in a short while aircraft crews reported that the eye wall was disintegrating.

Or had it? Joanne and Bob Simpson, who were on the navy Constellation controlling the experiment, thought they saw changes in the storm, but, as Joanne said later, "I could never claim with all the clouds around, all growing very high, that the seeding had actually intensified the clouds. We sort of celebrated when we got back. We knew it was an operational success, and then we had to determine whether it was a scientific success." Confirming the preliminary results took months of work. The Simpsons and their collaborators painstakingly drew cloud maps by hand, using photographs taken off the radar screens on the navy Super Constellation aircraft (which had the best radar of the airplanes) during and after the seeding, as well as notes they had made by hand in their scientific notebooks. The final results showed that the eye wall had indeed disintegrated and that the highest winds had decreased by about 20 percent and moved farther from the center. Promising news indeed. Also good news was the fact that this hurricane was moving northward when it was seeded and never approached land. While the scientists knew their seeding experiments wouldn't change a storm's course, they realized that a lot of people might not understand this.

Despite the encouraging results of seeding Beulah, six years passed before another hurricane was seeded. One key reason for the delay was the Stormfury criteria for selection of a target. The hurricane had to be a mature one, with a reasonably well-developed eye wall. Forecasters had to believe that it would remain within a reasonable operational range of aircraft operating from Puerto Rico, Bermuda, or Florida for at least twenty-four hours, and that it would remain well away from land for at least twenty-four hours, preferably forty-eight hours, after the seeding experiments. The last restriction stemmed not only from the Project Cirrus experience in 1947 but also from the Stormfury scientists' desire for the "cleanest" laboratory possible for their experiments. They wanted to ensure that the storm wasn't being affected by land because such effects would be difficult to separate from those that might be induced by the seeding. By this time, the politics involved with the project began to wear on Joanne Simpson, as a few scientists and forecasters in the Weather Bureau were quoted in newspapers deriding Project Stormfury, even though the National Science Foundation had made weather modification a centerpiece of its activities.

In 1965, Hurricane Betsy did look like a promising candidate for seeding, and several research flights were made into the storm, including the first hurricane flight by Bob Sheets, who had joined the project. But Betsy never met the Stormfury criteria, at first because it didn't have a well-formed eye wall and later because forecasters said it could hit land within forty-eight hours. It's probably just as well Betsy wasn't seeded. On September 5, the storm was about 300 miles east of Cape Canaveral, Florida, and a normal hurricane path would have taken it north, maybe to hit the Carolinas or to turn back out to sea. Instead, Betsy turned back to the south, hit Florida just south of Miami, crossed Florida into the Gulf of Mexico, and came ashore again near Grand Isle, Louisiana, with 135-mile-per-hour winds. The storm killed 75 people and did more than an estimated $7.5 billion damage (in year 2000 dollars). The turn was more unusual and the damage much greater than that of the 1947 hurricane that had caused so much controversy about seeding.

No storms suitable for seeding showed up over the next three years, but the Project Stormfury team would assemble several aircraft in Puerto Rico to run practice missions that included testing seeding devices on lines of clouds over the Caribbean Sea and monitoring the effects. Finally, after the six-year hiatus, a suitable storm came along in 1969 and actual seeding experiments resumed. By then, the methods for spreading the seeding agent had been greatly improved. The seeding generators were now small, shotgun-shell-size devices. Earlier experiments had used much larger generators, and many fewer of them than were tried now. The new generators were loaded in pods mounted on the outside of the aircraft, with each pod holding as many as 100 shells. As the airplane flew through the target cloud, the shells were shot well away from the aircraft. The material in the shell would then ignite and burn as it fell, giving off a plume of silver iodide smoke. These much more reliable devices enabled the researchers to seed a larger area of clouds. As the burning canisters fell, they spread silver iodide deeper into the clouds than previous techniques had done. A more massive and extended seeding period was also planned, with better control of the aircraft delivering the silver iodide. Most important, the experiment called for repeated heavy seeding of the first rain band outside the eye wall, with the hope of creating a second eye wall that would cut off the flow of humid air to the original eye wall.

The target for the new protocol was Hurricane Debbie, which moved into range of the project aircraft on August 18, 1969, when it was centered about 700 miles east of Puerto Rico and traveling toward the northwest. After five seedings at two-hour intervals on the 18th, the researchers determined that the maximum wind speed had decreased from 115 to about 80 miles per hour, a remarkable reduction of about 30 percent. For the next twenty-four hours the hurricane was left to its own devices, a pause that proved quite instructive, because the maximum winds returned to the original speed of 115 miles per hour. When the aircraft returned to the hurricane for the second round of seeding on August 20, Debbie was centered about 500 miles north-northeast of Puerto Rico, still moving toward the northwest but forecast to turn north and then northeast, which would ensure it wouldn't hit any land within two days. The second seeding then decreased the wind speeds again, this time to just under 100 miles per hour, a reduction of about 15 percent. An important bonus was that the forecast turned out to be correct, and Debbie never threatened land.

As it happened, this seeding activity had required a major portion of the best available navy reconnaissance and Weather Bureau research aircraft for the Atlantic and Gulf regions, leaving limited resources to monitor Hurricane Camille, which was driving toward the Mississippi Gulf Coast. Therefore, all the news stories about Camille also included news of the apparent success of seeding Debbie, holding out promise that such killer storms as Camille could be weakened. Subsequent analyses indicated that a portion of the wind speed reduction reported inside Debbie on August 18—but only for the 18th, not for the 20th—was probably caused by influences of large-scale weather patterns, but the studies also concluded that significant reduction on both days could reasonably be attributed to the seeding. In addition, although radar coverage was less than optimum, later analyses supported the hypothesis that the eye of Debbie had expanded after the seeding events. The results from the Hurricane Debbie experiments seemed so positive that many researchers believed the project should become fully operational and fully prepared to seed major hurricanes that threatened landfall. A team of scientists at Stanford Research Institute at Stanford University conducted a comprehensive independent "decision analysis" of all past seeding events that strongly endorsed the Stormfury research. The report said, "The Government may have to accept the responsibility for not seeding and thereby exposing the public to higher probabilities of severe storm damage and possible higher death tolls." James Matheson of that group stated, "We claim they should consider seeding now, if a big hurricane comes straight for Miami."

Ironically, perhaps, the Stormfury scientists themselves, although encouraged by the results, strongly disagreed with the idea that a proven technology had been developed. Robert Cecil Gentry, who was then the director of project, after taking over from Joanne Simpson, responded: "First, a hurricane naturally undergoes sharp changes as it crosses a land area." He obviously wasn't referring to Debbie, which never neared land, but was making the point that researchers who seeded hurricanes as they neared land would not be able to sort out what the seeding had accomplished and what nature had done. He could imagine a seeding experiment near land that was followed by a hurricane's growing stronger, in which case the lawyers would have a field day. Second, Gentry said, "It is still not a proven fact that Stormfury can weaken a hurricane." The major element missing from the Debbie experiments had been the ability to monitor and document the entire hypothesized sequence of events. That is, while the speeds and directions of the wind in different parts of the storm were reasonably well monitored, little was known about the small-scale physical changes in the clouds—the microphysics, as they were labeled—and the three-dimensional structure of the showers and thunderstorms. The DC-6 aircraft hadn't been able to fly high enough to monitor the highest cloud column to be seeded, and the jet fighter aircraft delivering the silver iodide had no instruments to make such measurements. In addition, the airborne radar available (which didn't supply images of the detailed structures that we now have from airborne Doppler radars) was able only to document gross changes in the eye wall and rain bands.

The Stormfury Advisory Panel, acting under the auspices of the National Science Foundation, agreed with the project scientists that more information was needed before the program became fully operational. The panel recommended that "top priority . . . be given to the acquisition . . . of aircraft and instrumentation necessary to obtain accurate and representative observations of liquid and solid water content of the eye wall and vicinity in the layer from approximately 20,000 to 35,000 feet, before, during, and after seeding." Another recommendation was the closer monitoring of unseeded hurricanes as a "control" mechanism. The scientists could then compare the natural variability of hurricanes with the behavior of seeded storms.

Congress endorsed these recommendations and appropriated $30 million to obtain the necessary aircraft and instrumentation to study more thoroughly the Stormfury hypothesis. One of the most important benefits of this endorsement and appropriation was the purchase of two new Lockheed WP-3D aircraft and state-of-the-art instruments, including Inertial Navigation Systems, which greatly improved wind measurements. The new airplanes carried several cloud physics instruments to more accurately measure liquid water contents, ice contents, and cloud particles. Digitized radar systems now incorporated the first airborne Doppler weather radar and recording system. It was the beginning of a whole new era in atmospheric and oceanographic data collection and research. These airplanes and their equipment earned their keep over the next few years, even though no storms were seeded, because their research flights revealed much about hurricane structure that had not previously been documented.

Because no hurricanes meeting the selection criteria formed in the Atlantic in the early and mid-1970s, Stormfury leaders once again considered moving operations to the western Pacific Ocean, operating from Guam, or to the eastern Pacific, operating from Mexico. They also looked into the possibility of combining Atlantic Ocean operations with operations from Australia, a cooperative arrangement that would allow Atlantic hurricanes to be seeded during the northern summer and those around Australia during the southern summer. Nothing came of any these ideas, however, because of potential political problems. One such problem was the fact that more than a quarter century after the Project Cirrus incident in 1947, every unusual movement by a seeded hurricane was likely to prompt someone with access to a microphone or a printing press to blame the seeding. Joanne Simpson recalls that, in the mid-1960s, "we were getting static from the State Department, very real static. Castro was saying we were using hurricanes as warfare against him. Mexico claimed we were seeding storms off the west coast of Mexico, depriving them of moisture and hurting their agriculture." It was true that some hurricane researchers made flights into storms off the west coast of Mexico when there were no hurricanes in the Atlantic to study, but not with aircraft equipped to seed. None of these storms was ever seeded. Elsewhere around the hurricane-prone world, critics were also uneasy about seeding hurricanes. In 1965, when the Simpsons attended a conference in Manila, the Philippines, to discuss moving Stormfury experiments to the western Pacific, where there are more storms than in the Atlantic, the Japanese raised the same objection: storms inadvertently steered away from Japan might deprive the islands of needed rain.

When Hurricane Fifi struck Honduras in 1974, taking perhaps 10,000 lives with floods and mud slides following torrential rains, a transplanted Cuban in Mexico, writing under the name "Dr. Vivo," wrote newspaper articles claiming that the United States had seeded the hurricane to divert it from Florida's beaches, thereby inadvertently steering it into Honduras. Bob Sheets, who was then the assistant scientific director of Project Stormfury, had to address this challenge at a lecture in Mexico City, where the packed house included reporters drawn by the growing controversy. The first question from the somewhat hostile audience concerned the alleged seeding and steering of Fifi. Sheets replied that no hurricanes had been seeded since 1971, and that, in fact, the United States had flown no research missions at all over the western Atlantic, the Caribbean, or the Gulf of Mexico in 1974. A large project sponsored by the World Meteorological Organization had diverted all available

U.S. research aircraft to the eastern Atlantic, where they operated out of Dakar, Senegal. Sheets was fortunate to find confirmation in the lecture hall from a Mexican scientist who spoke up to say that he had flown on one of the U.S. airplanes in Africa at the time of Fifi. The atmosphere in the room changed markedly, and apparently news of the testimony in Mexico City preceded Sheets to his next stop, Honduras, where the alleged chicanery involving Fifi was now a dead letter.

Sheets became the scientific director of Stormfury in 1977, and numerous research flights were conducted for the next three years. Still, no hurricanes suitable for seeding were tracking through the target zone over the Atlantic Ocean. This was discouraging. So was new research in cloud physics, which had been accelerated to investigate the critical "seedability" factor of clouds. The studies did confirm that there are zones of supercooled water where seeding would probably be effective, but they also revealed that other target areas that would qualify for seeding under the revised Stormfury protocol

Dr. Bob Sheets at the Chief Scientist position in the cockpit of the NOAA WP-3 Hurricane Hunter aircraft in 1979. Sheets flew through the "eyes" of hurricanes more than 200 times from 1965 through 1980.

already had numerous ice particles. Since natural ice particles are good seeding agents, their presence might make an artificial seeding agent redundant. How could the scientists know whether the natural or the artificial seeding agent, or some combination, had done the job?

Nor was Hurricane Debbie forgotten. In 1980 yet another study compared the results of that Stormfury experiment eleven years earlier with data from Hurricanes David in 1979 and Allen in 1980, two unseeded storms that gave evidence of natural changes similar to those recorded in Debbie. The studies again raised the question whether the Debbie changes had been caused by the seeding or had occurred naturally.

One could argue that the fact that the changes occur naturally is good for seeding, because seeding could perhaps induce them to take place when nature doesn't, for whatever reason. The bottom line would be beneficial: no matter whether nature or seeding changed the storm, wind speeds would be reduced. Still, the scientific questions about seeding, the costs of keeping aircraft and crews and researchers on standby from late July through October, the severe shortage of storms that fit the criteria for experimentation — all of these considerations finally reached a critical mass in 1980. A consensus developed that more needed to be known about the internal processes of hurricanes, and better criteria needed to be established to determine if change was from seeding or from natural causes, before the government should consider resuming modification experiments. Since suitable hurricanes are so rare, it might take hundreds of years to gather sound statistics simply based upon the changes in wind speed that would reveal whether the experiments are really working—a doubtful and politically difficult use of the taxpayers' money. So Project Stormfury was shut down in 1983.

Bob Simpson says, "I never personally felt we stood much of a chance of operationally proving the modification of a storm feasible until we leaned an awful lot more about the hurricane and its energy processes. But, we had to have a starting point." The real legacy of Project Stormfury is the knowledge that it generated and the resources it purchased, including the two NOAA's WP-3 airplanes, which are now in their third decade of service.

Nearly two decades after the demise of Stormfury, the question hangs over the hurricane community: Since seeding did seem to show promise, and since hurricanes still cause terrible loss of life and property, should seeding experimentation be revived? Did those involved give up too soon? Researchers now believe that hurricane-seeding projects should stay on hold for now. Both research and operational cloud seeding continue today, but the aim is to squeeze a little more precipitation from clouds than would otherwise occur, or to clear fog from runways at airports. The great majority of meteorologists don't think in terms of controlling hurricanes. At the present time and for the foreseeable future, money available for hurricane research would be better spent enhancing basic understanding, especially of the internal dynamics that cause storms to strengthen and weaken, and improving forecasts. Investments in better data-gathering and in improved computer models would almost assuredly pay bigger dividends than any hurricane modification program that any scientist can now propose. Future modification programs, if any, should await proven understanding and technology that is not only scientifically sound but logistically and economically feasible.

CHAPTER 8

THE 1970S AND '80S

FLYING AROUND hurricane country on his official duties, Neil Frank, the director of the National Hurricane Center from 1973 to 1987, liked the pilots of the Weather Bureau's DC-6 or the NOAA's WP-3 to cruise right along the coastline while he crouched by a window, clicking away with his 35-millimeter camera at all those coastal features—sand dunes, beach houses, beachfront restaurants, condos, and a lot more—that wouldn't be there the morning after a major hurricane struck the shore. He'd be sure to get the shot of a particularly egregious example of dangerous development, such as the four-story apartment building with only 100 feet of level beach between it and the ocean. The photographs were all grist for Frank's before-and-after-the-hurricane-hit slide show, which he delivered with urgency because coastal populations were increasing much faster even than our forecasting ability, and few of these coastal residents, including responsible local officials in high-risk areas, had actually experienced a major hurricane. He often traced his commitment to the cause of preparedness to an encounter he had while investigating the effect of Hurricane Betsy's storm surge in the Miami area, in 1965. Frank found a street with flooded houses on one side and dry houses on the other side. A woman walked out of one of the flooded homes and wasn't happy when the gregarious Frank introduced himself as a scientist collecting data on storm surge. She demanded, "Why didn't someone tell me I would have been safe on the other side of the street?"

Frank decided to do just that, every opportunity he had, up and down the Atlantic and Gulf Coasts. The number of strong hurricanes hitting the United States had decreased since the late 1960s, but this was almost a mixed blessing for preparedness: more people and fewer hurricanes meant that the newcomers weren't learning about hurricanes as quickly as they would have back in the 1950s. In many areas, no one really knew just how much time was required to evacuate vulnerable neighborhoods. Plans for coping with hurricanes were marginal at best, because most civil defense directors were still centered around Cold War plans for surviving a nuclear attack. Frank, other forecasters, and a few emergency management officials led the transition from a focus on nuclear attack survival to preparedness for natural disasters, such as hurricanes, as well as for man-made disasters such as toxic waste accidents. State and local governments began changing the name from "civil defense" to "emergency management," and the federal government eventually followed.

Naïve people thought a repeat of a disaster on the scale of the Great Galveston Hurricane of 1900 was impossible in more modern times, but they were mistaken. Galveston is now protected by a sea-wall and has in place one of the country's best evacuation plans, but long stretches of the Gulf and Atlantic Coasts were just as vulnerable in the '70s and '80s as they had been in 1900 (and just as vulnerable, or even more so, in the first decade of the twenty-first century) because they're packed with more people than ever—about fifty million—and more valuable property—an incalculable sum.

So when he became the nation's chief hurricane forecaster, in 1973, Frank decided to fill the role of Cassandra. If few of the thousands of families taking up residence on the coastal plains had any experience with hurricanes, Frank would attempt to substitute education. He spent much of his time traveling the hurricane-prone coasts, making speeches and giving radio, television, and newspaper interviews. Often accompanied by local forecasters of the National Weather Service, he met with local business people, government officials, and local and state emergency management officials. Almost always he set up his before-and-after slide show featuring Hurricane Camille: if this demonstration of the power of a storm to take lives and destroy property in the modern world didn't get everyone's attention, nothing would. He even visited new residential developments along the coast to talk in person with property owners, salespeople, and, when possible, the developers. At one such meeting in the late '70s in Hilton Head, South Carolina, an island that was evolving into a premier community of retirement homes and second homes, Frank asked one of the salespeople if this area had a hurricane problem. The man laughed. Frank then asked if the residents had any kind of evacuation plan, and the man replied he didn't see any need to evacuate. Then Frank said, "If I told you two thousand people died out here in 1893 when the islands went under water, would you change your mind?" The man's face turned ashen. Today, Beaufort County, South Carolina, where Hilton Head is located, has a highly regarded emergency management operation. Signs all around the county make clear how high the water from surge could be at that location, and "Hurricane Evacuation Route" signs dot the roads. When Hurricane Hugo headed for South Carolina in 1989, thousands of residents fled Beaufort County; if the storm had hit there instead of Charleston to the north, there would have been no repeat of the 1893 tragedy.

At a new development on the southwestern coast of Florida, Frank talked with a local official who said he wouldn't evacuate his home, which was only a street or two back from the beach: "We need to stay here since we know a hurricane is going to put water up in our homes. We need to be here so that when the storm goes away, we can open the doors and let the water out to minimize our flood damage." Frank replied, "Guess what? If this development had been here in Donna in 1960, you would have had at least eight feet of water in your living room. What are you going to do then, since your ceiling is eight feet high?" Again, since then emergency management departments in southwestern Florida have become among the nation's most active, because they know the dangers their residents face.

When Frank was making his rounds in the NOAA's state-of-the-art WP-3, the crew would open the hurricane-hunting airplane for public tours, and Frank, local forecasters, and local emergency management officials would be sure safety brochures were available. Local television and newspaper reporters interviewed crew members and photographed the airplane, inside and out. Some reporters were surprised to find in Neil Frank a public official who spoke candidly, admitting that forecast landfalls can be off by 100 miles or even more. He explained meteorology in understandable terms. He got a lot of ink, he got on the air, and the word spread, because Frank was an extraordinarily effective spokesperson for hurricane preparedness.

Human lives were the main concern of Frank's campaign, but the unnecessary loss of property was another, and the issue came into high profile in the hurricane community in 1983. On the night of August 14, thunderstorms developed along a frontal trough over the Gulf of Mexico south of Mississippi, Alabama, and Florida. By noon the next day the sustained winds had reached 45 miles per hour, and it was named as the first tropical storm of the 1983 Atlantic season: Alicia. By the following afternoon the storm was a modest hurricane. It hit the Texas coastline with 115-mile-per-hour winds and a storm surge of twelve feet. Alicia then pushed across Houston, fifty miles inland, where its winds blew gravel from the rooftops of downtown skyscrapers. The flying gravel crashed like bullets into the neighboring skyscrapers' windows, which had been designed to withstand a hurricane's winds but not flying gravel. Hundreds of panes shattered, while others remained whole but were "sucked" off the building or blown out when windows on the other side of the building shattered. Falling glass, in large and small pieces, was one of Alicia's urban hazards. The storm then weakened as it quickly moved north across Oklahoma and Kansas, where heavy rain eased a drought. Ironically, a weakening storm can be a dangerous storm for another reason: tornadoes. Alicia spawned at least twenty-three of them, most of which were weak, with winds between 40 and 72 miles per hour, but one that touched down near Tyler, in northeastern Texas, was strong.

Most hurricanes spawn few, if any, tornadoes. The twenty-three from Alicia were on the high side. They seem to be most prevalent in the United States but have been reported in all countries hit by tropical cyclones; sometimes it's difficult to confirm tornadoes because of the problem of distinguishing between their damage and damage from a hurricane's ordinary winds. What *is* known—thanks to the work of William Gray and his colleagues at Colorado State University in the 1970s—is that strong hurricanes that begin to rapidly weaken after hitting land are the most likely to spawn tornadoes, as the surface winds are slowed by friction with land and structures while winds aloft are still blowing at high speeds. Wind shear between the slower surface winds and faster winds above them creates a mini–spinning motion within the larger spinning motion of the whole storm. This aberration can become a tornado. "We had a forecast rule," Gray says. "If a hurricane has come in around you and the winds near the surface are weak, and you look up and the clouds are going by fast, you're in the environment that's favorable for tornadoes."

Alicia happened to be the hurricane that ended the three-year lull for storms making landfall on the mainland. (Hurricane Allen had hit Brownsville, Texas, on August 9, 1980.) In the aftermath of Alicia, attention was focused on the damage on Galveston Island, where the famous seawall built after the Great Galveston Hurricane of 1900 wasn't able to protect the beach itself. Alicia's storm surge, wave action, and attendant currents washed away 50 to 200 feet of some sections of the beach; that is, the beach was 50 to 200 feet narrower than it had been. Moreover, the Federal Emergency Management Agency (FEMA) dispatched a team of engineers to survey Alicia's property damage, and the report was a textbook of poor building practices. Texas has a "home rule" approach to such matters as building codes, giving local governments great power and, in the end, often encouraging inadequate codes, or even no codes. In many cases, the pilings that lifted houses above the storm surge weren't seated deep enough in the sandy soil to withstand the erosion caused by the same storm surge and waves. In other cases, the pilings were too small for the house or building they supported. When the pilings fell or broke, the building plunged into the water. The FEMA team discovered that, in many cases, the pilings weren't bolted or attached in any way to the floor joists or supporting beams. Gravity alone was supposed to keep the building atop the pilings—but it didn't. Even in structures in which hurricane "clips" had been used to connect the pilings to the floor joists and the supporting beams, the clips often weren't large enough for the job, or were so badly rusted that the wind snapped them, or were improperly installed and more or less worthless. Many buildings were merely nailed together.

Of course, the poor construction standards and practices exposed by Alicia were nothing new. In her book *Hurricane*, Marjory Stoneman Douglas wrote:

> From his earliest history man learned to shelter himself from the wildness of weather by building a house. The things which can be done to keep a roof from blowing away and house walls from crashing in under pressure have been studied and are simple enough. It is extraordinary that tens of thousands of people in countries subject to hurricane winds and waters live contentedly in houses that can give them no protection whatsoever. The shocking thing is not only that cities must have building codes and police powers to keep people ordinarily safe but that there are so few cities which have

Hurricane Alicia, Galveston, Texas. August 17, 1983.

and enforce building codes adequate to protect all of their people in hurricanes.

That book was published in 1958. A quarter century later, Alicia struck Galveston. Nearly two decades after Alicia, although some building improvements have been made, including better use of hurricane connectors, many of the FEMA team's strong recommendations for strengthening buildings' resistance to winds, such as by protecting windows from flying debris, *still* remain to be adopted in Galveston and many other areas along the coast.

In addition to helping illustrate a large variety of shoddy construction—as well as reminding Galveston of the dangers of hurricanes and prompting development of the city's highly regarded evacuation plan—Hurricane Alicia also highlighted the issue of who should pay for the damage of about $3.2 billion (in year 2000 dollars), which was greater than it should have been. After Alicia, insurance companies wanted to stop selling homeowners' policies for homes on the Texas coast, or to be allowed to charge rates that reflected their estimation of what future hurricanes would be likely to cost. The companies had a point. While no comparative property valuation figures exist for Galveston, we can assume that they're in line with the figures compiled for other locales in hurricane country. For example, during the 1980s the value of insured property in Dare County, North Carolina, increased by 111 percent. All along the coast the value of property was growing much faster than the population, as old-fashioned beach cottages were replaced by larger homes, larger motels, and apartment buildings.

In the end, the State of Texas wouldn't allow the insurance companies either to quit selling policies on the coast or to charge substantially higher rates. Instead, a coastal "wind pool" was created, which was funded by every company that insures structures *anywhere* in the state. Insurance companies were also told they could *not* require higher building standards, or window and door protection. Yet, as anyone who has ever studied hurricane damage will tell you, protecting windows and doors, especially sliding-glass doors, should be the first line of defense for a building owner. Even if a building is sturdy, debris smashing windows or doors sets off a cascading chain of events, all of them bad. First, the wind blows in rain. Even worse, when hurricane winds blow into windows or sliding-glass doors that have been smashed, the air pushes up on the roof, adding to the lifting force being created by the winds blowing overhead. In high winds, a roof is like a poorly designed airplane wing, but the wind can still create enough lifting force to send it flying.

Years ago, engineers and meteorologists believed that the higher pressure inside a building caused it to "explode" when low pressure, such as in a hurricane or tornado, passed over the building, and that the pressure inside couldn't equalize quickly enough with the lower outside pressure. Close study of damage and wind tunnel tests with models of different kinds of buildings have shown this is not what happens. Instead, wind flowing over a roof or around the corner of a building creates a low pressure area on the lee side of the flow, perhaps "sucking" off the wall on that lee side or even lifting off the entire roof. Once a roof is lifted off, the wind might blow a wall, or walls, outward, giving the impression that the building has exploded. Meteorologists and emergency managers now teach homeowners to ignore the old adage about opening windows to "equalize the pressure." It's not only a waste of time; it's counterproductive, since open windows allow the wind to blow in.

As Hurricane Center forecasters tried to give the warnings that the growing numbers of people in danger on the coastlines needed, they had the invaluable help of the new satellite images that became a television staple in the 1970s. The coherent formation of swirling white clouds sweeping across the vastness of the blue ocean was just so beautiful television producers and forecasters found it irresistible. The image was also awe-inspiring, and the most jaded coastal dweller could not dismiss out of hand the threat it might pose.

The images that so captured the public's fancy were taken from geostationary satellites. The science fiction writer Arthur C. Clarke had been the first to propose the idea in an article in the October 1945 issue of *Wireless World*, titled "Extra-terrestrial Relays: Can Rocket Stations Give World-wide Radio Coverage?" Clarke pro-

An ATS 3 satellite photo of Hurricane Agnes taken on June 18, 1972. This was one of the most destructive U.S. storms of record, with $8.4 billion (2000 dollars) and 122 deaths primarily from heavy rains in the northeast.

posed that three geostationary satellites in suitable orbits could serve as worldwide communications links. Clarke was far ahead of his time, of course. It was two decades before the United States launched a communications satellite, named *Syncom*, in time to provide coverage of the 1964 Olympics in Tokyo. The first geostationary satellite dedicated to meteorology was launched a couple of years later, on December 6, 1966.

The secret behind these satellites is that they maintain their position relative to the rotating Earth, and the secret behind this feat of science and technology is choosing the correct altitude for the orbit. Two issues come into play. First, for any satellite to maintain a stable orbit, centrifugal force, which tries to throw the satellite out into space, must exactly balance the gravitational force, which is trying to pull the satellite toward the Earth. The question then becomes: At what altitude above the planet does the centrifugal force *exactly* match the gravitational force when the satellite is traveling at a speed that *exactly* matches the Earth's rotational speed? The answer turns out to be an altitude of 22,238 miles. In this orbit, the satellite is traveling at 6,802 miles per hour.

So far, so good, but there's a catch when it comes to taking pictures from such a satellite. In order to maintain their stable orbits, the satellites of the 1960s had to spin, much like a child's top that stays upright as long as it's spinning, so the problem was designing a camera for a spinning platform. Enter Verner E. Suomi, the Weather Bureau's chief scientist, who had read in an electronics magazine in 1963 that NASA was going to launch a geostationary communications satellite. Suomi realized that such a satellite would have to spin, and he also believed he could invent a special kind of camera for the job. Suomi was a meteorologist, not an inventor, but he did create such a camera, and his first working model of the "spin-scan" camera worked well. He tested it in a California lab by spinning it as it would spin on the satellite while it took photos of Santa Barbara from a vantage twenty miles away.

In that Cold War era, a sure way to interest higher officials in any project was to tie it to the space race with the Soviet Union. Over dinner at a Chinese restaurant, Suomi explained his camera to his boss, Robert White, the chief of the Weather Bureau; showed him the photos of Santa Barbara; and then asked, "Why don't we beat the Russians on this one?" White immediately understood the importance of Suomi's work and took the pictures and the blueprint to NASA officials, who also grasped the value of such reconnaissance.

Suomi's first camera was lofted into orbit in 1966. Simply put, it worked by constructing the final image one narrow, horizontal strip at a time, something like a computer printer works. In the 5 percent of the time the spinning lens was pointed at the Earth, it recorded the image of a small east-to-west strip at the North Pole. The next spin around, Suomi's camera recorded an image of the strip directly below the first one, and so on "down" the Earth to the equator and on to the South Pole. Strip by strip, from pole to pole, the camera assembled one picture and then immediately started another one.

Suomi's technology eventually evolved into the first Geostationary Operational Environmental Satellite (GOES), launched on October 16, 1975, almost a decade after the first prototype had gone on duty. GOES scanned the entire Western Hemisphere, its cameras compiling a new image every thirty minutes, not just twice a day as the old polar-orbiting satellites did. Even though the word "camera" is often used in reference to the imaging devices on satellites, only a few military satellites ever used film like an ordinary camera does. Those rare satellites really did drop the film back to Earth over the Pacific, where an airplane snagged it as it drifted down under a parachute, but all other satellites, including weather satellites, record the strengths of various wavelengths of visible light and infrared energy in digital form and send this data back to Earth. NOAA computers translate this data into "gray scale," yielding images that look much like black-and-white photographs. In the early days, these photographs were then placed upon a copy stand and photographed in sequence with a 16-millimeter movie camera, with each image being photographed two or three times—all in all, a process similar to the one used for animated cartoons. A sequence of these time-lapse photographs now on movie film was then spliced together to form "loops" rather than reels of film. The loops then were run through a projector, which resulted in a repetition of the sequence over and over. They were stunningly beautiful and valuable—and not just as a good visual aid for television broadcasts, or for Neil Frank to use in his public relations and hurricane preparedness work.

The images from the geostationary satellites are unquestionably the greatest technological advance ever for researchers and forecasters in tropical meteorology. Conventional data, especially upper-air data, is sparse over the vast oceanic areas of the tropics and subtropics. There is only one upper-air station for more than four million square miles over the tropical and subtropical Atlantic between the southeastern United States and Africa. By comparison, there's one upper-air station for about every 40,000 square miles over the continental United States. This fact of life means that the weather satellites are the primary data source for most of the area where hurricanes form and grow.

Over the years, computer technology improvements transformed the mechanical process of creating time-lapse loops into an electronic one, which led to the false-color satellite images routinely seen on television today. Different image depictions from the Weather Channel, CNN, local television stations, and other sources may use whatever color the forecaster prefers. One common enhancement uses various shades of red to show the temperatures of the tops of clouds. We know these temperatures only because any substance in the universe, including "invisible" substances such as molecules of water vapor in the air, radiates infrared energy. The strength of the infrared energy detected at different wavelengths indicates the amount and the temperature of the water vapor. The satellite's so-called "vapor channel" images provide a general picture of how humid the air is at various wide bands of altitude. These images even show the humidity of the high-altitude jet streams, which are cloud-free—vital information for forecasters studying the winds that are steering a storm. These images also show otherwise invisible "rivers" of humid air flowing north from the tropics to feed a hurricane, or rivers of dry air from the west that can weaken a hurricane as this drier air flows in and replaces the humid air that powers all tropical weather. For the first time, forecasters could now see the middle- and upper-level low-pressure systems that can affect the formation, development, and track of tropical cyclones.

The images relayed to Earth from the geostationary satellites, particularly the time-lapse images, revealed that the atmosphere is even more complex than most meteorologists had imagined. The water vapor images, in particular, showed air movements in the tropical atmosphere that are very complicated. These observations have almost certainly improved long-term predictions. However, the satellite images do not and cannot directly measure the barometric pressure in the center of a hurricane, nor can they measure the speed and extent of its winds. This is a real limitation, but it was lessened to some extent in 1973, when Vernon Dvorak, a NOAA satellite meteorologist, developed a technique for estimating the strength of tropical cyclones using the cloud patterns and the temperature differences between the eye and the cold tops of the clouds around the eye. All of this data is revealed by the infrared spectrum. The wind speed and air pressure figures obtained with the Dvorak technique aren't as accurate as those obtained by airplanes, but they continue to provide forecasters with a way to roughly estimate the strength of storms that airplanes can't or don't fly into.

Tropical cyclone forecasters around the Pacific and Indian Oceans have to rely strictly on satellites to track storms; the United States is the only nation routinely to have flown airplanes into tropical cyclones in this region. Pacific typhoon flights ended in 1987 because of budgetary reasons and the U.S. military's belief that satellites provided sufficiently accurate data for their purposes. The Web site of the the Hong Kong Observatory announces this fact with ill-concealed annoyance and then states: "With the scarcity of direct data, the intensity of a tropical cyclone has to be inferred from analysis of cloud top temperatures as shown on enhanced infrared satellite pictures." Unfortunately, these Dvorak technique estimates can be off by at least one category of strength, and in some instances even the location of the center of the storm, based on satellite imagery, can be off by a hundred miles.

Thanks to a combination of the new satellite tools and all of the old tools, researchers in the late 1970s had pinned down a set of conditions that must be present for a storm to form. Meteorologists had known since World War II that warm water is needed; if an ocean's surface wasn't at least 79 degrees Fahrenheit, storms wouldn't form. Now they also discovered that in addition to being at least a few hundred square miles in area, the pool of warm water needed to be at least 200 feet deep. These criteria provide the "critical mass" necessary to provide fuel with sufficient octane for the potential storm to run on. If the warm water isn't at least 200 feet deep, for example, a growing storm may stir it up enough to bring cooler water from the depths to the surface, cutting off the energy supply. As the water grows warmer—the oceans warm to around 90 degrees in a few places—it doesn't cause more tropical cyclones or make them more likely to form. But, the warmer the water the stronger a storm can grow, if other conditions allow.

Large portions of the tropical Atlantic, Pacific, and Indian Oceans contain such large, deep areas of warm water all year, and these areas expand during the summer. In addition to suitable water, there must be a large layer of warm, very humid air extending from the ocean surface to around 18,000 feet. Without this deep layer of moist air, a budding storm could choke on air that's too dry. Finally, the pool of warm water and the deep layer of warm, humid air need some kind of initial disturbance to initiate a storm. The warm water and warm, humid air are like an engine with plenty of fuel, but which isn't running. The disturbance is the starter motor. In the eastern Atlantic, as we have seen, tropical waves moving west off Africa are the sources of most of the strongest hurricanes, but other kinds of disturbances can also be responsible. One of these is the end of a frontal trough, which is an elongated area of low pressure along the boundary between warm and cool air masses. Such boundaries may penetrate into the tropical latitudes from the middle latitudes and become nearly stationary; they are often the source of hurricanes that form over the Gulf of Mexico, the western Caribbean, or the Atlantic. Another possible source of the needed disturbance is a monsoonal trough, an area of low pressure associated with the seasonal monsoon rains that move over large areas of Africa and Asia.

Finally, the tropical disturbance taking shape over a sufficiently warm, deep, and broad pool of water must be in a region where the surrounding winds are either light, or at least *consistent* in direction and speed, from the surface to heights of 40,000 feet or more. Such winds are necessary if the clouds and thunderstorms of the nascent storm are to grow to great heights and persist for many hours and days. If winds aloft are blowing in different directions or different speeds from the winds at low and middle levels, they will tear apart the budding circulation of the storm. Meteorologists use the term "wind shear" to describe such winds, which can weaken or kill even a full-fledged hurricane.

Shearing is one key reason the South Atlantic doesn't produce hurricanes, even though the water there is nearly as warm as the water north of the equator, where many hurricanes do form. Satellite reconnaissance reveals many disturbances that seem to be on the verge of forming in this southern ocean but are then torn apart by the prevailing westerly winds of the middle latitudes, because in the South Atlantic these westerlies are closer to the equator—and to the developing disturbances—than they are in the North Atlantic. These winds literally shear the storms in half, and half a storm is soon no storm at all.

Much of the credit for this understanding must go to William Gray of Colorado State University, who put the whole package together in the late 1960s. A decade later Gray traveled the world for a study sponsored by the World Meteorological Organization. He visited twenty-two tropical cyclone forecasting centers, collecting reams of statistics, and he determined that about eighty tropical cyclones form somewhere in the world each year, with one-half to two-thirds of them growing to full-fledged hurricane or typhoon strength. What happens to the hundreds of other candidate disturbances, ones in which all conditions are "go," with the right water and the right winds? We don't know. Despite the intense scientific study of hurricanes for half a century now, despite the constant watch that satellites keep over the world's tropical oceans and the detailed study of these images, scientists and forecasters are still unable to say with certainty which disturbance will give birth to a cyclone and which will continue peacefully across the Atlantic, the Pacific, or the Indian Ocean, bringing no more than brief showers.

Gray's study determined that the Atlantic Basin, which includes the North Atlantic Ocean, the Caribbean Sea, and the Gulf of Mexico, ranks third in the total number of tropical cyclones. First is the western North Pacific, and second is the eastern North Pacific. The determination that more storms are formed in the western part of the North Pacific than anywhere else was not a surprise, but meteorologists working with the satellite images were very surprised to learn that the *eastern* Pacific Ocean off the Mexican and Central American coasts is in second place, generating an average of thirteen tropical storms a year, the majority of which grow into hurricanes. They had thought the number of these storms was about half as large as it is, but since this region is outside the normal shipping lanes and airways, many storms had gone completely unobserved before satellite reconnaissance. This seems hard to believe today, but it was true just a few decades ago. In fact, satellites showed that one particular region over the Pacific west of Mexico, a square measuring five degrees of latitude by five degrees of longitude, produces more tropical cyclones than any similarly sized region on the planet. Water temperatures here are favorable, and there are no large land areas to produce cold air masses and fronts to penetrate into these waters and produce the killer shears. In addition, tropical waves that travel all of the way from Africa across the Atlantic, the Caribbean, and Central America without developing into a storm provide an abundance of initial disturbances that can give birth to hurricanes in the Pacific.

The Atlantic Basin averages about nine tropical storms a year, with six becoming hurricanes, most of which miss the United States. Since the 1870s, when reliable records began, an average of about one and a half hurricanes have hit the Gulf or East Coasts every year, with about 40 percent classified as "major" storms with winds of 111 miles per hour or faster. Obviously, most areas go many years, even decades, between storms, though some areas, such as southern Florida, can expect one every few years. Along the U.S. Gulf and Atlantic Coasts, the highest odds are in the Miami–Ft. Lauderdale area, where twenty-six or twenty-seven hurricanes can be expected during 100 years, and ten or eleven are likely to be major. The lowest odds are for the Ocean City, Maryland, area, where only four hurricanes are to be expected in 100 years and only one likely to be major.

Many a hurricane season has passed with no hurricanes hitting the United States. Since reliable records began in the late nineteenth century, the longest period was three years and one week, from August 10, 1980, when Allen hit Brownsville, Texas, until August 17, 1983, when Alicia hit Galveston. This lull was part of a decrease in the number of hurricanes, especially major hurricanes, hitting the United States from the late 1960s until the late 1990s. But as we have seen, there have also been fluky times when the same area is battered again and again and again, such as in 1954 and '55.

While the biggest hurricane threat by far to the United States is on the Gulf and Atlantic Coasts, Hawaii and California aren't completely immune. However, easterly winds steer most hurricanes that travel as far west as Hawaii well south of those islands. Some eastern Pacific hurricanes will occasionally affect islands off the coast of Mexico, but most will die a harmless death over the cooler waters west of the upper Mexican coast, which is empty of islands and people, except for Hawaii. Each year, however, a few eastern Pacific storms turn northward to hit Mexico's Pacific Coast, and some of these bring heavy rain to California and to the Southwest. Unlike the East Coast, where the north-flowing Gulf Stream keeps ocean water warm near the shore as far north as the mid-Atlantic states, the Pacific Ocean off California is chilly, cooled by the north-to-south California Current, which is typical of the west coasts of continents. This cool water weakens or destroys the few Pacific storms that aim at the West Coast. On September 25, 1939, however, a tropical storm with 50-mile-per-hour winds moved ashore between San Diego and Los Angeles, killing forty-five people. In 1997 Hurricane Linda briefly threatened southern California but turned away. Linda's 185-mile-per-hour winds made it the strongest hurricane ever recorded over the eastern Pacific Ocean. Only three weeks after Linda turned away, Hurricane Pauline slammed into Mexico near Acapulco with 130-mile-per-hour winds and heavy rain, killing 230 people, mostly in floods on inland streams. Many of the hurricanes in the eastern Pacific that do hit northwestern Mexico quickly weaken, but with their extremely humid air they continue to the north or the northeast into the United States and cause floods in California, the Southwest, or as far away as Oklahoma.

From time to time a storm that forms in the eastern or central Pacific hits Hawaii. The worst such hurricane on record was Iniki, which passed directly over the island of Kauai in September 1992 with sustained winds of probably 115 miles per hour. The Red Cross estimated that 14,350 homes were damaged or destroyed, with total damage of about $2.3 billion (in year 2000 dollars). Considering the strength of the winds and the amount of damage, Iniki's death toll of six was low.

The North Pacific west of the International Date Line is the world's most active tropical cyclone region, with a yearly average of twenty-six storms, which are called "typhoons." The word "typhoon," for many people, carries more menace than the word "hurricane" or "cyclone," and with good reason. The larger Pacific Ocean provides the native cyclones with more time to grow before they move over land, and typhoon season runs all year, although most of the storms occur during the summer and early fall. Some of the cyclones in this region of the world are deeply rooted in national psyches, none more so than two storms that struck Japan more than 700 years ago.

In November 1274, Kublai Khan, the ruler of the Mongol empire that extended from Europe to northeastern China and Korea, set forth to attack the island of Japan with 40,000 troops aboard 1,000 ships. They never had a chance, as a powerful storm sank 300 of the ships and took the lives of about one-third of the invaders. Was this tempest, by today's standards, a full-fledged typhoon? It's impossible to know, but we do know that the maritime disaster only delayed Kublai Khan's ambition. Seven years later, in 1281, after consolidating his power in China, he again sailed forth to conquer the island stronghold, this time with a much larger force of around 150,000 men, and this time another storm struck Kublai Khan's great fleet, sinking 4,000 vessels and taking 100,000 lives. Japanese accounts of the day said that a person could walk across the entrance to Imari Bay on the wreckage of the Mongol ships. The Japanese believed that the two storms that delivered them from conquest in 1274 and 1281 were signs of divine protection. Centuries later, in the late stages of World War II, only when they faced the first serious threat of invasion since 1281, the Japanese turned to organizing squadrons of suicide pilots to crash bomb-laden airplanes into American ships. They called these men "kamikazes," after the name given the two fateful storms of yore. The word means "divine wind."

Typhoons strike islands and nations all around the western Pacific, and they are a major threat to Japan, Korea, China, Taiwan, the Philippines, and Vietnam. With their long coastlines on the western edge of the target zone, the Philippines and Japan suffer the most; each nation is often hit by four or more damaging storms a year. These are direct hits, while many of the storms that strike Korea, China, and Vietnam have been weakened by their passage over Japan or the Philippines. Even though typhoons have caused thousands of deaths in the Philippines and Japan over the years, both nations value the storms for the needed rainfall, even if it does come as deluges. The Japanese Meteorological Agency's Tokyo Typhoon Center is the World Meteorological Organization's Regional Specialized Meteorological Center for the northwestern Pacific Ocean, but individual nations also have typhoon forecasting centers, including the U.S. Navy's Joint Typhoon Warning Center at Pearl Harbor, Hawaii, which handles forecasting for U.S. interests around the Pacific.

Unlike the northern Pacific Ocean, the northern Indian Ocean is not a great incubator of cyclones, because that ocean is relatively small north of the equator. There's just not much room for storms to prosper before they strike either Bangladesh, the eastern coast of India, or Pakistan on the Arabian Sea. This ocean averages only six tropical cyclones each year. However, during the twentieth century these typhoons have been the deadliest of them all, especially in tiny Bangladesh. In this country, where normal tidal ranges are as much as eighteen feet, any cyclone thrusting north across the Bay of Bengal and arriving at the time of high tide pushes storm surge across the low-lying coast of the Ganges Delta, where more than three million people live in extreme poverty. In just the past three decades, tropical cyclones hitting Bangladesh are estimated to have taken more than 600,000 lives, mostly from drowning. When indirect effects such as famine and disease are considered, these cyclones may have taken more than 1.5 million lives in Bangladesh.

In 1970 what is believed to have been the deadliest tropical cyclone in history killed an estimated 300,000 people, maybe more, in what was then East Pakistan, now Bangladesh. In fact, dissatisfaction with aid by Pakistan's central government helped spur the unrest that led to East Pakistan's breaking away from the mother country. Since a 1991 cyclone killed more than 60,000 people, Bangladesh, which has a tropical cyclone forecasting center in Dhaka, has improved its warning services and built concrete shelters atop dirt mounds that are higher than storm surge levels. The precautions seem to be working. In May 1998, a storm with 125-mile-per-hour winds left 80,000 people homeless but killed fewer than 200 people.

Australia faces the threat of tropical cyclones along its entire western, northern, and northeastern coasts, a stretch of 5,000 miles. Since Southern Hemisphere seasons are reversed, the Down Under season is during the Northern Hemisphere's winter and spring. About ten storms take shape annually over the oceans to the north and west of the island continent, and another six organize over the Pacific off Australia's northeastern coast.

The most famous cyclone to hit Australia was Tracy, featuring 135-mile-per-hour winds that destroyed most of the city of Darwin on Christmas Day 1974, killing sixty-five people. Darwin is on the tip of Australia's northern coast; fortunately, this populated area is an unusual target for the strongest cyclones, which tend to hit the thinly populated coast to the west. Tracy destroyed more than 6,300 of the 9,000 houses in Darwin at the time, and another 1,800 were seriously damaged. In the week after the storm more than half of the 46,000 people who lived in Darwin were evacuated because it's in a remote part of Australia with no nearby towns that could shelter everyone whose home had been destroyed.

Tracy led to major improvements in building standards for the tropical parts of Australia. These included requiring stronger roof designs that can stand up to the gusty winds of a tropical cyclone, and making protection of windows and doors from wind-blown debris mandatory. A few storms hit Queensland on the populated eastern coast, but none of Australia's tropical cyclones has been a major disaster. The nation's worst death toll from a storm was in March 1899, when a storm destroyed a fleet of more than 100 pearl-fishing boats in Bathurst Bay on the northeastern coast of Queensland, killing 307 people. Australia has separate tropical cyclone warning centers at Brisbane for its northeastern coast, Darwin for the northern coast, and Perth for the western coast.

In addition to sometimes hitting eastern Australia, southwestern Pacific tropical cyclones also hit the islands of French Polynesia, Fiji, and Samoa. The tropical cyclone center in Fiji and the Australian center in Brisbane handle forecasts for this area. No tropical cyclones on record have struck New Zealand, which is surrounded by cool ocean water, but a few cyclones have metamorphosed into strong extratropical cyclones to bring New Zealand its worst floods and highest winds. The strongest wind ever recorded in New Zealand, 113 miles per hour near Wellington, came from such a storm on April 10, 1968. It sank an inter-island ferry in Wellington Harbour, drowning fifty-one people.

The southern Indian Ocean also produces tropical cyclones,

about eight each year, with most of them heading west to threaten or hit the small islands of Mauritius and Reunion and the very large island of Madagascar, which serves as a blockade for Africa. Sometimes the remnants of one of these storms will bring flooding rain to southeastern Africa.

No one knows how many men, women, and children have lost their lives in hurricanes, typhoons, and other tropical cyclones over the centuries. A conservative estimate of deaths for the entire last half of the twentieth century alone would approach three-quarters of a million, with the majority of these around the Bay of Bengal, in Bangladesh and India. But these figures are at best rough estimates. Even today, many nations aren't able to give a detailed accounting of a storm's death toll. Often bodies of victims are washed away by the retreating storm surge or buried under debris or mud slides. When a storm leaves hundreds of bodies, an exact count becomes impossible, as authorities rush to bury the dead as quickly as possible to avoid an outbreak of disease.

As well as conducting his hurricane and typhoon research around the world, William Gray was also teaching a course in tropical meteorology at Colorado State University. Of course one of the subjects was El Niño, that now-famous disruption in world weather patterns that begins when the water of the tropical Pacific off the coast of South America turns unusually warm and triggers a huge shift in the atmosphere above it. During ordinary times the Pacific's trade winds push warm water west along the equator, where it literally piles up; sea levels west of the International Date Line are normally a few inches higher than in the eastern Pacific. The huge pool of warm water energizes huge thunderstorms over the western Pacific. These, in turn, pump huge amounts of air upward, which affects the location and strength of jet stream winds that flow east high above the Pacific. An El Niño begins when the trade winds ease up, allowing the piled-up warm water in the western Pacific to move along the equator toward the east. As this happens, more thunderstorms grow over the central Pacific as the western Pacific air dries out, causing drought in Indonesia and Australia. Changes in the jet stream caused by El Niño affect weather far away, including over the United States, as everyone now knows, and also over the tropical Atlantic and the Caribbean.

One day in the late 1970s, Gray was looking through the National Hurricane Center booklet "Tropical Cyclones of the North Atlantic," which has separate maps showing the paths of tropical storms and hurricanes for each year since 1888. "I knew when the El Niño years were, and I knew when the active and inactive hurricane years were," he says. "Very few other people know this. People who were studying El Niños didn't know about hurricanes and the hurricane people didn't know about El Niño." As he looked through the book, Gray quickly realized that El Niño years tended to be years with few hurricanes. Later, when Gray studied more detailed weather records, he found that during El Niño years the upper-air winds over the Caribbean tended to be stronger than normal and blowing from the west, instead of from the east as during most years. Since hurricanes move toward the west, these winds would create wind shear that would weaken or even destroy hurricanes.

As Gray continued looking for other global factors that could affect the numbers of Atlantic Basin hurricanes, he discovered one other factor that seemed to be related to the hurricane count for a given season: more major hurricanes hit the Florida peninsula and mainland coastline to the north during years when the Sahel area of West Africa is wet. The Sahel is between the Sahara Desert to the north and the wet, tropical areas to the south. The tropical waves that are seedlings for many Atlantic hurricanes move over this area and then over the Atlantic. Gray found that during the twenty-five years from 1916 to 1940, when the Sahel was dry most of the time, nine major hurricanes hit the U.S. East Coast. From 1941 to 1965, when the Sahel was wet, seventeen major hurricanes hit the East Coast. The following twenty-five years, from 1966 until 1990, were dry in the Sahel, and only two major hurricanes hit the East Coast. The pattern held. The dry phase continued through the mid-1990s and then became less dry or more neutral toward the end of the decade. During this ten-year period, three major hurricanes made landfall on the United States: Andrew, Fran, and Opal.

However, Gray decided that the correlation between rain over the

Sahel in West Africa and hurricanes over the western Atlantic is not as simple as it might seem to be. West African rain would not some-how add energy to Atlantic hurricanes. Instead, Gray reasoned, the same long-running weather pattern that causes the Sahel to be wet somehow also helps strong hurricanes make it across the Atlantic to hit the United States. Moreover, the relation between Sahel wetness and major hurricanes doesn't hold up for the Gulf of Mexico. This makes sense, because quite a few of the strong storms that hit the Gulf Coast are born over the western Caribbean Sea or even over the Gulf of Mexico itself. Both Audrey in 1957 and Alicia in 1983 were born and bred right in the Gulf. Beginning in 1984, Gray began making objective, statistical forecasts, with some small subjective adjustments, for the number of storms in the upcoming season. He never tried to predict when or where hurricanes would hit, only how many tropical storms, hurricanes, and major hurricanes a season would bring. These seasonal forecasts are reasonably successful in most years.

By the 1980s the United States, which only fifty years before had been a backwater for the atmospheric sciences, was the world's pow-erhouse in hurricane research, with several universities granting doctorates in the subject. However, most American hurricane scien-tists or forecasters had little or no contact with their counterparts around the world, except for those in Mexico and around the Caribbean Sea. The American Meteorological Society had held some tropical cyclone meetings overseas, but the expense of overseas travel worked against extensive international cooperation well into the 1970s. Thus William Gray was breaking new ground when he traveled the globe for the World Meteorological Organization in 1978. He recalls, "When I visited Nouméa, New Caledonia, in the South Pacific, they told me I was their second international visitor in thirty years. The head of the Australian Bureau of Meteorology had visited ten years before."

In the rest of the world, almost all tropical cyclone research was conducted by national weather services, not by universities, as in the United States, and most of those national programs were, by U.S.

standards, small. Some had a longer history than any in the United States—Hong Kong Observatory, still a major typhoon forecasting center, was established in 1883, and the French and British empires had traditions of tropical cyclone forecasting in their many tropical colonies—but few could afford extensive research. None had anything approaching the huge amount of storm data our research and reconnaissance airplanes had been collecting since the Weather Bureau's Hurricane Research Program of the 1950s.

Since the 1980s, however, the lower cost of jet travel has opened up the world to tropical cyclone meteorologists, just as it has to vacation travelers. Computers have also enabled scientists to share information in ways they could have only dreamed of in the 1970s, transmitting the longest text and the most complex images around the world in the blink of an eye. The United States continues to be the leader, but tropical cyclone research has become truly international. At the American Meteorological Society's tropical cyclone conference in May 2000, about a quarter of the 200 papers presented had at least one author from outside the United States. Nor did the overseas visitors present papers just on the concerns of their particular regions of the world. Instead, scientists from Australia, India, China, Japan, France, Mexico, Germany, Canada, Cuba, Costa Rica, and the United States discussed topics in the mainstream of tropical cyclone research—year-to-year variations in numbers of storms, improving forecasts, understanding changes in storm intensity, ways to collect data, and, of course, the fascinating, vexing subject of computer modeling.

CHAPTER 9

COMPUTER MODELING

COMPUTERS, IT SEEMS, have changed just about everything in the modern world, and they've certainly changed how we study and forecast the great tropical cyclones. Hand in hand with the development of geostationary satellite reconnaissance and computer imaging, computer-aided forecasting (also known as "numerical forecasting," or "computer modeling") has transformed the field. A British weather observer, Lewis Fry Richardson, is credited with developing the basics of computer modeling during World War I, when he estimated that 64,000 human "computers" working in tandem would have been necessary to calculate his simple forecast. The first program to take advantage of electronic computers was written shortly after World War II by a group at the Institute for Advanced Study in Princeton, New Jersey, headed by the noted mathematician John von Neumann. This program was set up to develop computerized weather forecasting because, according to von Neumann, forecasting was "the most complex, interactive, and highly nonlinear problem that had ever been conceived of." In July 1954, the Weather Bureau and the navy set up the Joint Numerical Weather Prediction Unit, which began turning out routine operational computer forecasts a year later. These forecasts were very general ones, identifying areas of high and low air pressure and the flow of upper-air winds. They didn't include any detail, such as tomorrow's high temperature for a particular city—certainly not for what a hurricane might do. But they were a start.

Today, forecasters, especially hurricane forecasters, use three different kinds of computer programs, or models: statistical, dynamical, and the hybrid statistical-dynamical. The most simple, both in terms of the mathematics and the computer power required, are the statistical models. A simple, pure statistical model starts with information such as a storm's location and the time of the year. The program then searches its database for other storms in the same location at the same time of year, and it bases its forecast on what similar storms in the past have done. The program is not provided with any information about weather factors that might influence a specific hurricane.

The most simple statistical model for track predictions was, and still is, known as "CLIPER," an acronym for "climatology" and "persistence." It was developed in 1972 by Charles J. Neumann, who was at the National Hurricane Center at the time, and one of the basic assumptions of the program is that the manner in which a storm is moving at any given moment is likely to be the manner in which it will move for the next twelve to twenty-four hours. This is "persistence." Beyond about twenty-four hours, the storm is assumed to start moving more like similar storms in the same area at the same time of year have moved in the past. This is the "climatology" part of the forecast. An actual CLIPER forecast starts essentially as total persistence and then increasingly blends in climatology for the longer forecast periods through seventy-two hours. At times, this statistical model can produce forecasts that are quite accurate, but forecasters consider it a "no skill" model. In fact, it is used by meteorologists and forecasters today to judge the skill of other models and the official forecast. CLIPER doesn't exactly rule the roost anymore, but it does endure as a "quick and dirty" projection of where a hurricane may go over the next seventy-two hours, and as a standard against which to judge other forecasts. It is the type of simple model that many people now have on their home computers.

Dynamical models, on the other hand, disregard the historical data entirely and use as much information about the storm and surrounding weather conditions as they can digest. They use the basic laws of physics that apply to the atmosphere to predict where the storm will go. These models have a noble lineage, with ideas rooted in Isaac Newton's seventeenth-century laws of motion, but the specific mathematical equations that could be employed by computers to describe the Earth's atmosphere were mostly worked out early in the twentieth century. There are six of these equations. The three "hydrodynamic" equations use Newton's second law of motion to find horizontal and vertical motions of air caused by air pressure differences, gravity, friction, and the Earth's rotation—complicated stuff. The two "thermodynamic" equations calculate changes in temperature caused by water's evaporating into vapor, vapor's condensing into liquid, and the like—even more complicated. The sixth equation, known as the "continuity equation," accounts for the volume of air entering or leaving an area—just as complicated as all the rest.

This simple description of the equations only begins to convey the complexity of the job confronting the dynamical models and their programmers. An important breakthrough that helped make simple dynamical computer modeling possible with the slow computers of the 1950s was a method of simplifying the equations devised by Jule Charney, who had a doctorate in meteorology and who worked with von Neumann. Charney's brilliant insight was to use a very simplified "barotropic" atmosphere, which assumed frictionless airflow, greatly simplified the movements of warm and cold air, and averaged the wind speeds from different altitudes to one idealized norm, usually 18,000 feet above sea level, called the "equivalent-barotropic level." With these simplifications, Charney could combine the six basic equations of the atmosphere into one equation that early computers could handle.

In essence, a barotropic model moves weather patterns from one location to another with horizontal winds only, but it often gives some surprisingly good results in predicting basic flow patterns. It works best of all in the tropics, where the real atmosphere over oceans is often similar to the one assumed in the model—that is, until a storm begins developing. Then the barotropic models are *least* accurate, because cold or warm air moving across lines of equal air pressure is a dominant feature of any developing storm. Instead of being parallel as in the simplified model, real-world lines of equal temperature and of equal pressure (isobars) cross each other. This is called a "baroclinic" atmosphere, and it complicates models, increasing the computer power required to produce forecasts. Charney and Norman Phillips later developed a simple two-level, baroclinic model, which did allow for storm development and thus often produced superior forecasts to the barotropic models. However, these simple models still had great difficulties in trying to accurately predict anything more than basic flow patterns.

In the early years of numerical forecasting, the more complex dynamical models consistently lost the forecasting competition to the statistical models, but as data collection steadily improved and computer power grew almost exponentially during the 1970s and '80s, and even more so in the '90s, these dynamical models became better and better and showed considerable and rapidly improving skill. The simplest form of this kind of model sets up a three-dimensional grid of isolated points covering some given area of the Earth's surface. For each grid point, the computer is fed all pertinent data on the current atmospheric conditions, including temperature, air pressure, humidity, and winds. The Weather Bureau's first such operational model in the mid-1950s worked with grid points 248 miles apart and on only one level of the atmosphere, about 18,000 feet. Even though the model was restricted to one layer, it was able to make some useful forecasts, because 18,000 feet is the middle level (in terms of weight, half the atmosphere is above 18,000 feet, half below) and very important to storm growth, development, and movement.

Twenty years later, the Hurricane Center was using guidance from a model developed by John Hovermale and run at the National Meteorological Center with grid points only thirty-seven miles apart and encompassing *ten* layers of atmosphere, from the surface to the top. This model was exponentially more complex than the first ones—so complex, in fact, that no computer could handle such a fine grid for a large area, such as the Northern Hemisphere, so the model "moved," keeping the storm in the center of an area 1,860 miles on each side. For this reason, it was called the "Movable Fine Mesh model."

Another way to model smaller-scale features is by using "nested grids." These models use larger scale grids, perhaps one covering an entire hemisphere, for determining the "boundary" conditions around the area in which the forecaster is interested. Within that larger grid is "nested" a second grid with points closer together, and perhaps a third grid with still higher resolution is nested within the previous grid, progressing in this way toward a grid centered over a "smaller" feature such as a hurricane, and this finer grid "moves" with the storm, much like the entire Movable Fine Mesh model of the 1970s and '80s.

Clearly, the "tightening" of the grid for these sophisticated models required new means of gathering data. A key technology developed in the 1980s and early '90s was the dropwindsonde, a radical improvement over the old-fashioned radiosonde. Each dropsonde package was equipped to receive radio signals from the worldwide Omega navigation system, a set of ground-based radio stations. This system enabled the sonde to indicate the longitude, latitude, and altitude of every set of data collected about air pressure, temperature, and humidity as it drifted down to the ocean. The accurate positioning could also be used to calculate wind speeds and directions at various altitudes, as the sonde was buffeted this way and that. A marked improvement in this technology was the replacement of the Omega system with the Global Positioning System, which allowed for more accurate and frequent position measurements for use in wind calculations. In tests of the new technology, models run with the data from dropsondes were from 16 to 32 percent more accurate than models run for comparison purposes without the extra dropsonde data.

Today, the computer model that takes the best advantage of the dropsondes and other sources of data—including weather balloons, ground observations, satellites, and even automated reports of temperature and winds from airliners—is the GFDL (named after the Geophysical Fluid Dynamics Laboratory, an NOAA research center in Princeton, New Jersey, that develops models for both meteorologists and oceanographers). The GFDL model contains eighteen levels of the atmosphere and three nested grids. It obtains all of its initial and boundary conditions from the "Aviation run" of the National Weather Service's Medium Range Forecast (MRF) model. (The Aviation run is one of the first that's produced with a given set of data. It produces relatively short-range forecasts, which are useful to pilots, but it also has many other uses, such as providing boundary data for the GFDL model.)

In the GFDL model, the two innermost of the three inner grids move to follow the storm. The smallest grid is 345 miles on square, with data points 11.5 miles apart, for a total of some 900 points for each of eighteen levels of atmosphere. That's a grand total of some 16,200 points, each of them calculated in "time steps" of fifteen seconds. Yet even with its relatively high resolution, the GFDL model represents a hurricane with an idealized vortex based upon a few parameters of the real storm, such as the maximum wind and the distance of this maximum wind from the center.

In comparison with the inner grid of the GFDL model, the U.S. Navy's Operational Global Atmospheric Prediction System (NOGAPS) model has a horizontal grid resolution of about fifty-two miles, or only forty-five data points for each layer of a 345-mile square grid, as compared to 900 data points for GFDL. However, NOGAPS is just what the name says, a *global* model, and as such it has a very high resolution. Today, NOGAPS takes twenty minutes to produce a twenty-four-hour forecast while running on a sixteen-processor Cray C90 supercomputer. Neither that formidable machine nor any other on the market could run the GFDL's 11.5-mile grid for the entire globe in a timely manner. Crude calculations show that if the NOGAPS model *were* run with such a fine grid and with time steps of fifteen seconds for each calculation, as with the GFDL model, it would need approximately one week to produce a twenty-four-hour forecast. That is, if today is Monday and we want to know where the hurricane will be tomorrow, a global model working with a tight grid would not produce its prediction until next Monday—six days too late.

In addition to the statistical and dynamical models, forecasters also use the hybrid statistical-dynamical model. (The Cuban meteorologist Father Benito Vines intuitively understood the value of combining the two approaches. He combined the historical data he had collected about the tracks of past storms—his statistical model—with what he had learned about the motions of clouds at different levels of the atmosphere around a hurricane—his dynamical model.) Like the much simpler statistical models, hybrid models have often provided better forecasts of the tracks of some hurricanes than the more complex purely dynamical models. At the National

Hurricane Center, the statistical-dynamical NHC90 model combines forecasts from the statistical model CLIPER with dynamical model predictions of the strengths of high- and low-pressure areas that are most likely to affect the storm over the next seventy-two hours. The forecast starts off for the first twelve to twenty-four hours heavily weighted toward the "persistence" statistics of CLIPER, but then tries to improve on the simple "climatology" for the longer forecast periods by taking into account what the actual atmosphere looks like for this specific storm, rather than relying on some average condition based on past storms.

Even though some numerical models may represent such features as hurricanes as far as five days or more into the future, most specific hurricane forecasts released to the public are for no longer than seventy-two hours. Beyond that time, weather predictions become less and less accurate, especially for "smaller-scale" features such as hurricanes. And sometimes *all* of the models have been wrong. A notorious instance within the hurricane community were the forecasts generated on the evening of August 6, 1980, when Hurricane Allen was south of Haiti with 160-mile-per-hour winds. One of the four models crunching those powerful numbers decreed that Allen would cross Cuba and hit the mainland near Fort Myers, Florida, on the evening of August 8. The other three models had the hurricane still over western Cuba on the evening of the 8th. As it turned out, Allen moved south of Cuba, slipped between it and Mexico's Yucatán Peninsula, and entered the Gulf of Mexico on the evening of August 8. It subsequently hit Padre Island, Texas, with winds around 115 miles per hour and up to twelve feet of storm surge.

For forecast periods of thirty-six hours or longer, the rapidly improving dynamical models coupled with astronomical growth in computer capabilities have been the primary reason for improved forecasts of the track and forward speed of hurricanes. On the other hand, the models have yet to become as useful for predicting changes in storm *intensity*. Finding better ways to predict intensity is the biggest challenge facing researchers and forecasters in the twenty-first century. In the end, however, no increases in computer power or modeling skill are ever expected to lead to completely accurate weather forecasts. In addition to all the practical problems with data and grids, there's an insurmountable theoretical problem, which was first studied in depth by the theoretical meteorologist Edward Lorenz, working at MIT in the early 1960s. Lorenz had intended to become a mathematician, but he was one of those World War II Army Air Corps forecasters who became fascinated with the field and stayed in it following the war, always with an emphasis on mathematical and theoretical problems. At one point in his postwar work, Lorenz developed a relatively simple computer model that did a pretty good job of mimicking weather—not predicting specific weather, just mimicking weatherlike changes. One day in 1961, he decided to rerun the results of one particular run, starting halfway through the run with the numbers he had on his printout at that point. Soon the "weather" from this second run began deviating from the first run, and then it bore no resemblance at all to the first run. Yet both had used the same input. How could this be?

At first Lorenz suspected a bug in the program or a problem with his computer, but this wasn't the case. The explanation turned out to be quite simple, but with profound implications for many fields of science, not just meteorology. While his program took its calculations to six decimal places, the printout took the numbers to only *three* places. This relatively tiny change between, say, 3.461453 in the first run and 3.461 of the second run, when replicated in all the data in the program, yielded enormous differences. Lorenz referred to this aspect of his program as "sensitive dependence on initial conditions." He related his results to a set of "dishpan experiments" conducted at the University of Chicago that were attracting a lot of attention at the time among meteorologists and other scientists. In these, a large pan is filled with water and placed on a turntable. When the center of the pan is cooled and the rim is heated, the cold water sinks and migrates toward the rim, as we would expect, while the warm water rises and flows toward the center, as we would also expect. When the pan is rotated, the moving water develops wavy patterns that resemble jet stream winds, and as the speed of rotation is increased, the waves flip from one kind of pattern to another, with no apparent order—just like real jet streams, like the weather in general, and, in a way, like Lorenz's computer program if the input is just a tiny bit different.

This field of inquiry is now known as "chaos theory," one of the most exciting in theoretical mathematics and one with profound practical implications for almost every field of science, including meteorology. Perhaps no system is more "sensitively dependent on initial conditions" than the Earth's atmosphere, and perhaps no scientists are more severely restricted in their ability to establish those initial conditions. The grid for the computer models does keep getting smaller and smaller, but we're still talking in terms of *miles*, while the actual weather is taking place at the level of molecules. The adage "Does the flap of a butterfly's wing in Brazil set off a tornado in Texas?" was the title of a paper Lorenz gave in 1972. It is also an expression of the chaos inherent in the atmosphere. Even in a perfect world sometime in the distant, utopian future, the effect of chaos on their models would be one reason Hurricane Center forecasters would not want to depend on a single computer model, or even on a single kind of model.

Today, chaos theory writ large is one reason one model might predict that a Gulf of Mexico hurricane will move ashore in southern Texas thirty-six hours from now, and another might predict landfall for the same storm at the same time in the Florida Panhandle. That's a range of 600 miles, and of little value for a Gulf Coast resident. But that large discrepancy is not the end of the story for the forecasters, because they know their models, the principles each is based on, and the strengths and weaknesses of each. Forecasters mix and match their models, or decide which of half a dozen or more is most likely to be making sound predictions. Even though hurricane forecasting is a science and many forecasters have doctorates in the subject, the final decision about the official forecast is often as much art as science. Of particular importance is the forecaster's subjective and qualitative analysis of what is happening in the atmosphere surrounding the storm, with great reliance upon time-lapse satellite water vapor images. A forecaster draws on experience with scores of storms, an understanding of how the atmosphere works, and knowledge of the computer models, including how each model is handling the current storm, to plot the line on the map that represents the official forecast of a hurricane's path. History confirms that we have become much better at this over the past three or four decades, with a significantly greater rate of improvement during the past decade coinciding with improved computer modeling and data collection.

Beginning as much as thirty-six hours before expected landfall, forecasters and emergency managers begin to rely on storm surge models to issue warnings and order evacuations. By 1979, a decade after Chester Jelesnianski had developed the SPLASH model that predicted the enormous storm surge for Hurricane Camille, he had developed the SLOSH model, a nifty if somewhat tortured acronym for "Sea, Lake, and Overland Surges from Hurricanes." Unlike the much simpler SPLASH, which predicts how high the surge might be right on the coastline but makes no predictions about conditions inland, SLOSH calculates how far inland the surge from a particular storm might go and how deep the water there might be. Surge models, however, do not take into account possible flooding from a storm's heavy rain. As a tropical storm or hurricane threatens to move ashore in the United States, local and regional forecast offices use data from the National Weather Service's Hydrometeorological Prediction Center to predict how much rain the storm should produce and then issue predictions for "fresh water" flooding. These computer models also take into account factors such as how much water is already in rivers, streams, and lakes and how wet the soil already is, which determines how much rain will soak in.

In a cooperative effort with the Federal Emergency Management Agency, the U.S. Army Corps of Engineers, local and state governments, and other components of the Weather Service, Hurricane Center personnel ran the SLOSH model for the entire U.S. coastline from Texas to Maine. The basic information came from U.S. Geological Survey contour maps. Maps with accurate elevations were essential, but so was information about man-made features such as railroad embankments that raise the tracks a few feet above the ground and "gated" communities near the shoreline. These residential enclaves are often surrounded by walls; a six-foot brick wall will be an obstacle to an in-rushing storm surge, and openings within the wall will be outlets for the surge. Someone, such as the Army Corps of Engineers, has to survey this wall, including the openings for roads, and feed this data into the SLOSH model.

In return, SLOSH indicated which gated communities, which homes, strip malls, highways, roads, and farms were likely to be underwater, and which potential shelters should be out of the reach of a storm surge. As director of the National Hurricane Center, Neil Frank started using the SLOSH model to determine how the size, strength, and direction and speed of approach of a hurricane affects the impact of the storm surge on a given basin. As common sense and experience lead us to expect, the program confirmed that these factors can make all the difference.

Since forecast tracks and intensities are not perfect even twenty-four hours in advance, when evacuations often have to begin, a series of model runs were made for each basin along the coastline. SLOSH would make a surge forecast for a particular storm path and speed, and then an additional run would put landfall for the same storm a few miles up the coast, and another run would put landfall a few miles down the coast, and then another variation, then another, then another—hundreds of runs for each basin (in some cases more than 1,000), with each requiring from half a billion to one billion calculations. Then all of these runs were "composited," and the highest value from any of the runs for every location was plotted on a map, which became the Maximum Envelope of Water (MEOW) for that particular coastline for a specific storm's strength, size, speed, and direction of motion, pinpointing potentially dangerous areas.

MEOWs were generally produced to cover a county or group of counties that needed to coordinate evacuation plans, such as the Galveston Bay basin model, which covers several counties, including inland areas as well as complex coastlines. Traffic analyses and behavior studies determined how people would probably respond and how much time evacuations would require for various storm scenarios in each coastal area. Emergency planners designed their programs and plans accordingly. A selected set of MEOW maps are now routinely published in telephone books, hurricane prepared-ness pamphlets, and seasonal newspaper special sections for many coastal communities. Anyone who's thinking of buying property near the Gulf or Atlantic Coast should make the appropriate map a mandatory part of his or her pre-purchase research.

Without a doubt, the biggest *success* story of computer modeling and response has been the almost complete elimination of deaths from storm surge in the United States. From the beginning of good hurricane records through Hurricane Camille in 1969, storm surge was the leading hurricane killer in the United States. There's no question about this. But from Camille through the year 2000, storm surge took only five lives in the United States. The primary credit goes to the SLOSH program and to improved response planning based on its predictions. However, the threat remains large in vulnerable, densely populated areas such as New Orleans and the Florida Keys, where even the best warnings won't give people time to escape.

Among the experts, the vulnerability of New Orleans is legendary and scary because large parts of the city and its suburbs are below sea level. If the eye of a slow-moving, major hurricane roughly followed the Mississippi River up from the Gulf of Mexico and crossed right over the city, all the marshes to the south would be flooded. The highest surge on the storm's right side would push Lake Pontchartrain—north of the city—over the fifteen-foot levees and into a part of the city that's as much as five feet below sea level to begin with. The water on world-famous and famously vulnerable Canal Street, in the city's center, could be twenty feet deep while the high levee along the Mississippi River at the end of Canal Street stays above water.

Walter Maestri, the emergency management director of Jefferson Parish, Louisiana, is one of those whose profession includes worrying about saving people from hurricanes. Jefferson Parish includes some of the well-to-do suburbs adjacent to New Orleans, the area around the city's airport, and marshlands to the south where long-term residents who make their living trapping, shrimping, and working on oil rigs coexist uneasily with urbanites who are building large homes on the bayous. The parish ends at the Gulf of Mexico, which would drown much of Jefferson and surrounding parishes if the wrong hurricane came along. Maestri says, "The best guess is that we could get about sixty to sixty-five percent of the population out of the four-parish area around New Orleans if we had a seventy-two-hour window." That's 600,000 souls high and dry—and 400,000 in danger of being drowned by storm surge, if the evacuation started three days before the hurricane hit. In the twenty-first century, that's an incomprehensible number, and that's part of the problem. No one can imagine what it would be like, even in New Orleans, where ordinary afternoon thunderstorms can leave two feet of water around your house. Huge pumps scattered around the city and adjacent areas lift the water from ordinary rainstorms into the Mississippi River or into Lake Pontchartrain. They've handled the rain from weak hurricanes or the fringes of strong storms that didn't hit the city head on. But the pumps themselves would be covered or overwhelmed by the surge from a direct hit by a major hurricane.

In the past, emergency managers talked of "vertical evacuation" as the way to save those who were unable to escape a hurricane horizontally, so to speak. The idea was to shelter people in high-rise buildings as a last resort. No hurricane is going to blow over a high-rise building with a steel framework. But does this make such buildings safe? New research into the details of hurricane winds has found that they can be considerably stronger short distances above the surface. This discovery led engineers, and then emergency planners, to the conclusion that while the steel structure of many buildings would stand up to a hurricane, the winds only a few stories up could be strong enough to blow away the outside walls or cladding. Thinking about this scenario leaves Maestri with a mental picture of people on the upper floor of high-rise buildings trying to cling to something—anything—as winds rip away the walls. This happened at the nineteen-story Dockside Condominiums in Charleston, South Carolina, when Hurricane Hugo struck in 1989. The experiences of Alfred B. Hassell, a security guard at the building who was there that night, are described in the book *Hugo: Storm of the Century*, edited by William J. Macchio. Hassell tells of going from floor to floor pounding on doors to get people to join others in the lobby where he thought they would be safer. On the fifteenth floor, he thought he heard screams. By this time, the building was "weaving and wobbling" and the noise of the wind and the rattling of the doors in the corridor made it hard to discover where the screams were coming from. He finally found a nurse and her patient in an apartment, the nurse "scared to death, shaking and crying." He picked up the patient and carried him into the hall. Just as they left the apartment, its exterior walls collapsed and he watched as "the furniture was sucked out the hole where the wall had been."

The latest plan for New Orleans calls for sheltering people only on the fourth through the seventh floors of high-rises. These floors would be above any conceivable flood waters but low enough that surrounding buildings will help reduce the speed of the winds striking the floors. However, such shelters wouldn't be able to hold the 400,000 people who could be stranded in New Orleans in a worst-case hurricane, so area officials are talking about creating an "urban refuge" by building a flood wall to protect an entire part of the city from surge flooding. Such a wall would be expensive, but, Maestri notes, "there is a movement in the Federal Highway Administration to buffer neighborhoods adjacent to major highways against noise, so there's money in the federal budget to do the buffering. . . . Our point is simple: If you are going to buffer New Orleans, don't buffer it just aesthetically with aluminum. Let us buffer it with steel sheet piling, and we'll dress it up on the outside." The steel sheets would act as a flood wall, but the covering would make this impregnable wall look like the sound buffers seen along urban expressways across the country. Floodgates would be installed at all crossing streets.

The highest parts of New Orleans are along the Mississippi River, where the land was built up by sediment from floods before the city was built in the nineteenth century. The levees that now protect the city from floods on the river add to the elevation in this area, and they would serve as the southern boundary of the proposed urban refuge. The northern boundary that would hold off the storm surge from Lake Pontchartrain would be a dual-purpose sound buffer and flood wall running from near the French Quarter along U.S. Highway 61 (Airline Highway) west to New Orleans International Airport. The wall could even be extended to protect the airport, which would give relief airplanes a place to land in a worst-case scenario. The levees on the river to the south and the wall on the north would protect the city center, the Superdome, and several hospitals and universities from storm surge. Since this region is the high ground in a low city, it's where people caught by storm surge flooding elsewhere are most likely to head anyway.

There's some concern that such an urban refuge would entice people who would otherwise evacuate to stay put, knowing that if worse comes to worst, they'll have the refuge to head for. New Orleans, along with a few other places such as the Florida Keys, is an exception to the general idea that most people along the coast would be better off staying put than evacuating, as long as their homes are out of the way of surge or other flooding. In New Orleans and the Keys, no structure is safe from storm surge; even if New Orleans builds the urban refuge, most people in the city and its suburbs will still be in surge zones, and it's hard to imagine where the money could be found to create safe and comfortable shelters in the refuge that could hold everyone from outside the refuge. Even with a refuge, therefore, the best bet for most people around New Orleans is going to continue to be to get out of town when a hurricane threatens. Maestri thinks most residents will do this. He says, "A lot of the people are going to evacuate because of the comfort issue. They have come to understand this urban refuge isn't going to be a nice place. When I go out to talk to people, I exaggerate and tell them they'll be in a slum tenement, up to your knees in rats. If you go there you're going to be back-to-back, belly-to-belly, and up to your hips in water waiting for us to come and get you, and we can't promise when we're going to get there. That's the reality."

While the SLOSH models and MEOWs supply the firm numbers that emergency managers such as Maestri can use to plan measures such as an urban refuge, they're not perfect. No one should assume the map is accurate down to the level of which side of the street will flood, which the woman who confronted Neil Frank in Miami had wanted to know. When massive Hurricane Carla came ashore in southern Texas in 1961, it pushed a surge of thirteen feet on the coastline, but more than nineteen feet above normal *twenty miles inland* in Lavaca and Galveston Bays. Old-time residents of coastal areas know that flukes and aberrations are quite possible, but many newcomers may not, and if they focus on the latest MEOW or the specific hurricane track that is being forecast without considering the possible errors, they could be in trouble. Also, as the number of people living on and visiting low-lying coastal areas and the 295 barrier islands along the Atlantic and Gulf Coasts is increasing almost every year, the time needed to evacuate these areas gets longer and longer. Some industries and many communities now require more time to shut down or otherwise prepare than the Hurricane Center's standard twelve hours of daylight and good weather.

In the early 1980s, the National Weather Service looked at these problems and considered the options for dealing with them. One was to provide longer lead times by simply issuing earlier warnings — thirty-six hours or more in advance of landfall. However, this strategy would necessarily require that much larger areas of coastline be included in warnings; since longer-range forecasts become less and less accurate, this would result in higher "false alarm" rates. Systematic over-warning increases the costs of unnecessary preparedness, which have been estimated at as much as $100,000 per mile or more in some heavily populated or heavy industry areas. Even worse, it would likely lead many coastal residents to ignore all such warnings and wait until a storm's winds or tides were directly affecting their area before evacuating or taking other action. Such delays could lead to large death tolls if residents were then trapped by storm surge.

Another factor that forecasters and emergency managers considered was that most coastal residents do *not* need to be evacuated. These residents and businesses generally only need time to close shop and board up. The now-familiar system of issuing a hurricane "watch" for a larger area and a "warning" for a smaller area was generally adequate for these purposes. A hurricane watch advises that winds of 74 miles per hour or stronger are possible within the next thirty-six hours or less. Everyone in the designated area should closely monitor the storm and begin some preliminary preparation such as making sure that food and water supplies are in place and that covers for windows are ready to be installed if a warning is issued. A hurricane warning advises that hurricane-force winds are expected within the warned area within twenty-four hours or less. All those in the warning area should rush preparations to completion such as boarding up, and then evacuate, if recommended to do so, within the next twelve hours.

A major disadvantage of this system, especially for large businesses and industry as well as for some government operations, is that it permitted only a qualitative assessment of risk. That is, there was no way to mathematically balance the costs of various kinds of preparations against the possible losses if preparations aren't made and the storm hits. Many community officials and private industry decision-makers wanted to compare the costs of preparation against potential losses to determine where, what, when, or if action should be taken.

They wanted a cost-benefit analysis, in effect, and in 1985 they got it, when the National Weather Service decided to supplement its watch-and-warning program with a quantitative assessment of risk in the form of probabilities. Jerry Jarrell, who was then with the U.S. Navy, had developed a simple probability program, based upon past forecast errors, to compute the probability of hurricane strikes for various navy interests. Charles Neumann of the National Hurricane Center refined this technique to develop what is called the HUR-RISK model (for HURricane RISK). This model computes probabilities—or "the odds"—that a hurricane's center would pass within fifty-eight miles to the "right" or eighty-six miles to the "left" (looking along the track toward the coast) of selected coastal communities or other points. Those distances are the statute mile equivalents of fifty and seventy-five nautical miles, respectively. The HURRISK model recognizes that counterclockwise winds of a hurricane produce larger areas of strong winds and greater storm surge on the right side of the center, where the winds initially blow inland from the ocean, than on the left side, where they initially blow off the land toward the sea.

Every six hours (or less, if the hurricane's path or strength are rapidly changing), the National Hurricane Center issues a forecast that predicts the specific latitude and longitude for the center of a hurricane at various times in the future, between twelve and seventy-two hours. The differences between these forecasts and the actual storm track become the forecast error. The computer program generating these probabilities searches the data files for the forecast errors in similar situations in the past in order to calculate the range of error for *this* forecast. The program then calculates the odds of the storm's coming onshore with hurricane winds at various locations on the coast. Say a hurricane was forecast to move north through the Gulf of Mexico and strike the coastline just south of Mobile, Alabama, within twenty-four hours. According to all the probabilities forecast for that storm as it steamed north over the Gulf, there was a 9 percent chance that it would make landfall instead at New Iberia, Louisiana, almost 300 miles west. The chance that it would make landfall at New Orleans was 25 percent; at Buras, on the southeastern tip of Louisiana, 35 percent; at Gulfport, Mississippi, sixty-five miles west of the forecast landfall, 42 percent; at Mobile itself, 45 percent; at Pensacola, Florida, fifty-five miles east of the forecast landfall, 44 percent; at Panama City, Florida, 23 percent; at Appalachicola, Florida, 12 percent; and at St. Marks, Florida, 255 miles east of Mobile, 8 percent.

The map for the storm would not have a single line from the center's latest location over the Gulf of Mexico straight to Mobile, but rather lines that fanned out from the latest position to New Iberia, to the west of Mobile, and to St. Marks to the east. The highest probabilities for landfall are focused right along the forecast track, with probabilities decreasing outward to the east and to the west. It's important to note that the odds that the storm would hit exactly where it was forecast to hit south of Mobile are less than 50 percent—45 percent, according to the prediction.

These forecast "cones" were instantly adapted by news outlets because they were a visually compelling and effective way to reinforce the fact that the forecast is a *forecast*, and may be incorrect, and that the storm could hit anywhere along a long stretch of coastline. When Neil Frank retired as director of the National Hurricane Center in 1987, the new director of the center, Bob Sheets, was more optimistic about forecast improvements than Frank had been, but he realized there would be no instant cure to forecasting problems. Still, along with continuing Frank's public education efforts, Sheets pushed the technology that was likely to improve forecasts. He also began trying to help emergency managers realize that they shouldn't assume that everyone was going to get out. They should be thinking of ways to minimize evacuations.

The lull in hurricane activity that had begun in the mid-1960s was still continuing in the late '80s. Storms did hit the mainland, but not at the rate of the '40s and '50s. As hundreds of thousands of unsuspecting new residents moved to or bought second homes on the vulnerable coastlines, those who were experienced, who knew about hurricanes, wondered when the next cycle of increased activity would roll around. They wondered when and where another Camille would hit, with devastating and possibly tragic consequences.

CHAPTER 10

HURRICANE ANDREW

Sunday, August 16, 1992. It has been a generation since the last major hurricane—Betsy, in 1965—ripped through Miami, and even that hurricane had been well south of the city, with the eye passing over the upper Keys. In the interim, the forecasters at the National Hurricane Center have repeated again and again that southern Florida is, statistically, the most likely part of the United States to be hit by a hurricane. The center has its headquarters in a twelve-story office building in Coral Gables, a close-in suburb of Miami, but still the message has a hard time getting through to the local residents of this fast-growing paradise. Most think of tropical cyclones as something that happens to other people living along other vulnerable coastlines in other years. Few in Florida—or anywhere else, for that matter—give a second thought to the brief announcement on the late-night news on Sunday evening that the third tropical depression of the season has formed over the eastern Atlantic, 1,500 miles east of the Lesser Antilles, or 3,500 miles east-southeast of Florida. The trivial disturbance doesn't merit a name yet, so no one has any idea that Andrew is on the way.

Max Mayfield, the hurricane specialist on duty at the Hurricane Center, releases the bulletin at 11 P.M. after studying the unmistakable images from the European geostationary weather satellite: spiral bands of clouds around a low-level center, with towering clouds close to the center. Before issuing the first advisory, Mayfield follows the routine of placing a conference call to the computer model experts at the Weather Service's National Meteorological Center (NMC) in Camp Springs, Maryland. He also calls forecasters at the

U.S. Navy's Atlantic Meteorology and Oceanographic Centers at Norfolk, Virginia, and Jacksonville, Florida, respectively. According to policy and practice, the center will now release a new bulletin about this disturbance at least every six hours for the duration of its career. Every bulletin is keyed to the updated analysis and forecasts generated by the National Weather Service's various offices and computer models, and every bulletin is also preceded by the conference call to all concerned. If land is threatened, the number concerned gets larger, as the call is expanded to include National Weather Service headquarters in Silver Spring, Maryland, Weather Service regional headquarters, and the local offices for any areas likely to be affected.

At the beginning of these discussions, the NMC model expert provides a track forecast, which is copied down on a worksheet by the hurricane specialist in Coral Gables, who then gives his preliminary track and intensity forecast, which he has written down before the call. After discussion, an "official" forecast is arrived at. Even though he considers the opinions of his colleagues on the conference call, the center's specialist takes final responsibility for the forecast. Mayfield's advisory for tropical depression number three for 1992 states that it is moving toward the west at close to 20 miles per hour. Mayfield predicts the system will remain embedded in the "deep easterly flow"—the steady winds from right above the ocean's surface to several thousand feet—which is pushing it to the west. Only slow intensification is expected over the next few days.

At five o'clock on Monday morning, Hal Gerrish, who has replaced Mayfield as the specialist on duty, issues the newest bulletin, noting that the winds of this disturbance are now estimated at 40 miles per hour, which is just above the threshold for an official tropical storm—the first of the '92 season for the Atlantic Basin, because the first two disturbances had fizzled out. As such, this newborn storm needs a name, and Andrew comes from the list approved by the World Meteorological Organization's Western Hemisphere Hurricane Committee in 1981. (The original "A" name on the list had been Allen, but in August 1980 a hurricane named Allen had caused considerable damage in the islands of the eastern Caribbean and then had prompted the evacuation of 300,000 people from southern Texas, where it eventually killed twenty-two and did more than $1 billion in damage. When a hurricane causes large loss of life or property, its name is generally retired.)

In the eastern Atlantic, winds high in the atmosphere, 40,000 to 50,000 feet up—the top of the storm—are blowing from the southwest, while winds at lower altitudes are blowing from the east. This means the winds at the top of Andrew are trying to push the storm toward the northeast while the winds at the bottom are trying to push it toward the west. Such shearing forces can literally blow away a storm's top, as we have seen. In Andrew's case, the opposing winds aren't expected to be fatal. They should, however, stunt growth by disturbing the smooth, upward flow of warm, moist air. Therefore Gerrish, like Mayfield, expects only slow strengthening of this storm for the next three days, to wind speeds of about 65 miles per hour.

The morning runs of the computer models predict that Andrew will hit the northeastern Caribbean islands within about three days, and Gerrish issues a forecast predicting that the storm will be over Antigua early on Thursday morning. He and other Hurricane Center forecasters use a restricted telephone line to call their counterparts at meteorological offices in the potentially threatened nations of the Caribbean to discuss the threat and the timing of possible watches or warnings. Gerrish notifies John Pavone, chief of the three-person air force civilian unit at the National Hurricane Center, which schedules and coordinates all hurricane reconnaissance missions, that aircraft will probably be needed starting Wednesday morning. By then Andrew should be close enough for the special air force reserve's Hurricane Hunter unit to conduct flights out of Antigua. The forecasters certainly hope so; they're eager for the airborne reconnaissance to begin. The satellite images are indispensable—after all, they found the storm in the first place—but 22,238 miles above the Earth is a long way away. The images don't reveal the storm's exact center; this isn't unusual, because the center is hidden within and beneath the towering clouds. The Hurricane Hunter planes will be able to find this center and precisely measure winds and air pressure in all parts of the storm, giving forecasters a much more detailed picture of what's going on.

The Hurricane Hunters have been expecting this request, and

crews and ground support personnel are already preparing to fly two WC-130 airplanes to Antigua from their base at Biloxi, Mississippi, early Tuesday morning. A third crew will come along to ensure that everyone gets enough rest in the days ahead. This complicated transfer of resources is pulled off without a hitch, and the first reconnaissance flight heads east toward Andrew early Wednesday morning. The data uncovered is surprising. On its way into the center the aircraft encounters winds of only 30 miles per hour, and in the center it finds a surface air pressure of 29.71 inches of mercury, which is higher than expected. These measurements, coupled with satellite images showing a weakening storm, lead to talk among the crew and those back at the Hurricane Center who see the report that Andrew is already dying. But then the plane is directed into the northern part of the storm, where it finds sustained winds of 73 miles per hour at an altitude of 1,500 feet. So maybe Andrew isn't dying after all.

Starting with this flight, the Hurricane Hunters will fly into Andrew's eye at least once every six hours until it dies or is far out at sea and no longer a threat. If the Hurricane Center issues any watches or warnings for the storm, the planes will generally fly into the storm, obtain fixes, and collect data at least every three hours. In these crunch-time circumstances, it will be a hectic tour of duty for the flying crews and ground personnel. On a rotating basis, at least one air force reserve or NOAA plane will be in the air almost around the clock. As the storm moves closer to the United States, other air force reserve planes will fly from Biloxi or other bases closer to the storm, and NOAA P-3 planes will ferry researchers into Andrew while also providing regular reports to forecasters.

In the 5 A.M. bulletin Thursday morning, August 20, forecaster Richard Pasch in Coral Gables notes that the last C-130 crew surveying the storm hadn't been able to locate a center at 5,000 feet, and air pressures were relatively high, but they did find 62-mile-per-hour winds. Andrew is a poorly organized storm. Technically, it probably isn't a tropical storm at all now. However, air pressures around the storm are also high. This difference between "high" and "higher" is sufficient to account for the strong winds on the storm's northeastern side. Pasch notes in his bulletin that the Aviation run of the Medium Range Forecast model insists that the upper atmosphere "will become much more conducive for strengthening in about twenty-four hours." Pasch compares the model's forecasts with animated water vapor satellite images and upper-air data charts and feels that the forecasts "look realistic," which isn't always the case. The question now is whether Andrew will survive long enough to reach the more favorable environment, or die beforehand.

After everyone arrives at the office on Thursday morning, Bob Sheets and his colleagues consider whether to downgrade Andrew from a tropical storm back to a depression. They also try to make sense of the storm tracks the various models are calling for over the next seventy-two hours. The predictions vary greatly, but this isn't unusual. The models rarely completely agree with each other. In the end, Sheets decides that although Andrew technically might not be a tropical storm at this time, it's better to continue calling it one for the next twenty-four hours. He doesn't want to downgrade the system and then have to upgrade it again a few hours later. Such announcements would be scientifically correct, but they could erode public perception of Andrew's strength and possible future threat.

The official seventy-two-hour forecast issued on Thursday predicts that by 8 A.M. Sunday morning Andrew will still be a tropical storm with winds below 74 miles per hour, and that it should then be about 550 miles east of Miami. But it's not long before this forecast looks doubtful. On Friday morning, forecasters analyzing the time-lapse satellite data, the new surface data from the islands, and the upper-air data from the islands and reconnaissance planes find that the predicted favorable upper-level wind pattern is indeed helping air flow out of the storm's top, thus encouraging warm air to rise with renewed vigor. Andrew is strengthening. Its sustained winds hold steady at 60 miles per hour all day, but Max Mayfield revises the forecast: this storm will be a hurricane within twenty-four hours. It is about 470 miles north of San Juan, Puerto Rico, or about 930 miles nearly due east of Miami. It is moving toward the west-northwest at about 9 miles per hour.

The eight computer track prediction models routinely used at the Hurricane Center at this time are now becoming a little more consistent—or at least *three* of the models are. Instead of looking like spray from a fountain going in all directions, the track predictions of

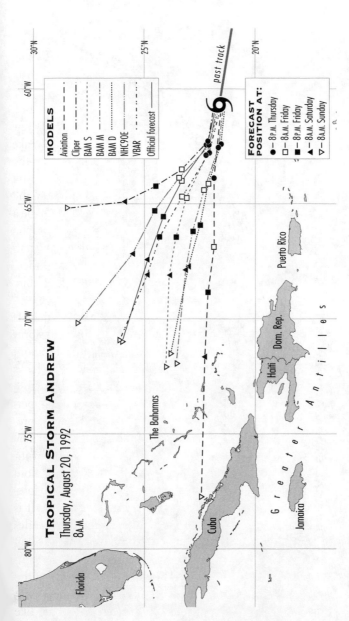

Computer model predictions for the future track of Tropical Storm Andrew initiated at 8 A.M. EDT on Thursday, August 20, 1992, while the storm was centered about 400 miles northeast of San Juan, Puerto Rico.

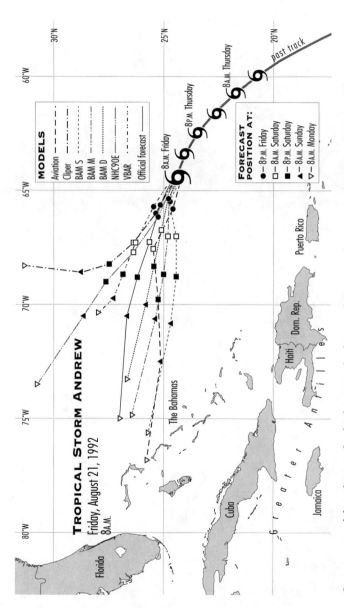

TROPICAL STORM ANDREW
Friday, August 21, 1992
8 A.M.

MODELS
Aviation
Cliper
BAM S
BAM M
BAM D
NHC90E
VBAR
Official forecast

FORECAST
POSITION AT:
● — 8 P.M. Friday
□ — 8 A.M. Saturday
■ — 8 P.M. Saturday
▲ — 8 A.M. Sunday
▽ — 8 A.M. Monday

past track

8 A.M. Friday
8 P.M. Thursday
8 A.M. Thursday

Florida
Cuba
The Bahamas
Jamaica
Haiti
Dom. Rep.
Puerto Rico
Greater Antilles

Computer model predictions for the future track of Tropical Storm Andrew initiated at 8 A.M. EDT on Friday, August 21, 1992. Note that all the models predicted that the storm would still be more than 200 miles from the Florida coast by 8 A.M. Monday. Andrew now had 60 mph winds.

these three, plotted on a map, are now in agreement that the storm will move rather slowly west-northwest to northwest over the next three days, positioning it more than 300 miles east of the central Florida coast by Monday afternoon. However, one model, the statistical model CLIPER, shows Andrew turning toward the north, which would take it away from any land. Two other models indicate slow movement generally toward the Carolina coast, with another model somewhere in between. The "outlying" prediction on the left, or to the south of the main set of predictions, is provided by the Aviation run, which shows the storm turning due west within twelve hours. This track would put Andrew's center between the islands of Great Abaco and Eleuthera in the northwestern Bahamas by 8 A.M. Monday morning, 220 miles east of Miami, and a distinct threat to southern Florida. However, the forecasters have their doubts about the Aviation prediction. Only twenty-four hours earlier, this same model said that Andrew would turn due west and that the storm would pass over Cuba, some 275 miles southeast of Miami. Can they trust a model that's already made such a large error on this particular problem? The three models moving the storm a little more toward the west-northwest or northwest have been the more reliable over the past few days.

After examining the forecasts, reconnaissance data, and satellite images and conferring with other meteorologists, Bob Sheets and Max Mayfield are relatively confident that Andrew will intensify and become a hurricane within twelve to twenty-four hours, but the major question is the effect of a ridge of high pressure that's building to the north. As this large high expands, its clockwise winds will speed up, turning Andrew more toward the west and increasing its forward speed. But the forecasters think that the ridge won't be able to have this influence for at least twenty-four hours, very likely forty-eight hours. What happens with Andrew in the meantime?

Sheets and Mayfield issue an official forecast that Andrew will continue moving toward the west-northwest at a speed and on a track that should put the storm's center about 300 miles due east of Fort Pierce, Florida, by Monday afternoon. This means Andrew would not strike Florida before late Tuesday, August 25, at the earliest, or more likely Wednesday. The forecast "cone" shows an 8 percent probability that instead of Andrew's center being 300 miles east of Fort Pierce, it could be within seventy-five miles of Fort Pierce or West Palm Beach. The cone also shows a 7 percent chance that it could be within seventy-five miles of Miami or Cocoa Beach by Monday afternoon.

After putting together the latest forecast on Friday afternoon for the 5 P.M. advisory, Sheets uses the National Warning System phone to brief emergency managers across Florida. He describes the atmospheric conditions and the storm's projected path and says he doesn't expect Andrew to affect Florida over the weekend. With this guidance, some officials let staff members take the weekend off. In his television briefings that evening, Sheets says Andrew is unlikely to affect the state before at least Monday, but he advises everyone to keep an eye on it over the weekend. Before going home for the night, Sheets calls Ken Lightbourne, the director of the Bahamian Meteorological Services, in Nassau, briefs him on the forecasts, and asks the Bahamians to start around-the-clock observations at some out-island weather offices, which are normally open only during the day.

At 4 A.M. Saturday morning, August 22, Hurricane Specialist Lixion Avila calls Sheets at home to tell him that in its newfound, favorable environment, Andrew has strengthened as expected. Also, Avila says, the forward speed may be picking up to around 12 miles per hour. This means that the ridge to the north of the storm has developed faster than expected, which would turn Andrew to a more westerly course toward the Bahamas and Florida, and with a faster forward speed.

Meanwhile, the computer models are disagreeing more than before, primarily about forward speed. The Aviation model moves Andrew inland near Fort Pierce, Florida, early Monday morning and has it clear across the state at Tampa by 8 P.M. This is the same model that thirty-six hours earlier had forecast the hurricane would pass over Cuba, and twelve hours earlier had predicted the storm would be in the northeastern Bahamas, well east of southern Florida on Monday. The inconsistencies prompt forecasters to discount this specific forecast. Nevertheless, the prediction of a faster forward speed is disturbing, because an increase of even two miles per hour in forward speed in the short term would mean an even faster for-

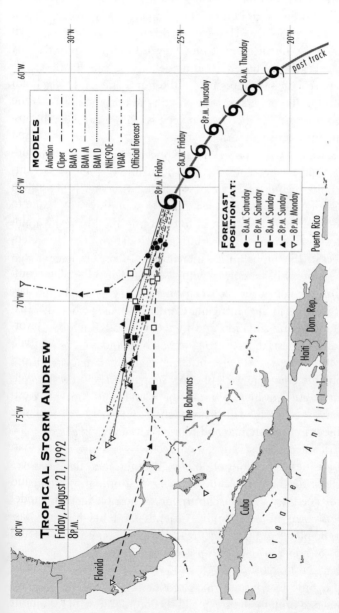

Computer model predictions for the future track of Tropical Storm Andrew initiated at 8 P.M. EDT on Friday, August 21, 1992. Note that only one model predicted that the storm would strike the Florida coast within the next three days. Andrew still had not yet reached hurricane strength.

ward speed later, possibly bringing Andrew onto Florida's eastern coast at least twenty-four hours earlier than previously expected, perhaps as early as Monday. However, at this time none of the models predict that the hurricane will move toward southern Florida, and with the exception of the Aviation model, all indicate that it will be more than seventy-two hours before the hurricane could reach the coast. Most of the predictions are pointing toward the north-central or northern Florida or the Carolina coasts, with CLIPER still indicating the hurricane will turn out to sea.

An hour after Avila's phone call to Sheets's home early Saturday morning, Andrew becomes the first hurricane of the 1992 season with sustained winds of 75 miles per hour. Its center is about 800 miles east of Miami, moving toward the west-northwest at about 12 miles per hour. The latest official forecast puts the hurricane about 135 miles east of Vero Beach, Florida, at 2 A.M. on Tuesday. With this forecast, the probabilities increase to 10 or 11 percent that Andrew's center will actually be within seventy-five miles of the coast at that time, and anywhere between Miami and Daytona Beach.

Sheets hurries to the Hurricane Center by 6 A.M., where he analyzes the changing situation and then again calls Lightbourne in Nassau and suggests that a hurricane watch should go up shortly for parts of the Bahamas. He also briefs emergency management officials using the emergency telephone system. With Andrew strengthening faster and advancing toward the islands and the U.S. coast faster than expected, the Hurricane Center and emergency management offices in the Bahamas and Florida have to begin catching up. The hurricane specialists know their decisions can save or cost people and businesses millions of dollars. At times, their decisions can mean life or death. With Andrew, for the first time in more than a quarter of a century, a powerful hurricane is possibly heading for the forecasters' own homes, families, friends, and neighbors. There seems to be plenty of time to get ready, if the forecast is correct, but the level of concern ratchets up a notch or two, there's no doubt about that.

It's also time to consider increased staffing levels, because the electronic and print media are quickly becoming aware of the changing situation, the increased tension, and are requesting more frequent Hurricane Center updates. Most areas on the coast will need twenty-four hours to prepare for such a storm, but the more populated areas in Dade and Broward Counties—the Miami–Fort Lauderdale area—and the Florida Keys will need thirty hours or more. On the plus side with Andrew is the fact that it is a small storm, with hurricane-force winds extending outward only about thirty miles east of the center and less to the west. Tropical storm winds—39 miles per hour—extend out only about eighty-five miles to the north of the center and less to the south and west. These numbers will make life easier for emergency officials: winds strong enough to make evacuations dangerous or impossible won't arrive well ahead of the center, as they do for large hurricanes, such as Hugo in 1989.

The Hurricane Center activates its "media pool agreement," in which all the broadcasters get together and provide a pool coordinator, a single camera and crew for the networks, and a second camera and crew for all local TV stations. The pool coordinator schedules all briefings under a plan that gives stations in threatened areas priority over stations elsewhere, including major cities not in the immediate threat area. Vivian Jorge, the center's administrative officer, and Herb Lieb, a retired National Weather Service public affairs official, take turns as the media coordinator. The set for the "briefing station" is to one side of the center's main forecast working area. It includes a large monitor displaying up-to-the minute satellite and radar images and maps. In the background are a large wall map and forecasters working at an oval table. This arrangement allows the individual conducting the media briefings to be involved in all the center's activities: receiving the latest reports, frequently making forecasts, and writing or helping to write advisories between interviews. This individual is usually the hurricane center director. The aim is to ensure that television viewers receive the most accurate and immediate information directly from Hurricane Center specialists, without intermediaries and possible misinterpretations of the message. Having a single individual provide most of the briefings helps to assure a consistent message and interpretation of that message.

In his first briefings, Sheets says that a hurricane watch will probably be issued for parts of the Florida coast on Saturday night or early Sunday morning. The government of the Bahamas issues a hurricane watch for the northwestern Bahamas at 11 A.M. Saturday, by which time Andrew's central pressure has dropped markedly and is now 28.76 inches of mercury. Wind speeds have increased to 90 miles per hour. The storm is moving nearly due west at a still higher forward speed of 14 miles per hour. At the same hour, the predictions of the computer models are agreeing more and more. All but one indicate that Andrew will hit Florida between West Palm Beach and Cape Canaveral. Some forecast that changes in deep-layer steering currents will slow the storm's forward speed, with landfall not before forty-eight hours, maybe as long as seventy-two hours. But again Aviation is the odd model out, predicting an even higher forward speed, up to 18 to 20 miles per hour, nearly twice the speed the model had predicted twenty-four hours earlier. The Aviation model shows Andrew's center passing over Miami at about 2 A.M. on Monday morning and over Naples on the western coast at 8 A.M.

This prediction surprises and concerns Sheets and the others at the Hurricane Center, but the model has been inconsistent over the past few days, and the extreme forward speed it's forecasting reduces their confidence that it has the right take on this storm. On the other hand, its predicted course is now somewhat more consistent with the others, though still showing a track well to the south of the predictions from the other models. Putting everything together, Sheets now believes that the hurricane will hit near West Palm Beach early Tuesday morning. However, he doesn't have a lot of confidence in this assessment, because of uncertainties about large-scale weather pattern changes that could turn the tables quickly. If the high pressure to the north continues to strengthen as quickly as it has in the last twenty-four hours, the forward speed will increase markedly and the track will be shifted farther south. That is what the Aviation model is predicting will happen.

At 5 P.M. Saturday, the Hurricane Center makes the danger official for the U.S. mainland. A hurricane watch is posted for a 375-mile stretch of Florida's eastern coast, from Titusville, 212 miles north of Miami, to Key West at the tip of the Keys, 164 miles south of Miami. Andrew's sustained winds are now 100 miles per hour. In the Public Advisory, Sheets states that "hurricane conditions could be experienced in the Northwest Bahamas late Sunday and in Florida sometime Monday." Even though neither Andrew's forward speed nor its strength have increased during the day, the ridge of high pressure to the north seems well established, and Sheets and the other forecasters think the storm will move faster and farther south than most of the models are predicting. Their official forecast reflects this thinking. It is also more consistent with the Aviation model's forecast, which now has Andrew hitting Florida just north of Fort Lauderdale about midday Monday. The "official" forecast calls for wind speeds to be 110 miles per hour at that time, just below major hurricane strength.

Issuing hurricane watches and warnings is a two-way, team process. As always, Sheets begins briefing emergency managers an hour or two before this watch is issued. He coordinates with them on zones to be included. These early briefings and discussions before the public release of the information allow for coordinated plans and help forestall piecemeal, confusing actions. Since the National Hurricane Center itself is in the watch area—the probability that Andrew will hit Miami and Coral Gables is 21 percent—a backup plan is activated to assure that forecasts and warnings will continue even if the Center is somehow disabled, which shouldn't happen. The building is designed to stand up to hurricane winds, and it is well away from the water. Shutters can be quickly closed over all of the windows of the sixth floor. The Center has its own emergency generator on the roof in addition to the building's generator in the basement, which could flood. With the fuel tanks topped off, the large roof generator could power all of the center's lights, equipment, and computers for nearly a week. It could even run an auxiliary air-conditioning system to keep sensitive electronic systems up to speed. Nevertheless, a team of hurricane specialists and support meteorologists prepare to fly to the National Meteorological Center near Washington D.C. They have already been assigned workstations at that facility, and the software programs they'll need for their work are installed on the computers they'll be using.

A dropsonde released by an air force Hurricane Hunter aircraft in the eye Saturday night measures a minimum pressure of 28.32 inches of mercury. Forecaster Miles Lawrence's 11 P.M. advisory states that Andrew's forward speed and direction of movement haven't changed for the past several hours, but that wind speeds have increased to 110 miles per hour, just below Category 3 status. With this increase in strength, Lawrence forecasts that storm surge heights in the north-western Bahamas will be ten to twelve feet above normal tide levels, accompanied by dangerous wave action. His forecast, which had been discussed earlier with Sheets, calls for the hurricane to move onshore farther south than previously forecast, in southern Dade County between Miami and Homestead, during the mid-morning hours on Monday with maximum sustained wind speeds of 125 miles per hour, which would make it a strong Category 3 hurricane.

Three hours after that advisory is issued, Andrew is indeed a major hurricane with 120-mile-per-hour winds. Latest reports from the Hurricane Hunters indicate that the pressure is continuing to fall, and the storm continues to move west at 14 miles per hour. The Bahamian forecasters extend their hurricane warnings southward to include the central Bahamas.

Hal Gerrish, the forecaster on early-morning duty Sunday, calls Sheets at home at 4 A.M. to discuss the possibility of upgrading from a watch to a warning for the Florida eastern coast in the upcoming 5 A.M. advisory. Considering the fact that there has been no major change in the hurricane's forward speed or track, Sheets decides that the "warning" decision should be held off until 8 A.M. This delay will allow emergency management and other officials a little more time to assess their situations and assemble personnel before the specific warning areas are designated. Posting warnings at 8 A.M. Sunday will still allow at least twelve hours of good daylight time for preparations and nearly twenty-four hours before the storm's center is expected to cross the coast. The delay will also give the forecasters a little more time to assess atmospheric conditions, with the hope of arriving at a more certain forecast, which would reduce the size of the warned area.

At 8 A.M. Sunday, the warning is issued for Florida's southeastern coast from Vero Beach south across the Keys, a stretch of 300 miles. The official forecast landfall is in southern Dade County. Andrew's center is expected to arrive at about 8 A.M. Monday morning, with hurricane-force winds moving in a few hours earlier. At the same time the warning is posted, a watch is issued for the western coast of the state from Bayport, north of Tampa Bay, south to Flamingo on the southern tip of the mainland. Now there's no doubt about Andrew. One week after the first bulletin about tropical depression number three, 3,500 miles away, the hurricane is finally for real.

On Sunday morning, August 23, residents of southeastern Florida scramble frantically to prepare. Some started the day before, but many have put it off. They soon strip supermarkets of food, toilet paper, and batteries, and hardware and lumber stores of materials to board up windows. Activity also accelerates at the National Hurricane Center. Volunteer ham radio club operators have been manning their station in the center's office for the past twenty-four hours, receiving reports from colleagues in the Bahamas and providing those operators with the latest advisories. Hurricanes frequently disable commercial communications systems, which leaves only ham radio as a link to islands and other countries throughout the region, as well as, sometimes, the only link to a few isolated communities on the mainland.

Bob Sheets instructs the standby team of hurricane specialists to fly to Washington, D.C., and get ready there. The team includes Jerry Jarrell, the deputy director of the center; Miles Lawrence, a hurricane specialist; two tropical analysts, Hugh Cobb and Jack Bevin; and John Pavone, chief of the center's air force civilian unit. These men finish preparing their families and homes and come to the Hurricane Center. Commercial airline reservations are impossible, because the flights are full with tourists and others fleeing Miami, so the backup team will fly north to Andrews Air Force Base outside Washington on one of the NOAA's WP-3 Hurricane Hunter research aircraft.

Just three hours after the first warning was issued, the next one, at 11 A.M. Sunday by Max Mayfield, is headlined DANGEROUS CATE-GORY FOUR HURRICANE HEADING FOR SOUTH FLORIDA. ALL PRECAU-TIONS TO PROTECT LIFE AND PROPERTY, INCLUDING EVACUATIONS, SHOULD BE RUSHED TO COMPLETION. Andrew has had a powerful and alarming growth spurt. Maximum sustained wind speeds are now 135 miles per hour, with gusts to 165. Reconnaissance aircraft measure a central pressure of 27.46 inches of mercury. If Andrew should come ashore with this pressure, it would be one of the strongest storms to strike the continental United States this century. Satellite loops show a very small, well-defined eye, and the hurricane is now moving due west at 16 miles per hour. At this hour, Andrew is centered a little over sixty miles east of the northern end of Eleuthera Island in the Bahamas, or about 330 miles nearly due east of Miami. It is still a small hurricane; sustained wind speeds on Eleuthera are just starting to exceed 40 miles per hour, with some stronger gusts as the first rain bands arrive. Estimates of the potential storm surge on the northwestern side of Eleuthera are increased to eighteen feet. Estimated storm surge heights for the Florida coast are forecast to be seven to ten feet above normal tides, with possible heights of nine to thirteen feet on the western shores of the shallow Biscayne Bay.

At noon, a reconnaissance aircraft reports a maximum wind at the airplane's 10,000-foot altitude of 195 miles per hour. Sustained surface winds are estimated to be 145 miles per hour, just 11 miles per hour below Category 5 status on the Saffir-Simpson scale. The minimum pressure has dropped even lower, to 27.34 inches of mercury. Such a number would make Andrew the third-strongest hurricane to hit the mainland this century.

The Hurricane Center team transferring to Washington takes off at 4 P.M. Sunday, leaving Bob Sheets, Hal Gerrish, Max Mayfield, Lixion Avila, Ed Rappaport, and Richard Pasch to handle all the forecasting duties at the Coral Gables office. All of the Hurricane Specialists are working at least double shifts, along with many other members of the staff who are collecting and analyzing data and performing their normal duties. Members of NOAA's Hurricane Research Division begin showing up at the center to assist in data collection and analysis, and to help with the phones. The media pool is going full blast with "hits" every three to five minutes. ("Hit" is the term used by broadcasters to describe each separate link to an individual station or group of stations.) Reporters from as far away as New Zealand are hounding the center for information. European media are especially interested because of the many European tourists in Miami.

By 5 P.M., Andrew's center moves over the northern end o

Eleuthera in the northwestern Bahamas. The staff at the center can only imagine the horrors that the residents on this low island are going through, since no reports are being received. Maximum sustained surface winds in a small area below the north eye wall are still estimated at 150 miles per hour, with gusts to 180. The latest Hurricane Hunter aircraft report gives a minimum pressure of 27.26 inches, just a little lower than previously. The strengthening phase may be at an end, at least for the time being. Now Andrew's spiral outer bands are starting to show up on the old-but-reliable 1950s-model weather radar whose antenna is on the roof of the Hurricane Center building. These bands are also just sweeping into view on a similar radar at West Palm Beach and on the National Weather Service's new Doppler radar at Melbourne, Florida. It's hard for the staffers at any of these offices to keep their eyes off the spiral rain bands and, soon, the eye wall itself.

The Hurricane Hunter aircraft are reporting their data every twenty minutes. They beam the news in bursts to an air force satellite, which relays the numbers to an antenna on the roof of the Hurricane Center as well as one at Kessler Air Force Base at Biloxi, Mississippi. The aircraft reconnaissance continues to show a very tightly wound storm, with weaker winds closer to the eye wall than in most hurricanes. Only thirty miles from the center the winds are less than 74 miles per hour—below hurricane strength. Knowing the wind speeds in different parts of Andrew helps forecasters estimate where the worst damage is likely to be when the storm hits land, and it also helps with storm surge forecasts. The information can also spur extra effort to get people out of the areas most likely to get the worst, and it alerts emergency managers to those areas that will probably need the most help as soon as possible *after* the storm has passed. The Hurricane Research Division has put extra efforts into measuring and forecasting winds at landfall with just this idea in mind.

The computer models now indicate that the western end of the high-pressure area centered to the north of the hurricane—the high that helped push Andrew onto its fast course to the west—will start to erode after about twenty-four to thirty-six hours, allowing the storm to swing back toward the north over the Gulf of Mexico. This could mean an increased threat to the northern Gulf Coast about forty-eight hours after Andrew crosses the Florida peninsula. Even as Andrew holds a steady course for them and their homes, the center's forecasters start thinking about New Orleans. Andrew could smash the Crescent City a couple of days after it wrecks southern Florida.

By 8 P.M. Sunday, the Hurricane Center's radar clearly shows Andrew's well-formed eye and intense eye wall as the center passes about forty miles north of Nassau and begins moving over the Berry Islands. The northwestern Bahamas are feeling Andrew's full force. A report from Eleuthera says that a gust of 120-mile-per-hour wind was measured as the eye wall passed over the island. The storm's center is now 185 miles east of Miami, where conditions remain good, with winds generally less than 20 miles per hour. All across southeastern Florida, residents and business owners and employees are boarding, nailing, taping, stowing, and buying whatever supplies are still left in the rush to finish preparations. The Hurricane Center, with assistance from other National Weather Service centers, provides the broad picture for the hurricane, with forecasts of the size, strength, track, rainfall, and storm surge. Local Weather Service offices use this information to prepare forecasts for their areas and to coordinate with local emergency management officials, who have the responsibility for ordering or recommending specific actions, such as evacuations. The news media are the vital third member of this team of forecasters and emergency managers. Radio and television stations provide up-to-the-minute information on the weather, the conditions of roads, which shelters are open, what actions are being ordered by local officials. Newspapers list the locations of shelters, specific actions to be taken as the storm approaches, and what to do in the wake of the storm.

In his 9 P.M. update, Ed Rappaport reports that the center of Andrew is 170 miles east of Miami. In addition to giving television interview after interview to the networks and local stations, for several hours now Sheets has been providing forty-five-second to one-minute updates at the beginning of each hour, which are beamed by satellite to stations all over the country and even overseas. Stations have even requested that these updates also be given at half past each hour. Sheets accommodates them, except when he's helping to pre pare the next forecast and advisory. On the television monitor on the set, a loop of satellite photos shows Andrew lunging toward the Florida coast. Behind Sheets the main forecast working area is buzzing with activity. At 10 P.M. the team that flew to Washington reports that they're in place and ready to take over operations if needed. News media crews had been waiting for their arrival at the nation's capital, and since the media demand in Florida has taxed the capacity of even the pool setup at the Hurricane Center, Jerry Jarrell, the deputy director of the National Hurricane Center, starts giving updates and interviews from the World Weather Building in Washington, supplementing those being given by Sheets in Florida.

Outside, the weather in southern Florida still offers no evidence of the threat which is now just over the horizon to the east. The sky is overcast, but the gentle wind holds no menace. The only hint of something amiss is South Dixie Highway, U.S. 1, which runs past the Hurricane Center. This main artery is almost empty; folks in Miami are hunkered down and waiting, not riding around getting their kicks. Three-quarters of a million residents have evacuated mobile-home parks and other neighborhoods in southern Florida that Andrew's storm surge could invade, including some neighborhoods just to the east of the Hurricane Center in Coral Gables. By 11 P.M. the Miami radar shows that Andrew's outer bands are finally getting close to the coast from West Palm Beach south through the Upper Keys. In the Bahamas, Nassau, on the weaker side of the hurricane, reports sustained winds of 85 miles per hour with gusts to 105. No information on Andrew's damage to the Bahamas will arrive until Monday. There is also some possibly good news for Florida residents. The hurricane is no longer strengthening and might be weakening. Radar images show the eye is expanding a little, and the minimum central pressure has risen to 27.67 inches of mercury, while the maximum sustained winds have decreased slightly to 140 miles per hour. The 1 A.M. Monday, August 24, advisory says ". . . outer rain bands of extremely dangerous hurricane . . . spreading across southeast Florida coastline. . . . Weather conditions will be rapidly deteriorating during the next few hours over southeast Florida. Tropical storm force winds [39 mph and faster] are already being observed at Fowey Rocks lighthouse." This landmark is about ten miles southeast of downtown Miami at the eastern edge of Biscayne Bay.

One of the Hurricane Hunter aircraft reports that the minimum central pressure has risen slightly again and is now at 27.79 inches. However, the forecast intensity at landfall still calls for maximum sustained wind speeds of 140 to 150 miles per hour, with gusts to 170 to 185. Andrew is now centered only eighty-five miles east of Miami and closing rapidly. As the first rain bands approach, technicians at the Hurricane Center make a smooth switch to the center's own emergency power. This is a standard practice, even for ordinary thunderstorms approaching the building, to avoid power fluctuations that could damage computers and other equipment. In this case, the Hurricane Center has no doubt that power will fail sometime that night. From now until commercial power is restored after Andrew has passed, the Hurricane Center will be using its emergency generators.

EXTREMELY DANGEROUS HURRICANE ANDREW CLOSING IN ON SOUTHEAST FLORIDA is the headline on the 3 A.M. advisory. Weather conditions are rapidly deteriorating over the area. This is expected, of course. Unexpected is the *decrease* in the air pressure measured by the reconnaissance aircraft. It's now 27.64 inches, reversing the earlier trend of slight weakening. Andrew has probably gained strength as it passed over the warm water of the Gulf Stream just off the Florida coast. Confirming this supposition are the radar images showing an intensifying and contracting eye wall. Andrew is now a very small but very strong Category 4 hurricane. The automated observing station on the Fowey Rocks lighthouse is reporting sustained winds of 59 miles per hour, with gusts to 69. It looks like the hurricane will make landfall during an intensifying stage, within two to three hours. Winds also continue to pick up as measured by the instrument on the roof of the Hurricane Center building. A blue flash lights the sky south of the center a little before 4 A.M. as an electrical transformer explodes. Commercial power fails outside, lights go out in the surrounding neighborhood, but the center's backup power is unaffected.

At 4:08 A.M., the wind gauge on the roof shows a sudden gust hits 107 miles per hour. Family members of the staff who have taken refuge at the center in the windowed offices of the administrative end of the office building are moved into the interior hallways, and the doors to the offices are closed. Even with shutters over the windows, there's a chance that the winds could shatter their glass. Very little noise from outside can be heard from inside the closed and shuttered sixth floor of the building, but when the heavy steel door to the emergency stairwell is opened on the exposed southwestern end of the building, a loud wind is heard and a strong suction felt. This suction is generated by the northeastern winds flowing around the building. Several individuals who aren't busy upstairs, including reporters, stand in the hallway on the ground floor, well back from the unshuttered glass doors. They occasionally open the door on the lee side of the building and peek out. On one such occasion, they see and hear pieces fly off the large satellite dishes on the building's east side. As planned, the center switches to receiving a basic set of satellite images through a dedicated, high-speed, underground line linking the center with Washington, D.C. With each passing gust, which are now coming about a minute apart, someone reads out the latest wind speed.

4:28 A.M.: "134 miles per hour."

4:30 A.M.: "126 miles per hour."

4:33 A.M.: "147 miles per hour."

Then a sudden *thud* shakes the building. No one says a word for a few seconds. Everyone looks at one another. What's happening? The radar stops working, so now the forecasters know that the sound must have been the antenna atop a ten-foot-high room on the building's roof. The one-ton dish must have blown over onto the main roof.

4:49 A.M.: "152 miles per hour."

4:52 A.M.: "164 miles per hour."

All eyes are glued on the wind dial. Suddenly, the speeds registered start to decrease rapidly, even though it is obvious from the noise level that the winds are actually increasing over and around the building. Apparently, the instrument has been damaged. And everyone at the center knows that these winds are not the strongest in the storm. The center of Andrew is about eighteen miles south-southeast of the Hurricane Center. The outer edge of the northern eye wall is about four miles south-southeast of the center. It now seems certain that Andrew's strongest winds, which are in that eye wall, will stay just to the south of the center itself. The staff can only imagine the incredible violence the storm is unleashing on Perrine, Cutler Ridge, Homestead, Florida City, and other areas only a few miles away, places where many of them and their families live. With winds gusting to 170 miles per hour and higher in the southern Dade County suburbs early Sunday morning, all anyone can do is hope and pray for survival of life, limb, family, and home.

About twenty miles southwest of downtown Miami in Whispering Pines, Tom Ochmanski and his wife, Laurie, have put their one-year-old son, Ryan, and two-year-old daughter, Caitlyn, to bed early in the evening. Whispering Pines is not in an evacuation zone, and the Ochmanski house is a strong one—they think. Around midnight, Tom and Laurie and Laurie's mother, Lee Bolander, finally try to get some rest, but the howling winds wake them two hours later. As the adults sit in the living room, watching reports on their battery-operated television set, squalls of heavy rain and high winds become more and more frequent and stronger. By 4:45 A.M., winds are probably gusting to more than 150 or 160 miles per hour, and debris slamming into the house creates an almost deafening roar. Above this roar, parents and grandmother hear breaking glass in Ryan's bedroom. Tom rushes in to find the window shattered by flying debris and scattered around the room, but, remarkably, Ryan is not cut or hurt. Tom grabs him and Laurie gets Caitlyn from her bedroom and the entire family huddles in the living room, close to the hallway entrance. They hear the other windows breaking on the north end of the house. As Andrew's eye wall moves directly over them, the screaming wind becomes even more terrifying. The Ochmanskis know when the wind shifts direction because the loud thumps of striking debris now come from the east side of the house.

Tom shines a large flashlight at the top of the front wall and sees it pulling away from the ceiling. This is a reinforced concrete tie beam connecting the walls to the roof, and these wind are doing their best to lift it right off the house. The family moves closer to the hallway door and starts praying. Suddenly, and with a tremendous crash, the entire front of their house slams inward, while the front half of the roof is ripped away. A large blunt object strikes Tom in the back, knocking him across the room. Laurie quickly crawls through the debris to the hallway, taking the two terrified children with her. She places Ryan and Caitlyn on shelves in the linen closet off the hallway and crouches in the open door to protect them with her own body. She is praying.

Where is Tom now? Where is her mother? Are they alive or dead? Laurie has only her fears, because she has her back toward the hallway. The noise is a steady, violent roar. Now her mother makes her way to the hallway and crowds into the open linen closet doorway behind Laurie, helping to cover the children with her body. Tom, after picking himself up, also makes his way there and crouches over all of them, trying to add more protection. They continue to pray and say good-bye to each other, certain that they will die. This seems like a pretty good bet when the wall behind them that separates the hallway from the living room starts to disintegrate. The soaked drywall and other debris pummel Tom's back, and the wall studs collapse onto the family. All the while, they can still hear the hurricane reports on the television in what used to be the living room. Tom shines his flashlight down the hallway toward Caitlyn's room, where he sees the closet nearly intact, to all appearances, except for the door, which is gone. The three adults crawl on hands and knees down the hallway, carrying the children through and over the fallen debris and beneath the flying debris. Laurie and her mother crowd themselves and the two children into one end of the three-by-five-foot closet. Tom grabs what is left of a door and uses it to partially shield all of them from the driving rain and flying debris. Laurie's wedding dress is still hanging in the closet. They use it and the other clothing in the closet to try to shield themselves from the chaos of Andrew.

Meanwhile, about seven miles farther south in the Naranja Lakes complex, Mike Shoemaker, an electronics technician with NOAA's Atlantic Oceanographic and Meteorological Laboratories, and his mother, Olive, have decided to ride out Andrew in her one-story, steel-reinforced, concrete-block, four-unit condo building. Because of the potential of storm surge flooding, the area had been recommended for evacuation, and most of the residents of this 1,600-unit complex have done so. Mike thought that the worst of the storm surge would be to the north—he was right about this—and he knew that the building is a simple design that usually stands up to wind well. When they hear a little after midnight that Andrew looks more and more as if it's coming right across southern Dade County— exactly where they are—Mike and his mother consider transferring quickly to Mike's home in Coconut Grove, some twenty miles to the north, near downtown Miami, but decide that it's too late to risk the drive. Rain squalls and high winds are already moving over Naranja Lakes.

By 3:30 A.M., the roar of the wind and rain drive Mike and Olive to the center hallway of her condominium. When the electricity fails, they crouch there with two flashlights, one battery-operated radio, and a gallon thermos of coffee. At about 4:25 A.M., they feel the wall they are leaning against begin to vibrate and then hear rumbling and "a loud ripping noise," as Mike later described it. This comes from the kitchen at the end of the hallway. He crawls in that direction and shines his flashlight just in time to see the corner of the ceiling lifting and tearing away from the interior wall. He yells for his mother to get into the bathroom, and he hurries in behind her. They lie facedown on the floor between the bathtub and the toilet with Mike covering his mother with his body. He hears "explosive and successive snapping sounds" as debris falls on his lower back and legs.

At the same time, John and Norah Bigelow are on their Belliure 40 sloop named *Mara Cu*, in Broad Creek thirty-five miles south of Miami. They had decided on a traditional strategy among owners of commercial and pleasure boats, taking the boat as far as possible up a small creek to a "hurricane hole," where it would be sheltered from the storm's worst wind, waves, and surge. By dusk on Sunday, John and Norah had anchored the boat in the creek and run three-quarter-inch nylon lines off both sides of the stern to the heaviest, thickest mangrove roots they could find.

At midnight, John starts a deck log, recording barometric pressure and wind velocity. At 3:05 A.M., the wind has risen to 70 miles per hour when the cell phone rings. On the line is a good friend who has been watching Andrew on television from his summer home in

Highlands, North Carolina, and he is astonished to hear where the Bigelows have chosen to ride out this Category 4 hurricane. He ends the short conversation with a terse "Hang in there, you guys!" The wind increases to 80 miles per hour at 4 A.M., and the pressure drops to 28.94 inches of mercury. "It was unbelievably loud outside," John recalled in his account of the event written shortly after the hurricane, based in part on entries in the log, "a constant, unnerving shrieking and moaning. . . . The boat moved about with short, violent jerks [and] torrential rain driven by the wind forced its way through the main companionway hatch." John and Norah begin reciting the Lord's Prayer. Within half an hour conditions deteriorate dramatically on board the *Mara Cu*. Judging by the anemometer reading, which had pegged at 114 miles per hour a few minutes before, and comparing the sounds and impacts on the boat between then and now, John estimates at 4:33 A.M. that sustained winds exceed 140 miles per hour with gusts to 170, "rendering an intolerable outcry in the boat's rigging."

Norah is wedged between the settee and main salon table in the violently pitching and rolling vessel, with a tear running down her cheek. "John, please tell me we're going to get through this," she says.

"The old girl is stronger than both of us," John answers. "We'll be laughing about this soon enough."

At 4:40 A.M. the pressure falls to 28.26 inches, and the broken anemometer still reads 114 miles per hour. At 4:46 A.M. John records a one millibar rise in the pressure and marks a large star in the deck log beside the reading. This slight increase in pressure means they have turned the corner; from now on the winds should begin to weaken, although the storm continues battering them for hours.

As Andrew's strongest winds rip apart communities south of the Hurricane Center, forecasters continue working with the radar images they still have, the ones from the Tampa and Melbourne radar arriving over high-speed, underground telephone lines. Ray Fagan, who is in charge of computer operations, is keeping the computers up and making sure that the satellite images continue to flow in from

Washington, D.C. Data from the airplanes are rerouted through the down link at Keesler Air Force Base in Mississippi. The winds have destroyed the center's microwave antennas used by the news media, so only voice connections are available for television reports except on NBC, which had installed a fiber-optics line to the Hurricane Center. The computer models indicate that the hurricane will move west across extreme southern Florida, weaken to a Category 3 storm, and then strengthen again with maximum sustained wind speeds of nearly 135 miles per hour once it is well over the Gulf of Mexico.

Warnings have been up for some time for southwestern Florida, so updating is all that is needed there. The urgent discussion now is when and where should watches and warnings be posted for the northern Gulf Coast. The computer models are indicating the continued erosion of the western end of the high-pressure area to the north of Andrew. If this happens, the hurricane will turn more to the north, increasing the threat to the central part of the northern Gulf Coast, including New Orleans. The consensus forecast brings the storm into Louisiana just southwest of New Orleans in about sixty hours; this worries Sheets and the other specialists, because they know how extremely vulnerable New Orleans is. A strong Category 4 hurricane coming in just to the south and west of New Orleans puts the city right in the middle of the northeastern quadrant of the storm, the most dangerous part of any hurricane. This eventuality could put the city under fifteen to twenty feet of water. On the other hand, Sheets knows that forecast errors are often large at seventy-two hours. They definitely had been when Andrew was far out over the Atlantic, and most of the models were calling for landfalls on Tuesday or Wednesday. This fact weighs heavily on the decision about issuing a hurricane watch for the New Orleans area at this time, and Sheets and his colleagues decide to wait at least one more forecast cycle, by which time they hope to have more confidence.

About two hours after the windows first broke in young Ryan Ochmanski's bedroom in Whispering Pines, the winds start to ease up a little. The inner edge of the northern side of the eye wall has passed directly over them. As dawn breaks and the winds begin to let up, the Ochmanskis find a haven at a nearby house, which has plywood covers over the windows and seems to be in good shape. A neighbor who is a registered nurse treats Tom's cuts and bruises, and the bruises the others have suffered. Miraculously, none of the family is severely injured. Later that morning, as the rain ends and the winds decrease, Tom and some neighbors return to their houses to see what's left of them—in several cases, not much, almost nothing at all. It turns out that the object that has destroyed the front of the Ochmanski house is a very large chunk of a concrete tie beam. However, it was not the beam from Tom's own house that he had seen the winds trying to lift, but one that had been lifted from a destroyed house about a block to the east. It had then sailed with part of the roof still attached over the tops of the houses across the street from the Ochmanski home before crashing into their living room wall. Damage caused by flying tie beams, which are supposed to hold buildings together, was an all-too-common sight in the aftermath of Hurricane Andrew.

At 5 A.M., the wind seems to be diminishing as Mike Shoemaker and his mother, Olive, huddle in the wreckage of her home in Naranja Lakes. Shoemaker thinks it's safe to roll over. When he does so and peers up, what he sees is "truly awe inspiring," as he recalls later. "The roof was totally gone . . . [and we see] the most amazing sight, the inside of the hurricane's eye wall with this churning mass of clouds lit by the half of the sky that was full of stars. It almost seemed as bright as twilight." The Shoemakers are in the calm eye of the hurricane in a roofless house that the storm has destroyed around them. Amazingly, they haven't been seriously injured, but Mike well knows that the second half of the hurricane is yet to come. When it arrives, the winds will be screaming at 150 miles per hour or more within a matter of minutes. There will be no gradual buildup with occasional squalls over a period of several hours, which had marked the hurricane's approach. The blast of incredible wind will begin immediately as the inner edge of the storm's eye wall passes overhead. Mike and his mother have to get out of the destroyed house and find shelter elsewhere, quickly.

As they stumble and climb through the debris toward the front

An aerial view of the Tom and Laurie Ochmanski home in South Dade County, Florida, after the passage of Hurricane Andrew. The Ochmanskis, their children, and Laurie's mother were in their home as it was destroyed around them.

door, they find a grandfather clock embedded in the wall and blocking their way. Mike pries the clock out and they reach the foyer, where they see what looks like the aftermath of an explosion. Furniture is strewn everywhere, wall decorations are smashed, and the entire front wall of the house is collapsed in the living room, supported by the crushed baby grand piano. Mike and Olive use the broken front door as a ramp to climb up the fallen exterior wall, shove the door down the other side of the pile of debris, and slide down to the yard. Outside, they see that roofs are gone from many neighboring buildings, which are destroyed. But one unit directly across the courtyard remains intact. Mike pounds on the door and he and his mother are immediately let in to this makeshift shelter. The family that lives in the house is taking refuge under an oak table in the hallway, and at least ten other people are already crammed in the bathroom. This leaves the living room for Mike and his mother. They fold out a sofa bed in the living room, shove its back toward a sliding-glass door, and then crawl underneath. At about 5:15 A.M., the back side of Hurricane Andrew slams into the condo and blows the front door off its hinges and into the kitchen.

"I think we're losing our second roof of the night, Michael," Olive Shoemaker says.

"Just keep your head down, Mom," he answers. His next recollection is waking up at dawn, lying on a water-soaked carpet under the bed with his mother. He had been so exhausted that he briefly fell asleep.

Elsewhere in the Naranja Lakes complex, sixty-seven-year-old widow Mary Cowan, who had installed storm panels for her windows and sliding-glass doors, believes she will be safe in her well-constructed home. Neighbors who have also decided to ride out the hurricane in their homes ask her to join them in their units, but she declines, saying she'll be fine. She'll stay with her cats. As the west side of the hurricane and the eye wall passes directly overhead and destroys some of her neighbors' homes, Mary Cowan's condo stands strong against the onslaught. After enduring the terrifying first half of the storm huddled in their bathroom, her neighbors take advantage of the calm of the eye and once again go to her door and urge her to join them. She has certainly been frightened, she admits, but since her house withstood those blows, she is even more confident that it will withstand whatever is to come. She'll stay home. But this eastern side of Andrew is even more powerful than the western half had been, and it destroys more buildings in Naranja Lakes, including the four-unit building where Mary Cowan lives.

As the winds start to die down at daylight, her neighbors dig out of the debris of the bathroom where they had taken refuge and go looking for her. They find her in her bathroom, impaled by a piece of two-by-four, but still alive. One of the neighbors does what he can to stop the bleeding and to comfort her. The telephone on one of the few remaining pieces of wall in Mrs. Cowan's condo still produces a dial tone, amazingly, but attempts to call 911 fail because the system is overloaded. Even though strong winds and rain continue, one of the neighbors tries to walk through the debris to South Dixie Highway about a mile away, with the hope of finding a police car or ambulance. But the highway is impassable, and no help is to be found. Mary Cowan dies about three hours later. Two other Naranja Lakes residents also die in Hurricane Andrew. Mike Shoemaker, his mother Olive, and the others in the condo in which they took refuge survive unharmed.

The *Mara Cu*, owned and sailed by the Bigelows, holds together, and John and Norah walk away later Monday morning, but another attempt to ride out Hurricane Andrew on a boat in a hurricane hole proves fatal to two men. Earlier on Sunday, Augustine Lorences, Tommy Vann, his stepson, and Stephen Suszek, a friend, had taken the forty-eight-foot sport-fishing boat that Lorences and Vann owned to Caesar Creek, where they think it would be safer than in the regular anchorage. Later, as Suszek told the *Miami Herald*, they tie up to the Ranger station on Adam's Key in southeastern Biscayne Bay. Sometime after 4 A.M., with the winds at their highest, a door at the rear of the boat breaks loose. Suszek holds a flashlight as his two friends try to secure it. The wind simply blows away sixty-two-year-old Augustine Lorences. "He was just gone, I couldn't see him anymore," Suszek told the *Herald*. Then, a two-by-six plank shoots

The concrete tie beam from the top of a wall of a home in the Naranja Lakes community lies on top of a car after the passage of Hurricane Andrew. The development of some 1500 units was destroyed and is vacant land today.

through the side of the boat and decapitates Tommy Vann, who was thirty-seven. Suszek hides in the boat's bait well until the wind calms down at daybreak. He is uninjured.

At 6 A.M. on Monday, August 24, Andrew's center is just to the west of Homestead in southern Dade County, about twenty-five miles southwest of Miami, and moving toward the west across the Everglades at 18 to 20 miles per hour. Because the hurricane is so small in area and moving rather fast, excessive rainfall and flooding are not expected. Maximum rainfall totals are forecast to be between five and eight inches, and that only in the area where the eye wall passes. By 9 A.M., Andrew is racing due west, weakening only slightly. It crosses the extreme southern part of the Florida peninsula in about four hours and is still a major hurricane when its eye wall passes over the Gulf of Mexico. At 10 A.M., it's time to issue the first watch for the northern Gulf Coast, and Sheets and the other forecasters at the center decide to include the stretch from Mobile, Alabama, on the east to Sabine Pass, Texas, near the Louisiana-Texas border, on the west—an expanse of 360 miles. All warnings for Florida's eastern coast are discontinued.

As the wind dies down and daylight begins to filter into the outer offices of the Hurricane Center, some shutters are opened on the west side of the building so the staff can study the damage below. Trees are down, but most houses and buildings in the area seem to be in good shape. Someone peeks out the south stairwell window and excitedly reports that a car is sitting upright with its front wheels on the hoods of two other cars and its back wheels on the brick wall around the parking lot. With none of the cars severely dented, it's a tableau that defies explanation. News photographers rush to get their cameras to take video to feed back to their stations. One cameraman looks out to find that the car on top of the pile is his. He can't believe this, because he had parked against the *east* side of the building. Later, the Hurricane Center team standing by in Washington sees this video on CNN, and Hugh Cobb realizes that one of the other cars is his. He had also parked on the east side of the building. Winds swirling around the building had shoved these cars 100 feet or more until they were stopped by the wall. One car was then lifted and dropped, right side up, on the other two. If you didn't know that a hurricane had just passed through, you might have thought that maybe some strong youngsters had played a practical joke on a teacher by stacking his car on top of the other two.

Someone from the center ventures onto the roof to find that the radar antenna had toppled over, as suspected. The wind had also lifted and shattered the fiberglass dome that covered the antenna and sent pieces of it flying into the swimming pool of the Holiday Inn next door. The offices of the Hurricane Center are becoming unusually warm, even though the auxiliary air conditioner has been running, powered by the Hurricane Center's emergency generators. Technicians figure out that water is not getting to the roof for the chillers. Nor is it getting up to the sixth floor offices, where 100 people are trying to work. Toilets can't be flushed. They can't be flushed on other floors either. The heat is taking its toll on the computers, and some start to fail as they begin to overheat. All but essential systems are shut down.

After seeing the damage outside, many at the center begin feeling queasy. They know the winds had been much stronger to the south, where many of their homes and, for some, their families are. Lixion Avila and Max Mayfield, who had been relieved the night before, have returned to the Hurricane Center to in turn relieve Rappaport, Gerrish, and Pasch, who try to go to check on their families and homes. Others are also making their way into the building, but several staff members cannot be contacted. Those who have made it in are from either Broward County or other localities to the north, or from only a few miles south of the center. Those from the south report considerable damage, but no one has arrived yet from homes as far south as Perrine, which the north eye wall passed over.

After posting the watch for the Gulf Coast, Bob Sheets, who has now been on duty since 6 A.M. Sunday, decides to take a couple of hours to check on his own home and those of his daughter and son, both of whom had evacuated inland, one to the safety of the family's second home in the middle of the state and the other to his in-laws in western Kendall. Sheets's own residence is about six miles south of the Hurricane Center, where the north eye wall had passed. His son's home is a little farther south, near the Ochmanskis, and would have been in the inner edge of the north eye wall—the most dangerous zone of all. His daughter Robin's home is another few miles south in an area that had been through the eye of the hurricane. Driving south in his daughter's small SUV, which he had parked in the center's underground garage, Sheets encounters downed trees, power lines, and other debris blocking the road, but he manages to drive over and along sidewalks and through edges of yards and around all the obstacles. Few other cars are on the streets. The farther south he goes, the more homes are heavily damaged, and some are nearly destroyed. There appear to be some swaths of nearly total destruction that are about 100 feet wide, taking off a corner of a house here, demolishing an entire house there, while the houses on either side of these swaths are much less damaged.

At his own house, Sheets finds that nearly all the fifteen to twenty large pine trees in the front and side yards are snapped off, some of them now on top of his house. In his backyard, many of the large mango and citrus trees are snapped off or simply ripped out of the ground, roots and all. The screen enclosure for the patio on the back of the house is gone, a large palm tree lays in the pool, streaks of roof tiles are missing, a tree limb sticks through the roof. But the wood panels over windows and glass doors have done their job—only one window behind the wood panels is broken—and the interior of the house is intact. After quickly checking his neighbor's house and closing a sliding-glass door that has vibrated open, he drives farther south to check on his son's and daughter's homes. Once again he's able to get around all the downed trees and power poles, but a large concrete power pole has crashed down across a bridge over a canal, cutting off that route. He tries others without success and returns to the Hurricane Center, by which time Andrew is well out over the Gulf of Mexico.

Large mobile satellite trucks have arrived at the Hurricane Center and the media pool continues, although less intensely than before the hurricane hit Florida. The federal General Services Administration and the building management are trying to bring the building support systems back to full operational power. Florida Power and Light has placed the Hurricane Center on its priority list to restore commercial power. Slowly, operations are stabilized. The team in Washington, D.C., tries to return to help the exhausted staff in Coral Gables, but they can't get flights into Miami International, so they fly into Tampa and rent a car to drive to Miami. They won't arrive until late Tuesday evening.

At 5 P.M. Monday, hurricane warnings are issued for the northern Gulf Coast from Pascagoula, Mississippi, west to Vermilion Bay, Louisiana. Andrew is centered about 470 miles southeast of New Orleans and is still moving west, but a gradual turn toward the west-northwest is expected within the next twelve hours. There has been no change in the storm's strength. The forecast cones put the probability of a strike at New Orleans actually higher than it had been a few hours earlier, up to 23 percent, the same as the probability for Miami on Saturday night, some thirty hours before the storm moved onshore in southern Dade County.

Sheets continues on duty until after midnight and then decides to go home to get a few hours sleep before the next intense period as Andrew approaches the Louisiana coast. Except for the two hours to check on his home, he has now been on continuous duty for some forty-two hours. He decides to drive down U.S. 1 rather than the route he took in the morning, because U.S. 1 will likely be more passable. There are no street or traffic lights. As he gets farther south he sees that buildings along the highway have also been heavily damaged or destroyed, but even though there are traffic lights, power lines, and debris on the road, it is passable. He misses his turn onto S.W. 144th Street, though, a route that he has taken for the past twenty years. Familiar landmarks are gone. The landscape has totally changed. Such an error will be a common occurrence for many residents of southern Florida over the next several days. After four hours sleep in the warm, humid house with no electricity, he welcomes the cold shower and returns to duty.

The sleep has been restless as Sheets worries whether New Orleans is in for a devastating tragedy. It's certainly possible. In the end, however, it doesn't happen; Hurricane Andrew makes its final landfall about forty miles south-southeast of Lafayette, Louisiana—a relatively unpopulated part of the state—at 8 A.M. Wednesday, August 26. Landfall is only 100 miles from New Orleans, but the storm is so tightly wound it doesn't reach even that far with hurricane-force winds, and the storm surge peaks at six to eight feet from Vermilion Bay south of New Iberia eastward to Dauphin Island, Alabama, south of Mobile. Along the north end of the causeway northeast of New Orleans, the rise is five feet. The levy system surrounding New Orleans is not seriously threatened.

Sheets, who once again has worked through the night, works his way to his son's home, which is basically in good shape, and later to his daughter's home, which is heavily damaged, her furniture and other items swept outside and scattered over the neighborhood. He then goes to his own house, where the phone is working, and calls his wife and daughter, briefly describing the situation and telling them to bring the family's van down to salvage what they can. Sheets's wife tells him later that Robin, who is an air-traffic controller at the Federal Aviation Administration's Miami Air Route Center, went into the bathroom, vomited, and then came out ready to go to work. They arrive on Wednesday afternoon and salvage what they can over the next two days. It is not much.

The Hurricane Center writes its final advisory on Andrew the following morning, Thursday, August 27, downgrading it to a tropical depression about seventy-five miles northeast of Jackson, Mississippi. Responsibility for further advisories is turned over to the National Meteorological Center in Washington, D.C. Andrew's remnants continue to produce severe thunderstorms, tornadoes, and heavy rain that causes flash floods as the storm moves northeast along the Appalachian Mountains. On Sunday, August 30, exactly two weeks after the first advisory had been issued on a tropical depression far out in the Atlantic, the National Meteorological Center writes the last specific storm summary on this particular atmospheric disturbance.

On the Thursday after Andrew hit Dade County, Bob Sheets took tornado researcher Ted Fujita on a tour of the damage. Fujita had started analyzing damage patterns when, as a young physicist in Japan, he visited Hiroshima and Nagasaki after World War II to study the destruction and estimate the height at which the atomic bombs had been detonated. Years later in America, he developed the theory of downbursts in thunderstorms and the Fujita scale for tornadoes. Colleagues stood in awe of two of the man's natural gifts, which were invaluable for his line of work: he never got airsick while examining wind damage in a bouncing small airplane, and he was a genius at observation in four dimensions (time being the fourth dimension).

In Miami, Fujita had already made a brief aerial survey and seen nothing that sparked his imagination, but Sheets urged him to take another look before leaving town for Chicago. In fact, Sheets *insisted.* On the way to the airport he drove Fujita and his former student and friend, Peter Black (now a researcher at the NOAA's Hurricane Research Division in Miami), out to the area of worst damage and pointed out the incredible streaks of essentially total devastation. Now Fujita got excited, and he ended up coming back two or three more times to study the patterns. He subsequently came up with the idea of "mini-swirls" as responsible for these "damage streaks" on the ground. Meanwhile, Black focused on the damage in the Naranja Lakes area, over which the eye of Andrew had passed, and he made a detailed examination of the time-lapse radar in Miami, until it was knocked out of commission, and in Tampa, where he believed he found evidence of structures in the inner edge of the eye wall that could have been responsible for the streaky damage in Naranja Lakes. He called such a structure a "mesovortex"—a term that has been applied to several different meteorological phenomena between ten and a hundred miles across. Black thought his mesovortex was on the lower end of that scale, about ten miles in diameter, but much larger than Ted Fujita's mini-swirls. Black thought it could also be responsible for the sudden, dangerous downdrafts and updrafts that aircraft sometimes encounter in hurricanes, including one in Hurricane Hugo in 1989 that Black experienced firsthand aboard a NOAA WP-3. Today, the jury is still out on both Fujita's mini-swirl and Black's mesovortex, but both—or neither—could have been responsible for some of the worst destruction in Dade County.

This much is certain: Hurricane Andrew hit southern Dade County with sustained wind speeds of 145 miles per hour, gusts to 175 miles per hour, and a minimum central pressure of 27.23 inches of mercury. It was the third-strongest hurricane of record to hit the mainland United States. Considering the storm's strength, the death toll was amazingly low—only fifteen in southern Florida, eight in Louisiana, and three in the Bahamas. Several other people died later from accidents that were indirectly related to Andrew. While the death toll was mercifully low, Andrew did more than $30 billion in damage, the most expensive natural disaster in U.S. history. Andrew reportedly destroyed 25,524 homes and damaged 101,241 others. The Dade County grand jury reported that 90 percent of all mobile homes in southern Dade were destroyed. In Homestead, more than 99 percent of all mobile homes (1,167 of 1,176) were destroyed. Estimates of people left without homes ranged as high as 300,000. The *Miami Herald* reported half a billion dollars in losses to boats in southeastern Florida, and the artificial reef system was extensively damaged. Before Andrew, the *Belzona*, a 215-foot, 350-ton barge, was sitting in sixty-eight feet of water on the ocean floor. One thousand tons of concrete lay on the deck. Andrew moved this barge 700 feet to the west and removed several large sections of steel plate sidings.

The $30 billion loss doesn't include the businesses that didn't survive the storm and the salaries they are no longer paying, or the goods and services that are not being purchased by the estimated 80,000 residents who moved away permanently. It certainly doesn't include the emotional costs to those whose homes were destroyed, often with irreplaceable mementos of their lives. For most victims who survive a hurricane without serious injury, what follows is almost as bad, maybe worse. The three or four hours of Andrew's violence were only the beginning of months or even years of frustration, financial strain, temporary living arrangements, and dealing with dishonest or incompetent contractors as they tried to rebuild. Eventually more than 20,000 national guard, army, and marine corps personnel moved into Dade County to guard against looting, set up tent camps, establish field kitchens, distribute food, and begin clearing downed trees and debris from roadways. The Federal Emergency Management Agency, the object of especially sharp criticism for its slowness to act, moved in with housing, emergency loans, and other aid.

It was one year and four days after Andrew hit Dade County before Laurie and Tom Ochmanski and their two children, Caitlyn and Ryan, moved into a new house on the same lot as the old one, which had been bulldozed out of the way. In the year of waiting, the Ochmanskis lived in five different places. The new house has steel-reinforced, poured-concrete tie columns and tie beams with steel straps connecting the roof trusses to the tie beam. It also has storm panels to cover all of the windows and sliding-glass doors and a built-in "safe" room. This is a central bathroom lined with three-quarter-inch-thick plywood for the walls and a second ceiling. When the next hurricane hits the area—not if, but when—the house should stand, and if it doesn't, the Ochmanskis will have a sturdier refuge than the closet that sheltered them during Andrew.

Olive Shoemaker was one of the estimated 80,000 who left southern Dade County after Andrew. She moved in with her son, Mike, for seven months, then she used insurance reimbursements for her destroyed home to buy a new one in Melbourne, Florida. The destruction of the Naranja Lakes complex was so great and so wide-

Mobile/manufactured home communities such as this located in the 20 mile wide swath covered by the "eye wall" of Hurricane Andrew during its passage over South Florida on August 24, 1992, suffered nearly total losses.

spread that the entire 1,600 units were cleared away, including the concrete slabs. It turned out that in many houses there were no tie columns connecting the tie beam that capped the outside walls to the foundation. Olive's claims for the building were settled very quickly, but all she has left from her share of the condominium development is a stack of legal papers two inches thick and a separate pile of letters between lawyers and owners, who continue to wrangle.

John and Norah Bigelow took the *Mara Cu* from the hurricane hole to the Miami Beach Marina, which had water and electricity. They had stocked the boat before Andrew for a trip to the Bahamas, a trip that was canceled. As John says, "It was with some sense of guilt that we lived there for over a month in air-conditioned comfort with a fully provisioned boat. We were reminded constantly that so many people to the south of us are far less fortunate." Norah decided to do something about that and went to work for the Red Cross in Homestead, commuting daily for the next two months. For the rest of their stay in Miami—four years—John reserved a slot up the Miami river in case of another hurricane threat. They used it twice between 1992 and 1996, when John retired from his position as a pilot with the European Airbus firm. The Bigelows then sailed away from Miami on the *Mara Cu* "with no clear idea of how far . . . or where we would go." Since then they've sailed across the Atlantic to the Mediterranean, visiting Israel, Lebanon, Turkey, and Greece. Both John and Norah say that their harrowing experience in Hurricane Andrew "brought us much closer together, and it remains this way."

Robin Sheets's home was severely damaged. Her parent's house and her brother's house had been protected by wood shutters, but her recently purchased home had not been. Although the small yard in this community of closely built homes was surrounded by a six-foot-high wood privacy fence, which, along with nearby houses, might be expected to provide some protection, she and her father had planned to prepare wood shutters for her windows and sliding-glass doors, but they had not done so before Hurricane Andrew. The window to the one room not "protected" by the privacy fence or adjacent house was boarded up, and Robin had moved some items such as electronic equipment to that room before she evacuated the area.

As Robin's father was able to confirm later from radar images, the Lakes-by-the-Bay community had been in the inner edge of the northern eye wall of the hurricane, the worst place to be. The north-western eye wall had approached the community about 4:35 A.M., and then minutes later the first wind peak struck, gusting to probably nearly 170 miles per hour, knocking down the privacy fence. Debris from upwind houses then broke all of the north- and east-facing windows and sliding-glass doors. The wind smashed debris through the house and broke the south-facing sliding-glass doors outward, and a lot of furniture soon followed the doors into the yard and beyond. The inside of the house was trashed, with glass embedded in couches, beds, and stuffed chairs. The master bedroom in the south-western corner of the house and the one sealed room on the western side held, but water coming over, under, and around the hallway doors flooded them anyway. The roof (except for the shingles) and the walls held. The northern part of the eye moved over the area, a lull that lasted ten minutes, until the northeastern eye wall slammed the community with winds once again pushing 170 miles per hour, but now from the southeast. This wind broke just about everything that had made it through the first wind and redistributed all the debris and furniture, yet the structure continued to hold.

At first, rebuilding for Robin Sheets seemed to be off to a good start, especially considering the magnitude of the disaster. After sev-eral weeks, she received an insurance adjustment that would be suf-ficient to repair her home. She paid $20,000 in advance for her contractor—who then left the scene after doing little work. She was not alone as a victim of such a fraud. Lawyers told her and others that they should be able to obtain a judgment against the man, but they are unlikely to ever recover even their legal fees. Dade County was also attempting to criminally prosecute fraudulent contractors, and had some success with the larger ones. However, the county had to prove "intent" to defraud, which was difficult, because in order to prove fraud the county had to *prove* that the contractor was not just an incompetent businessman.

Robin refused to simply let her mortgage holder foreclose. Instead, some six months later, after continuing to make large mort-gage payments for a house she could not live in, she took a chance on a couple who "rented" her house from her with the option to buy while they repaired the house to the point they could get a mortgage on it. After another six months, they were able to get the mortgage and purchase the house at a much reduced price. That money plus the remaining insurance paid off the original mortgage. Bottom line, Robin had lost all of her equity to the unscrupulous contractor. More than two years after Andrew had struck, she had accumulated enough money for a down payment on a new home, but she was more fortunate than many others who lost money to contractors, because she was able to live with her parents in the meantime.

After Andrew, insurance companies doubled homeowner's insurance rates in southern Florida and increased rates in other areas that face even a small chance of being hit by hurricanes. As it happened, Dade County had some of the most stringent building codes in the United States in 1992. With the exception of a lack of a requirement for windows and doors to be protected from flying debris (shutters, plywood, laminated glass), the codes were generally not the problem. Inappropriate design and poor construction accounted for a large amount of Andrew's damage.

At the Hurricane Center, lessons learned from the unexpected failures of the water supply, air-conditioning, and communications were applied to the design of a new building for the Center on the campus of Florida International University southeast of Miami. The new Center had been in the works before Andrew hit, as part of the National Weather Service's nationwide modernization program. Next-generation weather radars, with Doppler capability, are the keystone of the effort, and the leased building space in Coral Gables couldn't house the required equipment. When Andrew blew over the 1950s radar antenna on the roof, the Weather Service speeded up plans for installing a new Miami-area radar rather than trying to repair the damaged, obsolete unit.

The modernization program located new Weather Service offices at universities with meteorology programs, with the aim of encouraging cooperation among forecasters and university researchers. In the case of the National Hurricane Center, more than meteorology was considered. The Weather Service wanted to have the center on a campus where a multidisciplinary approach could be taken toward addressing the hurricane problem. To take advantage of the presence of the Hurricane Center on the Florida International University campus, the State of Florida's university system established the International Hurricane Research Center on the same campus to initiate and coordinate multidisciplinary hurricane-damage mitigation activities and studies. The combined program included such elements as community planning, structural engineering, emergency management training, behavior sciences, Caribbean studies, and communications, as well as meteorological studies.

The new Hurricane Center not only has emergency generators and air-conditioning but also an independent emergency water supply system. There's a self-contained toilet. Two independent sets of underground telephone lines enter the building from opposite directions and connect to different exchanges. If a storm or any kind of accident knocks out one exchange, the center stays connected through the other. Since the lines enter the building on opposite sides, one set should still function if a contractor accidentally digs up or breaks the other one. Underground fiber-optic lines are in place in case the television microwave systems go down. Shutters or hurricane panels can quickly be put over all the doors and windows. In addition to overall sturdy construction, the building's "safe area" provides extra protection against the worst a hurricane or tornado could do. It is in the central part of the building, in the area that includes the restrooms, and features steel-reinforced, poured-concrete walls and an interior, steel-reinforced, poured-concrete roof independent of the main building roof. Bob Sheets's insistence that the new building be strong enough to continue functioning even if hit by a storm stronger than Andrew led those who built the new National Hurricane Center to nickname it "Dr. Bob's Bunker."

CHAPTER 11

THE FUTURE

THE HEADLINE IN *Newsweek* asked: "Was Andrew a Freak—
Or a Preview of Things to Come?" The subhead answered: "Many
scientists say recent storms prove that global warming is changing
the world's climate." The story began: "They're called hundred-year
storms because they strike with a fury so enormous that meteorologists figure they can't come around more than once a century. Why
have the last three years seen both Hurricane Andrew and Hurricane
Hugo, which smacked into South Carolina in 1989 and was rated a
4 on the 5-point scale measuring storm intensity? And what about
Gilbert in 1988?" Gilbert's central pressure of 26.22 inches of mercury was the lowest ever recorded in the Western Hemisphere. It hit
the Mexican resort areas of Cozumel and Cancun with 160-mile-
per-hour winds, the first Category 5 storm to hit land in the Western
Hemisphere since Hurricane Camille in 1969. *Newsweek* said: "It
might be a horrible coincidence. Or it might be a harbinger."

The unwary concluded from this and many other hyperbolic, if
not hysterical, stories following Andrew that more hurricanes, especially strong ones, were suddenly hitting the United States and the
Caribbean. But this was wrong. In the five years from 1988 through
1992, Hugo and Andrew had been the only major storms to hit the
United States, and just three weak storms came ashore. In fact, Hugo
and Andrew had been only the second and third major hurricanes to
hit the U.S. Atlantic Coast since Betsy in 1965. (The first had been
Gloria, which hit Long Island, New York, and New England in
1985.) The years 1991 through 1994 actually turned out to have the
fewest Atlantic Basin hurricanes of any four-year period in half a cen-

tury, averaging less than four bona fide storms a year. Had Hugo, Andrew, and Gilbert been a "horrible coincidence" or a "harbinger"? There is not any reason to believe they were anything more than a horrible coincidence, and such coincidences are not all that unusual in the long history of hurricanes that have hit the United States.

Some of the confusion was caused by the media's wanting the most dramatic story possible, but there was, and still is, confusion over the meaning of "hundred-year storm." Meteorologists use this phrase to mean only that a hurricane of that strength has 100-to-1 odds of hitting a *particular* location in a year. It has nothing to do with the odds of such a storm hitting *anywhere* along the Atlantic Coast or around the Caribbean Sea, but that is often the interpretation. In fact, those odds are lower than 100-to-1 for some locations. If two 100-year hurricanes hit the same location the same year, this doesn't mean something has gone wrong, only that the location was unusually unlucky. It might go 150 years before the next such storm hits.

All that said, the idea that the numbers of tropical cyclones will increase because of global warming, and that they will be stronger, isn't unreasonable at first glance. If the world warms up, ocean temperatures will increase. In fact, NOAA scientists, using more than 5.1 million profiles of ocean temperatures collected since the 1950s by U.S., British, and Soviet submarines—and declassified with the end of the Cold War—have found that the top 1,000 feet of the world's oceans warmed by about a half a degree Fahrenheit in the last half of the twentieth century. Since warm oceans supply the energy for hurricanes, and since water temperature is one of the factors used to forecast whether a hurricane will gain or lose strength, it would seem to follow that warmer oceans will create more and stronger hurricanes. However, as with most questions about hurricanes and the global climate, the equations are not nearly as simple as that. In January 2001, the Intergovernmental Panel on Climate Change (IPCC), a large group of scientists from around the world who conducted an extensive study of climate change, concluded in a report that there is no evidence that the peak wind speeds or amounts of precipitation in tropical cyclones had increased during the last half of the twentieth century. In an earlier report, the IPCC had said: "The formation of tropical cyclones depends not only on sea surface temperature, but also on a number of atmospheric factors. Although some models now represent tropical storms with some realism for present-day climate, the state of the science does not allow assessment of future changes."

A study in 1998 concluded that it was impossible to say whether a warmer climate will bring more and stronger tropical cyclones. Publishing their work in the January 1998 *Bulletin of the American Meteorological Society*, the authors argued that the maximum potential strength of tropical cyclones could indeed increase by 10 to 20 percent in a warmer world, but "these predicted changes are small compared with the observed natural variations and fall within the uncertainty range in current studies." They took note of the argument that a warmer world would expand the areas of the world's oceans that are warm enough for spawning tropical cyclones, and therefore spawn more cyclones. But this will not necessarily be the case. Just one complication: climate change could raise or lower upper-atmospheric temperatures, which could increase or decrease the *difference* between the sea surface and upper-level temperatures. This difference in turn could change today's threshold of 79-degree water for hurricanes. With global warming, there's a good chance that some regions could see *more* tropical cyclones while other parts of the world could see *fewer*. Most predictably, perhaps, if a warmer world has more El Niños, the numbers of storms in the eastern and central Pacific might increase, but the numbers might decrease around Australia and in the Atlantic Basin. Moreover, some computer models have shown that a warmer world could have generally stronger upper-altitude winds that could weaken or kill hurricanes.

All in all, this group argued, the computer models making global climate predictions fail "to capture environmental factors that govern cyclone intensity. . . . Little, therefore, can be said about the potential changes of the distribution or intensities as opposed to maximum achievable intensity. Current knowledge and available techniques are too rudimentary for quantitative indications of potential changes in tropical cyclone frequency. The very modest available evidence points to an expectation of little or no change in global frequency." In the January 2001 report the IPCC said there's a chance that the peak intensity and rainfall from tropical cyclones could increase in some areas, but the areas couldn't be defined. Nothing was said about an increase or decrease in the number of storms.

In short, no one knows about the future global picture, and it seems unlikely anyone will know anytime soon. On the other hand, scientists may have discovered why Atlantic Basin hurricanes, especially strong hurricanes, run in the cycles that brought the mainland United States a rash of major storms in the 1940s and 1950s and then few strong storms from the mid-1960s to the mid-1990s. As we've seen, in the 1980s William Gray of Colorado State University untangled various large-scale climate signals, such as rainfall in West Africa, that he uses to make reasonably successful forecasts of roughly how many hurricanes, including how many major hurricanes, a coming season should bring. But as Gray points out, knowing about the statistical relationship is not the same thing as *understanding* it. From the beginning, he felt that the relationship between rainfall in the Sahel and hurricanes in the Atlantic was not as simple as the first causing the second. More likely, Gray thought, these two phenomena reflect the influence of a larger-scale factor that shifts over periods of two or three decades. But what could that factor be?

In the early 1990s, one of Gray's daughters, Sarah, a marine geologist, sent him some papers about the "North Atlantic conveyor belt," including one by Wallace S. Broecker of the Lamont-Doherty Earth Observatory of Columbia University, who first proposed that such a belt exists. Broecker's hypothesis describes what happens as large amounts of warm water moving north in the Atlantic Ocean, mostly in the Gulf Stream, evaporate as westerly winds blow across this water. In the first place, the winds carry the heat to Europe, making that continent warmer than it otherwise would be at those latitudes. In the second place, the evaporation cools the water slightly and also increases the relative salt content, because only water, not salt, evaporates. The salt and the cooling make the water denser, and as it flows north toward Iceland and the Labrador Sea it becomes so dense that it begins to sink to the bottom of the Atlantic, where it flows back toward the south, still near the bottom of the ocean, al the way to Antarctica, while more water flows north near the surface to replace it. The sinking of the relatively cool, salty water is like a motor that drives a conveyor belt, only in this case the "belt" is made up of massively large ocean currents of different densities, circulating on the surface and in the depths. If for any reason less water evaporates, the water isn't cooled as much, or more fresh water is added to the Atlantic from heavier rain or melting Arctic ice, the water wouldn't be as heavy when it reaches the area around Iceland. It would sink at a slower rate, which would slow down the global conveyor belt. Water that sinks in the North Atlantic can take a couple of thousand years to flow to the south deep under the Atlantic, move through the Drake Passage between Antarctica and South America — still far below the surface — into the Pacific, and then return to the Atlantic by the same route, but on the surface.

The scientific name for this phenomenon is a "thermohaline circulation," from the Greek and scientific terms for "heat" and "salt." There is no similar circulation in the Pacific Ocean, because the water in the North Pacific isn't as salty as in the North Atlantic, and the Indian Ocean is too warm for a thermohaline circulation. Broecker and many other scientists are trying to determine whether the conveyor belt could have been responsible for huge swings in temperatures around the world during the ice ages, and then again when the ice ages were ending around 12,000 years ago, and whether it could cause similarly large changes in the future.

William Gray had different questions. He and his colleague John D. Sheaffer wondered whether smaller changes in the speed of the conveyor belt might be the cause of climate shifts that could account for the twenty- to thirty-year cycles in the numbers of hurricanes. If the sinking rate of the cooler water speeds up, the conveyor belt speeds up, more warm water flows north, and the near-surface waters of the North Atlantic become warmer. If the sinking rate slows, less warm water flows north, and the Atlantic cools. Could this be the cause of some of the apparent multidecade hurricane cycles? There are no direct measurements of the conveyor belt, but records of salinity and temperature in various parts of the Atlantic Ocean were found that indicate the conveyor belt did slow down after the early 1960s, cooling the North Atlantic slightly. Gray and Sheaffer and others argue that the slower Atlantic circulation is associated with more and longer dry periods in West Africa, and fewer Atlantic Basin hurricanes. Specifically, a slowing of the conveyor belt might help decrease African rainfall, because changed ocean temperatures off West Africa shift air-pressure patterns. These shifts, in turn, reduce the amount of humid air that winds carry over the Sahel to fall as rain and weaken the West African monsoon trough, an area of low pressure off Africa that plays a large role in initiating the intense hurricanes over the eastern Atlantic.

There are indications from temperature and salinity measurements that the Atlantic thermohaline circulation speeded up in the 1990s. If so, and if Gray's theory is correct, the African monsoon will change back to the pattern that made the Sahel relatively wet during the 1940s and 1950s, and the Atlantic Basin will enter, if it has not already entered, a period of more hurricane activity than in the previous quarter century, a new era on a par with the active decades of the '40s and '50s.

While Gray's theories about the reasons for hurricane cycles are still debated, few hurricane scientists doubt the existence of the cycles. There is certainly no reason to think that the world's climate has changed in some way since the 1960s to permanently reduce the number of Atlantic hurricanes. The thousands of people who moved to their dream houses along the Atlantic Coast during the hurricane lull of the 1970s and 1980s could be in for some unpleasant times. In fact, the hurricane seasons from 1995 through 2000 give every indication that the Atlantic Basin has already entered an era of more hurricanes. And this six-year record occurred despite the 1997 El Niño, which was one of the strongest of the century and was probably why the Atlantic Basin produced only seven tropical storms, three hurricanes, and one major hurricane that year.

While the Atlantic Basin became more active from 1995 through 2000, the number of storms decreased over the Pacific Ocean north of the equator, both east and west of the international date line. From 1989 through 1994 the North Pacific produced 301 named storms. This dropped to 252 from 1995 through 2000. The total number of hurricanes (east of the date line) and typhoons (west of the date line) was 230 during the earlier period, only 183 for the later period. The number of major storms dropped from 100 to 73.

Even though the Atlantic Basin has produced more hurricanes during the past six years, fewer storms are hitting the United States than would be expected. From 1900 through 2000, the records show 221 major storms in the Atlantic Basin, with seventy-three of them, or about one-third, hitting the United States. From 1995 to 2000, only three of the twenty-three major storms hit the United States, much lower than the long-term ratio. Why? For a good part of the six hurricane seasons since 1995, an upper-air trough—an elongated area of low pressure—has often been parked over the eastern U.S. mainland. An eastern trough is usually part of a continent-wide pattern that has a countervailing high-pressure ridge over the West. With this setup, the upper-air winds turn clockwise around the northern end of the ridge in the West, then dip south over the middle of the country as they swing around the southern end of the trough, and then flow northeasterly around the eastern side of the trough, more or less parallel to the East Coast. A hurricane under the influence of these winds would also turn toward the northeast, sometimes far away from the coast.

The next question is why the trough has been in this position, providentially protecting the United States from hurricanes. It's probably related to various kinds of decade- or decades-long patterns involving the ocean and atmosphere that scientists are just beginning to understand. Whatever the reason, William Gray says, "We have been lucky. But this luck can not be expected to continue. Very few residents of the southeastern U.S. coastline are likely aware of how fortunate they have been over the last three or four decades."

If you consider only the Florida peninsula—the state's eastern and western coasts—and the East Coast from Florida to Maine, the numbers are even more skewed. From 1961 through 2000, only six major hurricanes hit the Florida peninsula and the East Coast, compared with the thirty-one that hit during the sixty-year period 1900 through 1960. "This long downturn in U.S. major hurricane landfalls along the Florida peninsula and East Coast is unlikely to continue," Gray says. "Climatology will eventually right itself and we must expect a great increase in land-falling major hurricanes in the coming few decades."

On April 13, 1994, the newest generation of the Geostationary Operational Environmental Satellite (GOES) was introduced, giving forecasters more frequent and more detailed views of the weather thanks to improvements in both satellite and sensor technology. One of the first major assignments for the new satellite was to keep a close eye on the storms of the busy 1995 hurricane season, including Tropical Storm Opal when it formed over the southern Gulf of Mexico on September 30, 1995, and began drifting toward the north. It became a minimal hurricane the morning of October 3 and then exploded overnight from a 97-mile-per-hour Category 1 hurricane at 11 P.M. to a 132-mile-per-hour Category 4 storm by 7 A.M. the following morning. It then reached its greatest strength of 150 miles per hour by 11 A.M., with forward speed increasing to nearly 20 miles per hour. Forecasters scrambled to keep up with Opal as it bore down on the northern Gulf Coast between Louisiana and Florida. Many residents and vacationers who had expected to ride out a weak Category 1 hurricane fled the shore at the last minute, causing traffic jams. Fortunately for all concerned, forecasting that a storm will *weaken* is just as hard as forecasting that it will *intensify*. By the time a WP-3, which was going to investigate the storm, flew into Opal, now centered about 140 miles south of Mobile, Alabama, the scientists saw telltale signs of disintegration. Opal no longer had an eye wall all the way around the center, and a second eye wall seemed to be forming. Both developments are signs of a weakening hurricane. When Opal came ashore southwest of Pensacola, Florida, around 7 P.M., it was listed as a Category 3 storm with 125-mile-per-hour winds, but they were restricted to only a small part of the hurricane.

As we'd expect, the Opal experience triggered an intense scientific investigation into the causes of its sudden changes in intensity. In the early morning hours of October 4, when Hurricane Opal grew from a 95-mile-per-hour storm to a 150-mile-per-hour storm in fourteen hours, it had moved over an eddy of deep, warm water about 200 miles in diameter; such eddies drift with the currents in the Gulf o

Mexico and other oceans. These eddies are so deep—maybe 300 yards—that the churning action of a storm fails to bring cooler water to the surface, so nothing dampens the strengthening process. Fortunately, Opal had passed the eddy and was rapidly weakening over cooler water when it hit the Florida panhandle with diminished winds. (The oceanographic data from satellites that identify these deep pools of warm water are collected over days, in order to eliminate effects from clouds, so they aren't immediately available to forecasters, as a rule.)

Scientists were also interested in what had happened in the top of Opal as it weakened. Time-lapse water vapor images showed cool, dry air wrapping in toward the center of the storm on the western side at the middle levels, and upper-air winds that were first enhancing and then restricting air flow out of Opal's top. As with many questions involving hurricanes, scientists were far from agreement on the causes of Opal's radically fluctuating strength, and scientific papers were written on all of the factors involved. Bob Sheets believes that the dry air was the primary factor contributing to the rapid weakening of the hurricane, because the water over which the storm was

The University of Oklahoma's Doppler-on-Wheels (DOW) system that is used to chase and investigate tornadoes and hurricanes.

traveling when it weakened was still sufficiently warm to maintain the hurricane, though not as warm as the eddy that probably contributed to the rapid strengthening. Either way, researchers and forecasters had something new to think about.

They also had something new to think about following Hurricane Fran that year, when a research team at the University of Oklahoma took its "Doppler-on-Wheels" to the Wilmington, North Carolina, area as Fran approached. That instrument is exactly what the name says: a Doppler radar, including the antenna, mounted on a truck. Led by Joshua Wurman, the team had developed this mobile radar to get close-up views of tornadoes in Oklahoma and the rest of Tornado Alley, and success on the Great Plains led the team to believe that its truck-mounted Doppler could collect a lot of useful information about hurricanes on the coast as well. They were right. In fact, they discovered a new phenomenon, labeled "wind rolls," which could possibly be responsible for the narrow wind streaks that may have produced the incredible damage following Hurricane Andrew.

Thanks to the new GPS dropsondes, which are more accurate and produce more detailed data on winds inside storms than the older dropsondes, researchers had already learned that winds only a few hundred feet above the ground might be blowing 50 miles per hour faster than those on the ground, which are slowed by friction. But, what brings the faster winds aloft down to the ground? Strong downdrafts in thunderstorms can do this, but the thunderstorms in hurricanes generally don't have the strong downdrafts sometimes found in thunderstorms over land. The radar images from the Doppler-on-Wheels images indicated that wind rolls circulating parallel with the ground can begin to form when a storm moves onshore and the winds at the surface are slowed by friction. As these tubes of air rotate, they bring down the faster winds from higher up, which hit the ground in a devastating blast before friction slows them as well. After Hurricane Andrew, meteorologists talked about different kinds of vertical swirls, which they called mesovortexes and mini-swirls, causing the worst damage. While the horizontal wind rolls are well documented thanks to Doppler-on-Wheels measurements in Fran and later storms, mesovortexes and mini-swirls could also exist, and all three might have been responsible for some of Andrew's incredible destruction.

Since the 1980s Bob Sheets, who was then director of the Hurricane Center, had started urging the government to buy and equip a mid-size jet that could fly higher and farther than the WP-3 and WC-130 aircraft to collect data over the oceans for hundreds of square miles around storms and even in the tops of storms, which should improve forecasts. As it happened, the new Gulfstream jet made its debut in 1997, a slow hurricane season in the Atlantic, with only seven tropical storms, three hurricanes, and one major storm—the El Niño effect. The jet made only three operational flights over the Atlantic, but the Pacific, as is normally the case, proved a more hospitable climate for cyclones, and just one flight into Hurricane Linda in the eastern Pacific proved the plane's value to forecasters. Linda was the strongest hurricane ever recorded in the eastern Pacific, almost surely a direct result of that year's El Niño. (It's no coincidence that the only tropical storm on record as hitting the West Coast of the United States came ashore between San Diego and Los Angeles in an El Niño year, 1939—as scientists determined years later when they went back to the records after the El Niño phenomenon was confirmed.)

On September 13, 1997, Linda was estimated to be a Category 5 storm—an estimate based on satellite images, because airplanes usually do not fly into hurricanes in the eastern Pacific except for possible research purposes. The official forecast showed the storm heading for southern California, which would have been an extremely rare track. Forecasters did expect Linda to weaken markedly when it moved over the chilly water off the California coast, but it could still cause major damage in an area not used to strong winds, and its heavy rains could cause the mud slides and floods that have always been the nemesis of coastal residents in California. Linda had the forecasters "really jumping out of their skins," in the phrase of Naomi Surgi, who was the Hurricane Center's manager of the Gulfstream jet. When the storm was a little more than 800 miles south of San Diego, local Weather Service offices were starting to mention the possibility of some effects from this hurricane within the next three days, but data gathered by the Gulfstream convinced the computer models, and then the forecasters, that Linda would turn away far out to sea. No watches or warnings were issued, and Linda did turn away from southern California.

Following the 1997 season, scientists ran their forecast models both with and without the data from the jet, for the storms it had flown around. The models run with the jet's data showed forecasting improvement of 31 percent for twenty-four-hour forecasts and 32 percent for thirty-six-hour forecasts. These improvements at the critical forecast periods were greater than the accumulated improvements over the previous twenty years.

The following year the Atlantic Basin hurricane season picked up markedly, following the trend which had begun in 1995. Hurricanes Bonnie, Danielle, and Earl either hit or threatened the United States. The Gulfstream aircraft was frequently used, including several days during Hurricanes Bonnie and George. In fact, the last week of August and first week of September brought researchers more detailed views of hurricanes than ever before, thanks to a whole fleet of airplanes, including the new jet, more powerful computers, satellites, two Doppler-on-Wheels units, and new improved dropsondes. These 1998 storms, especially Bonnie and Danielle, were probably the most intensely studied hurricanes ever. The air force reserve WC-130 turboprops made regular reconnaissance flights into each, gathering data mainly for Hurricane Center forecasters, as they always do. Two NOAA WP-3's carried their onboard Doppler radar and other instruments into the hearts of the hurricanes, and the Gulfstream jet flew around the storms at altitudes as high as 40,000 feet. For the first time in the Atlantic (there had been one similar navy project in the Pacific), a NASA DC-8 flew through the upper levels of this hurricane at about 35,000 feet, and a NASA ER-2—a version of the U-2 spy plane—flew well above the storms at 65,000 feet. "The two WP-3's did a minuet," as Hugh Willoughby, director of NOAA's Hurricane Research Division, describes one experiment. "They sort of danced around each other so their Doppler radar beams would cross." That kind of coordination made it possible for the computer to create a three-dimensional picture of the storm's winds. Evaluations from all these flights and others through the 1999 season have generally shown marked improvements over model predictions without this data, and experience is helping to refine the best flight patterns in and around storms for collecting data the models need.

During the Gulfstream jet's first two years of operation, NOAA officials were not about to fly it through the core of a hurricane at lower levels, where the horrendously heavy rainfall can rob power from jet engines, and where long periods of severe turbulence could batter the airplane. Finally, on August 14, 1999, the crew of the Gulfstream flew through the center of Hurricane Dora in the central Pacific near Hawaii at an altitude of 45,000 feet—an impossible height for any of the turboprop research planes—where it encountered thick cirrus clouds in the eye wall with no significant turbulence. Eventually the jet will routinely fly through the upper levels of storms, collecting data that are not now available. For its basic reconnaissance work, the air force reserve has also put new and better equipment on line—ten new WC-130 "J" models in 1999, which can climb faster and fly higher (altitudes up to 39,000 feet) than the older WC-130s, but not as quite as high as the Gulfstream. Their higher altitude data should also help forecasters predict changes in hurricane intensity.

But airplanes, no matter how high and fast they fly, cannot collect all of the data researchers need to learn the details of how hurricanes work. In the not-too-distant future, improved remote-sensing systems will be mounted on these high-flying aircraft, including lightweight and small Doppler radar systems, and sounding systems that can give nearly continuous detailed vertical readings of temperature and moisture. These readings will be combined with "spot" dropsonde data, and instruments that can see through the rain to the surface by detecting and precisely measuring microwave energy emitted by the ocean (a version of this instrument is already on a NOAA WP-3); the amount of energy depends on the ocean's roughness, which in turn depends on surface wind speeds. These advances will allow airplanes to collect data through the entire depth of the hurricane, including a storm's turbulent lower levels, without flying at those low levels. Some researchers think that a large drone (pilotless) aircraft could be used for reconnaissance in conjunction with mid-size jet aircraft, although a lot of questions remain. With or without the drones, it's entirely possible that perhaps five jets like the Gulfstream could someday handle all hurricane reconnaissance at a greatly reduced operational cost over the current fleets, and at the same time provide much improved forecasts.

Willoughby expects the advances of the last decade of the twentieth century to lead in the first decade of the twenty-first century to dramatic improvements in forecasting intensity changes in storms, much in the same way research begun in the mid-1980s led to the rapid improvements in track forecasts. But even a more gradual process as a result of dynamical model and computer technology advancements coupled with an improved understanding of the dynamics of the hurricane and its interaction with its environment will significantly improve forecast accuracy. Five-day track predictions during the first decade of the twenty-first century will be as accurate as the three-day predictions of the mid-1990s. Those five-day forecasts will soon become part of the publicly released forecasts, but will need to be used with caution. Advancements in satellite technology will play a heavy and important role in these model prediction improvements by providing more accurate data than they currently do, covering large areas that complement the more accurate but necessarily limited area coverage data collected by aircraft. All of these possible improvements will not simply materialize because of technological advancements, but will require dedicated, highly trained, and innovative men and women to take advantage of the improved technology. Even with all of these advancements and any others that we might reasonably anticipate, there will be no equivalent to the Salk vaccine cure for polio. There will always be forecast errors, and sometimes those errors will be quite large, although such events should become less frequent.

In September 1999, news reports showed satellite images of a hurricane approaching the U.S. mainland that appeared to be as large as the entire southeastern United States—a monstrous hurricane. Excited broadcasters reported on Floyd's 150-mile-per-hour or faster winds. Dan Rather, who got his break on the national scene reporting from Galveston during Hurricane Carla in 1961, set up shop on the coastline for CBS News. Of course, these satellite images were misleading for those viewers who think that the entire mass of clouds hides 150-mile-per-hour winds. The strongest winds were confined to a small area around Floyd's eye, but that didn't detract from the fact that this was a dangerous hurricane that could imperil anyone near the coast within fifty or 100 miles of where the eye comes ashore. Awareness of the danger was especially high in southern Florida, where many residents remembered the ravages of Hurricane Andrew only seven years before. And Floyd was a little stronger than Andrew, and much larger.

As Hurricane Floyd moved into the Bahamas and then along the East Coast, the National Hurricane Center posted hurricane watches, and later warnings, at various times for areas from Florida City, twenty-five miles south of Miami, to Plymouth, Massachusetts, thirty miles south of Boston. The warnings prompted more than two million people to flee these coastal areas, the largest evacuation in the nation's history. No estimate is available for the direct costs of this evacuation, much less for the costs of the economic disruption. When the eye finally came ashore near Cape Fear, North Carolina, at 2 A.M. on September 16, Floyd had weakened to a Category 2 storm with maximum winds of just over 100 miles per hour, but its rain caused major flooding from North Carolina to New England, including the worst in history for parts of North Carolina. Floyd was blamed for fifty-six deaths: inland flooding was responsible for forty-eight of them, and felled trees claimed the other eight.

The experience with Floyd didn't reassure hurricane forecasters, researchers, or those entrusted with making sure their communities are ready for the next hurricane. Their attitude was like that of someone who hears a bullet whiz overhead and wonders whether the shooter's aim will improve with the next shot. The concern prompted the American Meteorological Society to convene a forum in Washington, D.C., in June 2000. More than a hundred hurricane forecasters, researchers, television weather broadcasters, other journalists, and emergency managers from local, state, and federal agencies took part, and the discussions led to several conclusions that were summed up in a policy statement issued in September, which says:

In 1992, Hurricane Andrew wreaked broad devastation over the southern tip of Florida and inflicted approximately $26.5 billion in damages (1992 dollars). Economic recovery continues today, eight years after the event. In 1999, Hurricane Floyd caused massive inland flooding and triggered the largest evacuation in the nation's history. In that mobilization, the region's highways and major transportation arteries were overwhelmed, as many—not in any announced danger but nonetheless concerned—chose to leave. Other citizens refused to clear mandated evacuation areas, leaving themselves in potentially life-threatening situations. Andrew and Floyd do not approach the catastrophic losses of life and property the nation will face when a major hurricane makes landfall at a large population center such as Miami, New Orleans, Tampa–St. Petersburg or New York City. Death tolls could once again be in the thousands, figures not seen since the Galveston hurricane a century ago or the Lake Okeechobee, Florida, hurricane of 1928. Economic losses could exceed $100 billion. It could take up to six months to reestablish basic infrastructure. Overall economic recovery could require decades.

"Today's hurricane warning and response system is more capable than ever before but is inadequate to avert such a major catastrophe with its attendant large loss of life, enormous property destruction and business disruption, and long recovery times. One of every five people in the United States is at direct risk of hurricane impact, and the number is growing daily.

Everyone in the hurricane community agrees that better forecasts won't be enough to avoid hurricane disasters in the future. Coastal populations are growing so rapidly that no likely forecasting improvements will make it possible to predict landfall in time to evacuate *only* the areas that surge will flood, and not evacuate nearby locations that turn out to be safe. Everyone in the hurricane community also understands that shorter evacuation times would achieve the same purpose as more accurate forecasts. If evacuation times could be reduced to twelve to eighteen hours instead of today's standard, which is twenty-four to thirty hours or more, hurricane warnings would be substantially more accurate—which is to say, the warning area would be *smaller*, and therefore require less evacuation.

Hurricane Floyd provided a perfect example of this relationship. If Hurricane Center forecasters had been more confident in their forecast, and waited just a few more hours to issue hurricane warnings for extreme South Florida, they wouldn't have issued any warnings at all, and no evacuations would have been necessary for that area. Waiting a few hours would also have allowed the Hurricane Center to include in its warnings for central Florida north across Georgia the advisory that only the storm's weaker west side would affect the coast. Again, the number of people evacuated would have been much lower.

Ever since Columbus, mariners have struggled to read the skies to know when these great storms might be approaching. Nor were they alone in their quest. Part-time and amateur scientists such as Benjamin Franklin and William Redfield, engineers like Reed and soldiers like Piddington, even clerics like Father Benito Vines and Father Frederico Faura all contributed to our hard-earned ability to discover, track, and forecast hurricanes. The fact that two strong hurricanes such as Andrew and Floyd blew across several islands of the Bahamas and then hit the United States with fewer than one hundred deaths combined illustrates how much we've learned about these monster storms in the past half a millennium.

The establishment of the National Hurricane Research Project in the late 1950s, for the first time in history, provided for a group of scientists whose sole work was studying hurricanes. The scientists organizing that project initially thought that data collected by a fleet of three instrumented aircraft flying through several hurricanes during a three-year period would reveal the secrets of how hurricanes formed, strengthened, moved, and, maybe, even how humans could modify hurricanes to reduce their destructive forces. They thought that after approximately five years of studying the data, the Hurricane Project scientists and their collaborators at several leading universities around the country—along with collaborative efforts with other leading atmospheric scientists from around the world—would solve the mysteries of hurricanes and greatly improve forecasts.

Indeed, some of the mysteries were solved and forecasts did improve. For the first time, the basic three-dimensional structure of a mature hurricane was documented, showing not only the distribution of winds at the surface, as had been observed to a limited extent as far back as the early nineteenth century by Redfield, but also the basic structure of how winds, temperatures, pressure patterns, and clouds changed with height. However, the scientists discovered that while the basic characteristics remained the same in all mature hurricanes, there were many differences in detail from one to another and even within a particular hurricane from one day to another. New questions proliferated. The studies that were supposed to be a five-year project in the 1950s continue today.

Some tropical storms would grow to very strong hurricanes in a day or two, while other apparently similar tropical storms might travel across the entire Atlantic Ocean for days, maybe a week, and never strengthen. Why? We don't know. Why do some hurricanes go through rapid intensification while others do not, and more important, how can we predict in advance which ones will go through such changes and where and when those changes will take place? Why was Hurricane Andrew so destructive? When will we be able to predict with confidence where a hurricane will strike thirty-six to forty-eight hours from now, and just how strong will it be?

New technology, including the mind-boggling advancements in computer power, will greatly aid in the effort to find the answers. The advancements in computer power, combined with a better understanding of how the global climate system works might also answer the questions of whether a changing climate—be it completely natural or caused at least in part by human activities—will bring more or fewer hurricanes; whether future storms will be stronger or weaker; and whether we can expect a continuation of the increases and decreases in the numbers of storms that we've seen since Europeans first encountered hurricanes more than 500 years ago.

One thing we know for sure is that a hurricane at least as strong as Andrew is going to hit the United States again. It could be this year or it could be twenty or fifty years from now; it could hit one of the few remaining undeveloped places along the Gulf or Atlantic coasts, or it could hit a major city. How many suffer, how many die, and the costs to the economy will be determined over the coming years by men and women deciding whether to live near the coast and, if so, how to protect themselves and their homes from hurricanes; and by public officials and others writing building codes, development rules, and insurance regulations, and deciding how much to invest in research, planning, and emergency management. These decisions will determine how families will endure experiences like those of the Ochmanskis, the Shoemakers, the Bigelows, and Robin Sheets on August 24, 1992, and how many families will survive them.

APPENDICES

APPENDIX A: TROPICAL CYCLONE TERMINOLOGY AND SEASONS

TERMINOLOGY

Hurricanes are tropical cyclones with winds of 74 mph or faster over the Atlantic Ocean and the Pacific Ocean north of the equator and east of the international date line.

Typhoons are tropical cyclones with winds of 74 mph or faster over the northwestern Pacific Ocean north of the equator and west of the International date line. Elsewhere, the storms are called **tropical cyclones,** with "severe tropical cyclone" used in some areas for storms with winds of 74 mph or faster. Nonscientific, especially older books and articles sometimes call South Pacific tropical cyclones "typhoons."

SEASONS

Atlantic Basin: The official season is from June 1 through November 30. The season peaks from August through October. On the average, 87 percent of the Category 1 and 2 and 96 percent of the Category 3, 4, and 5 hurricanes occur during this three-month period.

Northeastern Pacific: The season runs from May 15 through November 30, with a peak in late August through early September.

Northwestern Pacific: Tropical cyclones occur all year, with a distinct minimum in February and the first half of March. The main season is from July to November, with a peak in late August through early September.

North Indian Ocean: There is a double peak of activity, first in May and then in November, although tropical cyclones are seen from April to December.

Severe tropical cyclones, with winds of 74 mph or faster, occur almost exclusively from April to June and from late September into early December.

Southwestern Indian Ocean, Australia–Southeastern Indian Ocean: These basins have very similar annual cycles, with tropical cyclones beginning in late October or early November and reaching two peaks, with the first in mid-January and the second in mid-February to early March. The season ends in May.

Australia–Southwestern Pacific Basin: Tropical cyclones begin forming in late October or early November and reach a peak in late February or early March. The season ends in early May.

Globally: September is the most active month, and May is the least active month.

Source: Christopher W. Landsea, NOAA Hurricane Research Division

2001–2006

2001	2002	2003	2004	2005	2006
Allison	Arthur	Ana	Alex	Arlene	Alberto
Barry	Bertha	Bill	Bonnie	Bret	Beryl
Chantal	Cristobal	Claudette	Charley	Cindy	Chris
Dean	Dolly	Danny	Danielle	Dennis	Debby
Erin	Edouard	Erika	Earl	Emily	Ernesto
Felix	Fay	Fabian	Frances	Franklin	Florence
Gabrielle	Gustav	Grace	Gaston	Gert	Gordon
Humberto	Hanna	Henri	Hermine	Harvey	Helene
Iris	Isidore	Isabel	Ivan	Irene	Isaac
Jerry	Josephine	Juan	Jeanne	José	Joyce
Karen	Kyle	Kate	Karl	Katrina	Kirk
Lorenzo	Lili	Larry	Lisa	Lee	Leslie
Michelle	Marco	Mindy	Matthew	Maria	Michael
Noel	Nana	Nicholas	Nicole	Nate	Nadine
Olga	Omar	Odette	Otto	Ophelia	Oscar
Pablo	Paloma	Peter	Paula	Philippe	Patty
Rebekah	Rene	Rose	Richard	Rita	Rafael
Sebastien	Sally	Sam	Shary	Stan	Sandy
Tanya	Teddy	Teresa	Tomas	Tammy	Tony
Van	Vicky	Victor	Virginie	Vince	Valerie
Wendy	Wilfred	Wanda	Walter	Wilma	William

ATLANTIC STORMS RETIRED INTO HURRICANE HISTORY

Experience shows that the use of short, distinctive given names in written as well as spoken communication is quicker and less subject to error than the older, more cumbersome latitude-longitude identification methods. These advantages are especially important in exchanging detailed information between hundreds of widely scattered stations, coastal bases, and ships at sea, as well as communicating with the general public.

Since 1953, Atlantic tropical storms have been named from lists originally drawn up by the National Hurricane Center and now maintained by an international committee of the World Meteorological Organization. The lists featured only women's names until 1979, when the international committee established a policy of rotating six lists of names, alternating both men's and women's names—of English, Spanish, and French origin. Thus, the 2001 list will be reused in 2007. However, if any individual storm has caused major damage or loss of life, that storm's name may be "retired," and replaced by a like name on the list.

Agnes (1972): Florida, northeastern U.S.

Alicia (1983): northern Texas

Allen (1980): Antilles, Mexico, southern Texas

Andrew (1992): Bahamas, southern Florida, Louisiana

Anita (1977): Mexico

Audrey (1957): Louisiana, northern Texas

Betsy (1965): Bahamas, southeastern Florida, southeastern Louisiana

Beulah (1967): Antilles, Mexico, southern Texas

Bob (1991): North Carolina, Northeast U.S.

Camille (1969): Louisiana, Mississippi, Alabama

Carla (1961): Texas

Carmen (1974): Mexico, central Louisiana

Carol* (1954): Northeast U.S.

Celia (1970): southern Texas

Cesar (1996): Central America

Cleo (1964): Lesser Antilles, Haiti, Cuba, southeastern Florida

Connie (1955): North Carolina

David (1979): Lesser Antilles, Haiti, Dominican Republic, Florida, eastern U.S.

Diana (1990): Mexico

Diane (1955): Mid-Atlantic U.S., northeastern U.S.

Donna (1960): Bahamas, Florida, eastern U.S.

Dora (1964): northeastern Florida

Elena (1985): Mississippi, Alabama, western Florida

Eloise (1975): Antilles, northwestern Florida, Alabama

Flora (1963): Haiti, Cuba

Fran (1996): North Carolina

Frederic (1979): Alabama, Mississippi

Georges (1998): Lesser Antilles, Haiti, Dominican Republic, Florida Keys, Louisiana

Gilbert (1988): Lesser Antilles, Jamaica, Yucatán Peninsula, Mexico

Gloria (1985): North Carolina, northeastern U.S.

Hattie (1961): Belize, Guatemala

Hazel (1954): Antilles, Carolinas

Hilda (1964): Louisiana

Hortense (1996): Puerto Rico

Hugo (1989): Antilles, South Carolina

Ione (1955): North Carolina

Inez (1966): Lesser Antilles, Haiti, Dominican Republic, Cuba, Florida Keys, Mexico

Janet (1955): Lesser Antilles, Belize, Mexico

Joan (1988): Curaçao, Venezuela, Colombia, Nicaragua

Keith (2000): Mexico

Klaus (1990): Martinique

Luis (1995): Lesser Antilles, Virgin Islands

Marilyn (1995): Virgin Islands, Puerto Rico

Mitch (1998): Central America, Nicaragua, Honduras

Opal (1995): Florida

Roxanne (1995): Mexico

*"Carol" was used again to denote a hurricane in the mid–Atlantic Ocean in 1965. However, because the name does not appear after that time, it is assumed that the name was retired retrospectively for the damages caused by the 1954 storm of the same name.

Source: National Hurricane Center

The Saffir-Simpson classification is based on the hurricane's intensity at a particular time, such as when a forecast is issued. It gives an estimate of the potential property damage and flooding expected along the coast from a hurricane landfall. Wind speed is the determining factor in the scale, as storm surge values are highly dependent on the slope of the continental shelf in the landfall region. As an aid to emergency managers and the general public, the kinds of damage that can be expected, as well as wind speeds and potential surge heights, are part of the scale.

Category 1 Hurricane:
Winds 74–95 mph (64–82 kt or 119–153 km/hr). Storm surge generally 4–5 feet above normal. No real damage to building structures. Damage primarily to unanchored mobile homes, shrubbery, and trees. Some damage to poorly constructed signs. Also some coastal road flooding and minor pier damage.

Category 2 Hurricane:
Winds 96–110 mph (83–95 kt or 154–177 km/hr). Storm surge generally 6–8 feet above normal. Some roofing material, door, and window damage of buildings. Considerable damage to shrubbery and trees with some trees blown down. Considerable damage to mobile homes, poorly constructed signs, and piers. Coastal and low-lying escape routes flood 2–4 hours before arrival of the hurricane center. Small craft in unprotected anchorages break moorings.

Category 3 Hurricane:
Winds 111–130 mph (96–113 kt or 178–209 km/hr). Storm surge generally 9–12 feet above normal. Some structural damage to small residences and utility buildings with a minor amount of curtain-wall failures. Damage to shrubbery and trees with foliage blown off trees and large trees blown down. Mobile homes

and poorly constructed signs are destroyed. Low-lying escape routes are cut by rising water 3–5 hours before arrival of the hurricane center. Flooding near the coast destroys smaller structures with larger structures damaged by battering of floating debris. Terrain continuously lower than 5 feet above mean sea level may be flooded inland 8 miles (13 km) or more. Evacuation of low-lying residences within several blocks of the shoreline may be required.

Category 4 Hurricane:
Winds 131–155 mph (114–135 kt or 210–249 km/hr). Storm surge generally 13–18 feet above normal. More extensive curtain-wall failures with some complete roof structure failures on small residences. Shrubs, trees, and all signs are blown down. Complete destruction of mobile homes. Extensive damage to doors and windows. Low-lying escape routes may be cut by rising water 3–5 hours before arrival of the hurricane center. Major damage to lower floors of structures near the shoreline. Terrain lower than 10 feet above sea level may be flooded, requiring massive evacuation of residential areas as far inland as 6 miles (10 km).

Category 5 Hurricane:
Winds greater than 155 mph (135 kt or 249 km/hr). Storm surge generally greater than 18 feet above normal. Complete roof failure on many residences and industrial buildings. Some complete building failures with small utility buildings blown over or away. All shrubs, trees, and signs are blown down. Complete destruction of mobile homes. Severe and extensive window and door damage. Low-lying escape routes are cut by rising water 3–5 hours before arrival of the hurricane center. Major damage to lower floors of all structures located less than 15 feet above sea level and within 500 yards of the shoreline. Massive evacuation of residential areas on low ground within 5–10 miles (8–16 km) of the shoreline may be required.

Source: National Hurricane Center

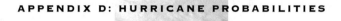

Below are probabilities of any hurricane and of a major hurricane with winds of 111 mph or faster passing within 75 miles of various locations in any year. The numbers are a measure of the relative danger.

The numbers can also be read as the number of storms to be expected in an average 100-year period. For example, Biloxi has a 10 percent chance of any hurricane passing within 75 miles and a 3 percent chance of a major hurricane coming within 75 miles each year. During an average century Biloxi can expect 10 hurricanes and 3 major hurricanes.

Location	*Any hurricane*	*Major hurricane*
CONTINENTAL U.S.		
Brownsville, Tex.	7.1	2.2
Corpus Christi, Tex.	6.7	2.3
Port O'Connor, Tex.	11.1	3.1
Galveston, Tex.	14.3	4.2
Port Arthur, Tex.	11.1	3.1
New Iberia, La.	8.3	1.9
New Orleans, La.	12.5	3.2
Biloxi, Miss.	10.0	3.0
Pascagoula, Miss.	11.1	3.3
Mobile, Ala.	10.0	3.0
Gulf Shores, Ala.	12.5	3.7
Pensacola, Fla.	12.5	3.7
Panama City, Fla.	14.3	3.7
Appalachicola, Fla.	14.3	3.3
St. Marks, Fla.	6.7	1.4

Location	Any hurricane	Major hurricane
Cedar Key, Fla.	11.1	2.4
Tampa, Fla.	17.5	4.8
Venice, Fla.	17.2	4.8
Port Charlotte, Fla.	17.0	4.6
Fort Myers, Fla.	17.5	5.6
Naples, Fla.	18.9	6.3
Key West, Fla.	19.6	7.7
Marathon, Fla.	22.2	9.1
Miami, Fla.	26.3	11.1
Ft. Lauderdale, Fla.	27.0	10.0
West Palm Beach, Fla.	18.2	7.1
Lake Okeechobee, Fla.	14.3	5.3
Ft. Pierce, Fla.	16.7	5.6
Cocoa Beach, Fla.	14.3	4.2
Cape Canaveral, Fla.	14.3	3.9
Daytona Beach, Fla.	11.1	2.6
Jacksonville, Fla.	9.1	1.9
Savannah, Ga.	7.1	1.3
Charleston, S.C.	10.0	2.2
Myrtle Beach, S.C.	10.0	2.6
Wilmington, N.C.	10.0	2.1
Morehead City, N.C.	12.5	2.7
Cape Hatteras, N.C.	21.3	5.3
Virginia Beach, Va.	6.7	1.3
Norfolk, Va.	4.8	0.8
Ocean City, Md.	4.2	0.9
Cape May, N.J.	7.1	1.9
Atlantic City, N.J.	4.8	1.2
New York City, N.Y.	6.3	1.6
Montauk Point, N.Y.	6.3	1.5
Providence, R.I.	10.0	2.9
Newport, R.I.	6.3	1.4
Nantucket, Mass.	12.5	3.2
Hyannis, Mass.	10.0	3.2
Boston, Mass.	5.9	1.3
Portland, Me.	2.9	0.3
Bar Harbor, Me.	12.5	2.9

Location	Any hurricane	Major hurricane
CARIBBEAN, BAHAMAS, BERMUDA		
Antigua	20.0	6.7
Barbados	8.3	2.3
Belize City	10.0	2.9
Bermuda	25.0	9.1
Bonaire	2.2	0.6
Guantanamo, Cuba	6.3	1.9
Havana, Cuba	16.7	6.3
Kingston, Jamaica	14.3	5.9
Merida, Mexico (Yucatán)	9.1	3.0
Nassau, Bahamas	22.2	9.1
San Juan, Puerto Rico	12.5	4.2
Santo Domingo, Dominican Republic	11.1	3.9
U.S. Virgin Islands	16.7	5.9

Source: National Hurricane Center

APPENDIX E: THE STRONGEST HURRICANES TO HIT THE U.S. GULF AND EAST COASTS 1900–2000

Strengths are measured at the time each storm hit the United States; many were stronger at other times. Central pressure readings, not wind speeds, are used because pressure is a more accurate representation of a storm's power.

Locations that the storm affected most are given before 1950. After 1950, when naming began, storm names are given.

Strength	Hurricane	Year	Category	Pressure
1.	Florida Keys	1935	5	26.35
2.	Camille	1969	5	26.84
3.	Andrew	1992	4	27.23
4.	Florida Keys, Texas	1919	4	27.37
5.	Lake Okeechobee, Fla.	1928	4	27.43
6.	Donna	1960	4	27.46
7.	Galveston, Tex.	1900	4	27.49
7.	Grand Isle, La.	1909	4	27.49
7.	New Orleans	1915	4	27.49
7.	Carla	1961	4	27.49
11.	Hugo	1989	4	27.58
12.	Miami, Fla.	1926	4	27.61
13.	Hazel	1954	4*	27.70
14.	southeastern Florida	1947	4	27.76
15.	northern Texas	1932	4	27.79
16.	Gloria	1985	3*†	27.92
16.	Opal	1995	3†	27.82
18.	Audrey	1957	4‡	27.91
18.	Galveston, Tex.	1915	4‡	27.91
18.	Celia	1970	3	27.91

Strength	*Hurricane*	*Year*	*Category*	*Pressure*
18.	Allen	1980	3§	27.91
22.	New England	1938	3*	27.94
22.	Frederic	1979	3	27.94
24.	Northeast U.S.	1944	3*	27.97
24.	Carolinas	1906	3	27.97
26.	Betsy	1965	3	27.99
26.	southeastern Florida	1929	3	27.99
26.	southeastern Florida	1933	3	27.99
26.	southern Texas	1916	3	27.99
26.	Mississippi, Alabama	1916	3	27.99

The first three notes show why category listings do not agree with category central pressure values.

* Moving more than 30 miles an hour, which means winds on the storm's right side would place the storm in a higher category than winds on the left side.
† Winds and tides did not justify 4.
‡ Classified 4 because of extreme tides.
§ Reached Cat. 5 intensity three times along its path across the Caribbean and the Gulf of Mexico.

APPENDIX F:
BILLION-DOLLAR HURRICANES

Hurricanes listed as having done more than
$1 billion damage in year 2000 dollars.

Rank	Hurricane	Year	Category	Cost (in year 2000 dollars)
1.	Andrew	1992	4	$34.3 billion
2.	Hugo	1989	4	$10.9 billion*
3.	Agnes	1965	1	$8.4 billion
4.	Betsy	1965	3	$8.4 billion
5.	Camille	1969	5	$6.8 billion
6.	Dianne	1955	1	$5.4 billion
7.	Frederic	1979	3	$4.9 billion
8.	New England	1938	3	$4.7 billion
9.	Floyd	1999	3	$4.6 billion
10.	Fran	1996	3	$3.6 billion
11.	Opal	1995	3	$3.5 billion
12.	Alicia	1983	3	$3.4 billion
13.	Carol	1954	3	$3.1 billion
14.	Carla	1961	4	$2.5 billion
15.	Juan	1985	1	$2.4 billion
16.	Donna	1960	4	$2.4 billion
17.	Iniki	1992	Unknown	$2.3 billion
18.	Celia	1970	3	$2.1 billion
19.	Elena	1985	3	$2.0 billion
20.	Bob	1991	2	$2.0 billion
21.	Hazel	1954	4	$1.9 billion
22.	Miami, Fla.	1926	4	$1.7 billion

Rank	Hurricane	Year	Category	Cost (in year 2000 dollars)
23.	Marilyn ([†])	1995	2	$1.7 billion
24.	Galveston, Tex.	1915	4	$1.5 billion
25.	Dora	1964	2	$1.5 billion
26.	Eloise	1975	3	$1.5 billion
27.	Gloria	1985	3	$1.5 billion
28.	Puerto Rico	1928	4	$1.3 billion
29.	Northeast U.S.	1944	3	$1.2 billion
30.	Beulah	1967	3	$1.1 billion

*Includes damage in Puerto Rico, Virgin Islands, and the U.S. mainland
[†]Damage in the U.S. Virgin Islands and Puerto Rico. The storm did not hit mainland U.S.

Source: National Hurricane Center

Death figures are the best estimate of fatalities in the mainland United States. All storms with an official death toll of 50 or more since 1900 are included. Locations most affected by each storm are included. Names are given for storms from 1950 on when naming began.

Rank	Storm name, location affected	Year	Category	Deaths
1.	Galveston, Tex.	1900	4	8,000*
2.	Lake Okeechobee, Fla.	1928	4	1,836
3.	Florida Keys and Tex.	1919	4	600†
4.	New England	1938	3	600
5.	Florida Keys	1935	5	408
6.	Audrey, in La. and Tex.	1957	4	390
7.	Northeast U.S.	1944	3	390‡
8.	Grand Isle, La.	1909	4	350
9.	New Orleans, La.	1915	4	275
10.	Northeastern Tex.	1915	4	275
11.	Camille in Miss., La., Va.	1969	5	256
12.	Miss., Ala., Miami and Pensacola, Fla.	1926	4	243
13.	Diane, in the Northeast	1955	1	184
14.	southeastern Fla.	1906	2	164
15.	Miss., Ala., Fla. Panhandle	1906	3	134
16.	Agnes, in the Northeast	1972	1	122
17.	Hazel, in the Carolinas	1954	4	95
18.	Betsy, in southeastern Fla., La.	1965	3	75
19.	Carol, in the Northeast	1954	3	56
20.	southeastern Fla., La., Miss	1947	4	51

Rank	Storm name, location affected	Year	Category	Deaths
21.	Donna, in Fla., S.C. to New England	1960	4	50
22.	Ga., the Carolinas	1940	2	50

*The total actually may have been as high as 12,000.

†More than 500 of the deaths were on ships at sea; the toll could have been as high as 900.

‡344 of these were lost on ships at sea, with 247 of them occurring when the USS *Warrington*, a U.S. Navy destroyer, sank in the Atlantic.

The deadliest Atlantic Ocean, Caribbean Sea, or Gulf of Mexico hurricanes from 1492 through 2000. Storms listed are estimated to have each killed at least 1,000 people. In many cases, especially before the twentieth century, the figures are estimates. "Offshore" refers to deaths on ships away from any land.

Rank	Locations most affected	Dates	Estimated deaths
1.	Barbados, St. Eustatius, Martinique, offshore	Oct. 1780	20,000–22,000
2.	Mitch: Honduras, Nicaragua, El Salvador, Guatemala, Belize	Oct. 1998	9,086 dead, 9,191 missing
3.	Galveston, Texas	Sept. 1900	8,000–12,000
4.	Fifi: Honduras	Sept. 1974	8,000–10,000
5.	Dominican Republic	Sept. 1930	2,000–8,000
6.	Flora: Haiti and Cuba	Sept.–Oct. 1963	8,000
7.	Guadeloupe	Sept. 1776	6,000
8.	Newfoundland Banks	Sept. 1775	4,000
9.	Puerto Rico and Carolinas	Aug. 1899	3,063–3,433
10.	Martinique, Guadeloupe, Puerto Rico, Turks and Caicos, Florida	Sept. 1928	3,375–4,075
11.	Cayman Islands, Jamaica, Cuba,	Nov. 1932	2,500–3,107
12.	Central Atlantic offshore	Sept. 1782	3,000
13.	Martinique	Aug. 1813	3,000
14.	El Salvador and Honduras	June 1934	2,000–3,006
15.	Cuba	June 1791	3,000
16.	Barbados	Aug. 1831	1,500–2,500

Rank	Locations most affected	Dates	Estimated deaths
17.	Belize	Sept. 1931	1,500–2,500
18.	Haiti, Jamaica, Honduras	Oct. 1935	1,000–2,168
19.	David: Dominica, Dominican Republic; United States	Aug.–Sept. 1979	2,063–2,068
20.	Offshore Florida	1781	2,000
21.	South Carolina and Georgia	Aug. 1893	2,000–2,500
22.	Eastern Gulf of Mexico	Oct. 1780	2,000
23.	Cuba	Oct. 1870	1,000–2,000
24.	Louisiana	Oct. 1893	1,800–2,000
25.	Guadeloupe and Martinique	Aug. 1666	2,000
26.	Martinique	Aug. 1767	1,600
27.	Mexico	Aug. 1909	1,000–1,500
28.	Cuba and Florida Straits	Oct. 1644	1,500
29.	Guadeloupe and Puerto Rico	July 1825	1,300
30.	Offshore Nicaragua	1605	1,300
31.	Gordon: Costa Rica, Haiti, Dominican Republic, Florida	Nov. 1994	1,145
32.	Jamaica and Cuba	Oct. 1780	1,115
33.	Florida Straits	Sept. 1622	1,090
34.	Gulf of Mexico	Nov. 1590	1,000
35.	Offshore Barbados	Sept. 1694	1,000
36.	Florida Straits and Bahamas	July 1715	1,000
37.	Cuba	Oct. 1768	1,000
38.	Veracruz, Mexico	1601	1,000
39.	Hazel: Grenada, Haiti, U.S., Canada	Oct. 1954	1,000
40.	Inez: Caribbean and Mexico	Sept.–Oct. 1966	1,000

Source: Edward N. Rappaport and José Fernandez-Partagas, "The Deadliest Atlantic Tropical Cyclones, 1492–1998," published by the National Hurricane Center.

This chart shows the general decade-by-decade trend of the death rate decreasing while the cost of hurricanes has been increasing.

Deaths	Years	Costs (in year 2000 dollars)	Dollars per death
8,734	1900–1909	$1.447 billion	$165,674
1,036	1910–1919	$3.504 billion	$3.382 million
2,124	1920–1929	$2.223 billion	$1.047 million
1,146	1930–1939	$6.059 billion	$5.287 million
216	1940–1949	$5.521 billion	$25.679 million
880	1950–1959	$13.362 billion	$15.184 million
585	1960–1969	$25.221 billion	$43.113 million
235	1970–1979	$20.610 billion	$87.702 million
129	1980–1989	$21.426 billion	$166.093 million
249	1990–1999	$56.659 billion	$227.546 million

In a 1998 study, Roger Pielke Jr. of the National Center for Atmospheric Research, and Chris Landsea of the NOAA Hurricane Research Division calculated what past hurricanes would cost if these same storms hit the same places today. They took into account inflation, increases in population, and increases in personal property in areas the storms hit. Below are the ten hurricanes that would cost the most today.

Rank	Hurricane	Year	Category	Damage in millions (year 2000 dollars)
1.	southeastern Fla., Ala.	1926	4	$87,170
2.	Andrew (southeast Fla., La.)	1992	4	$39,900
3.	Galveston, Tex.	1900	4	$32,090
4.	Galveston, Tex.	1915	4	$27,190
5.	southwestern Fla.	1944	3	$20,330
6.	New England	1938	3	$20,050
7.	southeastern Fla.	1928	4	$16,630
8.	Betsy (southeastern Fla., La.)	1965	3	$14,990
9.	Donna (Fla., East Coast)	1960	4	$14,530
10.	Camille (Miss., La., Va.)	1969	5	$13,220

Chapter 9 describes the use of computer models for forecasting hurricanes, including the differences between statistical and dynamical models. The information here has more details about the various models the National Hurricane Center uses. Discussions that are issued as part of the Center's regular forecast bulletins on storms often refer to the various models using the names given in boldface below.

STATISTICAL TACK FORECAST MODELS

NHC90/NHC91 and **CLIPER** are statistical track forecast models. The predictors for CLIPER (CLImatology and PERsistence) include the initial latitude and longitude of the storm, the components of the storm motion vector, the day of the year, and the initial storm intensity. The CLIPER forecasts are often used to normalize the output from other track models and as a benchmark for evaluating track forecasting skill. NHC90/NHC91 are combination statistical and dynamical models that use the output from CLIPER in combination with vertically averaged winds through the atmosphere and upper atmosphere air pressures from the Aviation run of the MRF model as predictors. NHC90 is used for the Atlantic Basin and NHC91 for the eastern Pacific.

DYNAMICAL TRACK FORECAST MODELS

AVN is the Aviation run of the National Weather Service's National Centers for Environmental Prediction Medium Range Forecast (MRF) model. The MRF is a 28-level global model. It includes parameterizations of convective, radiative, and boundary layer processes. For tropical cyclone forecasts, it uses synthetic observations of a storm's core that are constructed from estimates of central pressure, radius and pressure of the outermost closed isobar, the radius and value of the maximum low-level winds and the radii of 34-knot winds. Synthetic winds are included at about 50 locations within about 200 nautical miles of the storm center from the surface to the maximum level of the storm circulation (typically around 30,000 feet). An automated tracking algorithm provides a track forecast out to 72 hours.

NOGAPS (the U.S. Navy's Operational Global Atmospheric Prediction System) is a global forecast model with 18 levels, parameterizations of physical processes and a tropical cyclone bogussing scheme. Generally speaking, the NOGAPS bogussing scheme is similar to that of the MRF model, where synthetic observations that represent the storm circulation are added to the data assimilation system. Similar to the MRF scheme, the observations are created from the sum of an environmental flow and a symmetric vortex.

UKMET is the global forecast model run by the UK Meteorological Office. Similar to NOGAPS and the MRF model, it includes extensive physical parameterizations and a tropical cyclone bogussing system.

GFDL (Geophysical Fluid Dynamics Laboratory) is a limited area baroclinic model developed specifically for hurricane prediction. It includes 18 levels and uses three nested grids. The two inner grids move to follow the storm, and the resolution of the inner domain is ⅙ of a degree of latitude. The GFDL model includes convective, radiative, and boundary layer parameterizations and has a specialized method for initializing the storm circulation. The initial and boundary conditions are obtained from the Aviation run of the MRF model. The representation of the storm circulation in the global analysis is replaced with the sum of an environmental flow and an idealized vortex. This idealized vortex is based upon a few parameters of the observed storm, including the maximum wind, radius of maximum wind and outer wind radii. The environmental flow is the global analysis modified by a filtering technique that removes the hurricane circulation.

LBAR (Limited area BARotropic) is a two-dimensional track prediction model that is initialized with vertically averaged winds and upper atmospheric air pressures from the Aviation run of the MRF global model. An idealized symmetric vortex is added to the global model analysis to represent the storm circulation. The boundary conditions are obtained from the global model forecast.

The **BAM** (Beta and Advection Model) follows a trajectory from the Aviation run of the MRF model to provide a track forecast. The model incorporates a correction known as the "Beta effect" to account for the fact that the Coriolis force resulting from the rotation of the Earth is greater toward the poles, so the winds in the northern side of a Northern Hemisphere hurricane are turned more than those in its southern side. If no other winds were steering a hurricane the Beta effect would cause a westward-headed storm to drift toward the north in the Northern Hemisphere and to the south in the Southern Hemisphere. The three versions of the BAM model are based upon the depth of the vertically averaged winds each uses. The shallow version, **BAMS**, averages winds from about 5,000 to 10,000 feet; the medium version, **BAMM**, uses winds up to 24,500 feet; and the deep version, **BAMD**, uses winds up to 40,700 feet. For a tropical storm or even a weak hurricane that does not have a well-developed eye wall extending well up into the upper-level winds, it may be predominantly steered by lower-level winds and thus, the shallow version might produce the best forecasts. Also, the combination of these three model predictions are quite useful to the forecaster for diagnostic purposes. If the forecast tracks from the three versions of the BAM model are essentially the same throughout the forecast periods, then forecasters have greater confidence in the predictions. If there are large differences, forecasters have less confidence. Large differences also indicate large wind shear factors, which could affect intensity forecasts. Of course, any and all assessments using the BAM models depend on how well the Aviation run of the MRF model has captured the initial state of the atmosphere and predicted its future state.

STATISTICAL INTENSITY FORECAST MODELS

SHIFOR (Statistical Hurricane Intensity FORecast) is a simple statistical model that uses climatological and persistence predictors to forecast intensity change. Analogous to the CLIPER track model, it is often used as a benchmark for evaluating more general models. However, the developmental sample for SHIFOR excluded cases where storms made landfall, so it is only valid for storms over the ocean.

SHIPS (Statistical Hurricane Intensity Prediction Scheme) is a statistical model that uses climatological, persistence, and synoptic predictors. The primary predictors include the difference between the maximum possible intensity (MPI) and the current intensity, vertical shear of the horizontal wind, persistence (the previous 12-hour intensity change), a measure of the relative angular momentum at about 40,000 feet, and winds and temperatures at this altitude within 1,000 kilometers of the storm center. The MPI is estimated from an empirical relationship between sea surface temperature (SST) and intensity. The SST's are obtained from a weekly analysis. The MPI and vertical shear are averaged along the storm track, where the forecast positions are obtained from the LBAR model. Similar to SHIFOR, SHIPS was developed from cases where the storm track did not cross land. A version of SHIPS is available for the Atlantic and east Pacific.

DYNAMICAL INTENSITY FORECAST MODEL

The **GFDL** model has shown limited skill in producing intensity forecasts, but these forecasts are not nearly as good as the model's track forecasts.

BEFORE BUYING OR BUILDING A HOME IN A HURRICANE-PRONE AREA:

1. View flood maps at the local emergency management office to choose a home site that is not subject to flooding.
2. Obtain information on hurricane-resistant construction from FEMA, State Farm Insurance and the Florida Alliance for Safe Homes (www.flash.org). Choose a style that is wind resistant, such as with a hipped-roof (all roof edges come down to the outside walls) instead of a gabled-end (inverted V) roof.
3. If building, use the Miami-Dade County, Fla., or the new Florida coastal high-wind standard, not just local standards.
4. Include a safe room in your home to provide refuge during hurricanes and tornadoes.
5. Determine whether your home can be freely insured or must be in the "wind pool." Learn what premium reductions are available for various types of construction.
6. Obtain brochures from your local emergency management office on hurricane preparation. Learn the plans for your community in case a hurricane threatens.

BEFORE THE HURRICANE SEASON:

1. Develop a family action plan for preparing your home, and determine where you will seek refuge if you evacuate. Prepare an evacuation or survival kit with enough nonperishable food, water and prescription medicines for two weeks, a first-aid kit, and flashlights. (Don't include candles).

If possible, arrange to stay with friends or family in a substantial home safe from possible flooding that is as close as possible to your home to avoid long highway trips.

2. Fit covers to protect your windows and doors if they do not contain impact-resistant glass or other permanent materials that have passed the State of Florida or Miami-Dade County impact standards tests. Practice putting up your covers. If you have a gabled-end roof, check that it is properly braced.

3. Check your insurance policies to ensure adequate coverage.

WHEN A HURRICANE WATCH IS ISSUED FOR YOUR AREA:

1. Listen to directions from local emergency management officials.
2. Ensure your hurricane survival kit is current.
3. Make sure your window protection covers are ready. Install those that are most difficult to put up now.
4. Fill your automobile gas tank with fuel.
5. Obtain cash since credit card and ATM computers may not work for some time.
6. Continually monitor the progress of the storm on local media outlets.

IF A HURRICANE WARNING IS ISSUED FOR YOUR AREA:

1. Implement your "family action plan."
2. Quickly install window shutters, panels, or other protection.
3. If you are evacuating, pack clothing, toiletries and your evacuation kit, including valuable papers and other belongings in water-tight containers.
4. Notify family or friends where you will be going or if you are riding out the hurricane at home. Have a common point of contact for family and friends outside of the potential hurricane strike area.
5. If you are evacuating, leave as soon as possible. Turn off the main circuit breaker for the house and shut off gas and water at the exterior shut off valves. Notify your central contact point when you arrive at your destination.

DURING THE HURRICANE:

1. Stay indoors away from windows and doors.
2. If debris starts striking the house, seek refuge in a safe room or in an interior bathroom, closet or under a stairwell. Take your emergency kit with you.

3. Do not go outside until announcements on the radio indicate the hurricane has clearly passed. Don't go out when winds die down as the eye passes.

AFTER THE HURRICANE:

1. Do not return from an evacuation until officials announce that your area is clear for reentry.
2. If power is out, shut off the main circuit breaker for power entering the house. Do not turn it on until power lines have been repaired and your own circuits are in good working order.
3. Stay away from dangerous areas such as downed power lines and fallen trees as you inspect your home.
4. Protect property from further damage using tarps from your hurricane supply kit. Do not attempt repairs or major cleanup at which you are not skilled, such as operating chain saws or climbing on roofs.
5. Stay indoors and at home as much as possible to let emergency crews do their work.
6. Contact your insurance company to arrange for an adjustor to visit your home.
7. Make sure that any repairs are done by licensed and insured contractors and that local building permits are obtained.

GLOSSARY

Advisory: For the United States, official statements issued by the National Hurricane Center in Miami or the Central Pacific Hurricane Center in Honolulu, Hawaii, describing any and all active tropical cyclone watches and warnings along with tropical cyclone location, intensity, and movement, and precautions that should be taken to protect life and property.

Anemometer: An instrument used to measure wind speed.

Atlantic Basin: The Atlantic Ocean north of the equator, the Caribbean Sea, and the Gulf of Mexico. The National Hurricane Center in Miami tracks, provides forecasts, and issues advisories for tropical cyclones in this region. Also known as the North Atlantic Basin.

Barrier island: A narrow, sometimes long island lying just offshore that separates and protects the mainland from the open sea.

Beaufort Wind Scale: The scale used to describe wind speed, devised in 1806 by British Admiral Francis Beaufort to classify winds at sea.

CDO: See **Central Dense Overcast.**

Center: The axis or core of a tropical cyclone. It is usually determined by pressure and cloud and wind rotation.

Central Dense Overcast (CDO): The solid mass of rainy clouds that makes up the dense, circular body of a tropical cyclone.

Central North Pacific Basin: The Pacific Ocean north of the equator between 140 degrees west longitude and the international date line. The Central Pacific Hurricane Center in Honolulu, Hawaii, tracks, provides forecasts, and issues advisories for tropical cyclones in this region. Also known as the Central Pacific Basin.

Central Pacific Basin: See **Central North Pacific Basin.**

Central Pacific Hurricane Center (CPHC): Division of the U.S. National Weather Service in Honolulu, Hawaii, responsible for tracking and issuing watches and warnings for tropical cyclones in the Central North Pacific Basin.

Central pressure: The minimum surface pressure at the center of a tropical cyclone, used as a measure of intensity.

Cloud seeding: The artificial insemination of clouds with foreign particles which alter the clouds' natural formation, usually enhancing and accelerating the development of precipitation. Experiments conducted during the 1960s tried to temporarily reduce a hurricane's intensity by altering its structure.

Concentric eye: See **Double eye wall.**

Coriolis force: An apparent curving motion of anything, such as wind, caused by the Earth's rotation. It deflects moving objects to the right in the Northern Hemisphere, and to the left in the Southern Hemisphere. It was first described by French scientist Gustave-Gaspard Coriolis in 1835.

Cyclone: An area of low atmospheric pressure with winds blowing around it, counterclockwise in the Northern Hemisphere and clockwise in the Southern Hemisphere.

Dangerous semicircle: The side of a tropical cyclone where the storm's winds and the forward motion are in the same direction, increasing the total wind speed.

Doldrums: A nautical term for the region of light winds that straddle the equator (an equatorial trough) between the trade winds of the Northern and Southern Hemispheres.

Double eye wall: A second ring of thunderstorms with intense winds forming around the main eye wall in a concentric configuration (not side by side). Observed in intense hurricanes and typhoons, a concentric eye often goes through life cycles with the outer eye wall, constricting and replacing the inner eye wall.

Dropsonde: A tubular package of instruments, dropped from Hurricane Hunter planes and lowered to the ocean with a parachute. Measures temperature, pressure, and humidity inside hurricanes.

Dropwindsonde: See **GPS dropsonde.**

Dry ice: Solid carbon dioxide that is ground up and used for cloud seeding.

Easterly wave: See **tropical wave.**

Eastern North Pacific Basin: The Pacific Ocean north of the equator and east of 140 west longitude. The National Hurricane Center in Miami tracks, provides forecasts, and issues advisories for tropical cyclones in this region. Also known as the Eastern Pacific Basin.

Eastern Pacific Basin: See **Eastern North Pacific Basin.**

El Niño: The Spanish name (meaning "boy child") given to a periodic warming of the central and eastern Pacific Ocean along the equator that usually shows up on the coast of Peru around Christmas. The warm water generates abundant thunderstorms that enhance tropical cyclone activity in the eastern Pacific, while redirecting strong upper-air winds that can inhibit tropical cyclone development in the Atlantic.

Explosive deepening: A drop in the central pressure of a tropical cyclone of 2.5 millibars an hour for at least twelve hours, or five millibars an hour for at least six hours. See **rapid deepening.**

Extratropical cyclone: A large-scale storm that forms outside the tropics with winds blowing around a low-pressure center, and a temperature contrast between warm and cold air masses. Extratropical cyclones draw their power from contrasting cold and warm air masses. They have warm and cold fronts; tropical cyclones do not.

Eye: The calm center of a tropical cyclone that is more than one-half surrounded by a wall of cloud.

Eye wall: A ring of thunderstorms with intense winds surrounding the eye of a tropical cyclone.

Feeder band: See **Spiral band.**

Fujiwhara effect: Occurs when two tropical cyclones less than 850 miles apart begin moving around a common point between them; the common point might not be the halfway point, depending on the strength and size of each cyclone.

Global Positioning System (GPS): A series of geostationary satellites and receivers used to triangulate the position of a transmitter to within a few feet anywhere on the Earth.

GPS dropsonde: A dropsonde that uses GPS satellite tracking to determine hurricane wind speed and direction at different altitudes. Also measures temperature, pressure, and humidity.

Hurricane: A tropical cyclone in which the fastest sustained surface wind near the ground is 74 mph (64 kt or 119 km/hr) or more. The term "hurricane" is used for cyclones in the Central and Eastern Pacific and the Atlantic basins. The term "typhoon" is used for Western Pacific tropical cyclones north of the equator. The term "severe tropical cyclone" is generally used in the Indian Ocean and around Austrailia. See **Appendix A.**

Hurricane Hunters: The fleet of U.S. Air Force and National Oceanic and Atmospheric Administration planes that fly into tropical storms and hurricanes to determine intensity, center location, and movement. U.S. Navy planes flew these missions in the past. See **reconnaissance flights.**

Hurricane season: The time of year when hurricanes are most likely. In the Atlantic and Central Pacific basins, hurricane season is from June 1 to November 30; in the Eastern Pacific Basin, it's from May 15 to November 30. See **Appendix A.**

Hurricane warning: An alert stating that sustained hurricane force winds of 74 mph (65 knots or 119 km/hr) or faster are imminent or expected on a coastline in about twenty-four hours or less. A hurricane warning can remain in effect when dangerously high water or a combination of dangerously high water and exceptionally high waves persist, even though winds may be less than hurricane force.

Hurricane watch: An alert stating that a coastline may be hit by a hurricane in about thirty-six hours or less.

Intertropical Convergence Zone (ITCZ): A narrow, discontinuous belt along the equator where the convergence of trade winds from both hemispheres triggers tropical showers and thunderstorms. The ITCZ shifts north and south of the equator with the seasons and can breed tropical cyclones.

Isobar: A line on a weather map connecting places with equal atmospheric pressure. Patterns created by isobars show areas of high and low atmospheric pressure.

Knot: A measure of wind speed in nautical miles per hour, where 1 knot (kt) is equal to 1.15 mph.

Landfall: When and where the center of a tropical cyclone or hurricane crosses from the sea onto land.

La Niña: The Spanish name (meaning "girl child") given to a periodic cooling of the central and eastern Pacific Ocean along the equator, opposite of El Niño. Unlike El Niño, whose effect on weather and climate is nearly global, La Niña has a less-pronounced effect on world weather. Still, the cooler water tends to inhibit the formation of tropical cyclones in the eastern Pacific, while weaker winds aloft over the Atlantic favor the development of tropical cyclones across the Caribbean and tropical Atlantic.

Latent heat: Energy stored when water evaporates into vapor or ice turns into liquid. It's released as heat when vapor condenses or water freezes.

Major hurricane: A hurricane with sustained winds faster than 110 mph (95 kt or 178 km/hr); Category 3, 4, and 5 hurricanes.

Maximum sustained wind: See **wind.**

Millibar: A metric measure of air pressure; 34 millibars (mb) is about 1 inch of mercury.

National Hurricane Center: Division of the U.S. National Weather Service Tropical Prediction Center responsible for tracking and issuing watches and warnings for tropical cyclones in the Atlantic Basin and the Eastern North Pacific Basin.

North Atlantic Basin: See **Atlantic Basin.**

Peak gust: Highest instantaneous wind, usually of a 1 to 3 second duration. For hurricanes, this is generally 1.3 times faster than sustained winds, but the ratio can vary widely. See **wind.**

Radiosonde: A small balloon-borne instrument package equipped with a radio transmitter that measures temperature, pressure, and humidity as the balloon rises through the atmosphere. When tracked using directional radio techniques it becomes a **rawindsonde** as wind speeds and directions can also be determined.

Rapid deepening: A drop in the central pressure of a tropical cyclone of 1.75 millibars an hour, or 42 millibars in twenty-four hours. Also see **explosive deepening.**

Reconnaissance flights: When land is threatened, Hurricane Hunter planes fly into tropical storms and hurricanes every three to six hours to determine intensity, center location, and movement. On each pass through the storm, instruments gather wind, temperature, pressure, and humidity information and determine the extent of winds of different strengths. Other aircraft, including the National Oceanic and Atmospheric Administration's Gulf-stream jet, collect data in the storm's environment to help forecasters predict movement and intensity changes.

Recurvature: The transition of the generally westward movement of tropical cyclones in the deep easterly steering winds of the tropics to an eastward movement in the westerly steering winds of higher latitudes. This general motion occurs in all basins, both north and south of the equator. In the Atlantic Basin, this movement is reflected in the parabolic track of a hurricane from the deep tropics toward North America and then out to sea over the North Atlantic. At times, this recurving may take place too far west and a storm may strike the eastern United States.

Relocated: A term used in an advisory to indicate that a storm's latest position compared to its previous position does not reasonably represent its movement. Most often occurs when the first reconnaissance aircraft enters a storm that was previously being tracked solely using satellite imagery, especially for "weak" or "sheared" storms.

Return period: The average time, usually in years, between hurricanes of equal intensity at a specific place. This "number" can be very misleading in assessing potential future impacts, because hurricanes affecting an area do not typically occur at regular intervals.

Saffir-Simpson Hurricane Potential Damage Scale: A 1–5 scale developed by Herbert S. Saffir and Robert H. Simpson that measures hurricane intensity. See **Appendix G.**

Seeding: See **cloud seeding.**

Spiral band: Tightly curved banding of humid air, clouds, and often precipitation that spiral toward the tropical cyclone's center and form the dense wall of clouds that surround the eye. Spiral bands often "feed" moisture into mature hurricanes from hundreds of miles away, earning them the alternate name feeder bands.

Storm surge: The dome of water that builds up as a hurricane moves over water. When it comes ashore with the hurricane, the quickly rising water causes widespread coastal flooding, sometimes a mile or more inland.

Storm tide: The astronomical tide combined with storm surge.

Storm track: The path that a tropical storm or a hurricane takes.

Storm warning: An alert for sustained surface winds of 55 mph (48 kt or 88 km/hr) or faster that are not from tropical cyclones.

Subtropical cyclone: A low-pressure system that develops over subtropical waters and initially has nontropical features, such as a cold core, strongest winds aloft, and contrasting air masses, but does have some element of a tropical cyclone's cloud structure (located close to the center rather than away from the center of circulation). While some of these may be rather small, subtropical cyclones at times evolve into tropical cyclones.

Subtropical depression: A subtropical cyclone with fastest sustained surface winds less than 39 mph (34 kt or 63 km/hr).

Subtropical storm: A subtropical cyclone with fastest sustained surface winds of 39 mph (34 kt or 63 km/hr) or more.

Subtropics: Areas roughly between the tropics and the temperate zones in both hemispheres.

Sustained wind: See **wind.**

Temperate zones: Areas from roughly 30 degrees to 60 degrees latitude in both hemispheres.

Tornado: A strongly rotating column of air extending from the ground to at least the base of a thunderstorm.

Tropical cyclone: A storm that forms over a tropical ocean with a core warmer than the surrounding atmosphere. Winds blowing around central low pressure, unlike in storms outside the tropics, are strongest near the surface and just outside the storm's center.

Tropical cyclone plan-of-the-day: Schedule of the day's reconnaissance flights into tropical cyclones in the Atlantic, Eastern Pacific, and Central Pacific basins. Identifies possible requirements for the succeeding day as well.

Tropical depression: A tropical cyclone with fastest sustained surface winds less than 39 mph (34 kt or 63 km/hr).

Tropical disturbance: Often the earliest stage of a developing tropical cyclone. An organized area of thunderstorms forming in the tropics and persisting for more than twenty-four hours. Low pressure might form at the surface, but there is no closed surface circulation.

Tropical storm: A tropical cyclone with fastest sustained surface winds of 39 mph (34 kt or 63 km/hr) to 73 mph (63 kt or 118 km/hr).

Tropical storm warning: An alert stating that tropical storm winds of 39 mph (34 kt or 63 km/hr) to 73 mph (63 kt or 118 km/hr) are expected on a coastline in about twenty-four hours or less.

Tropical storm watch: An alert stating that a coastline may be hit by a tropical storm in about thirty-six hours or less. A tropical storm watch will not be issued if a system is forecast to reach hurricane strength; a hurricane watch will be issued instead.

Tropical Upper-Tropospheric Trough (TUTT): An elongated area of relatively low atmospheric pressure aloft (at about 30,000 feet, or the 200–300 millibar level) over the tropics.

Tropical wave: A kink or bend in the normally straight flow of surface air in the tropics, which forms a low-pressure trough, or pressure boundary, showers, and thunderstorms. Can develop into a tropical cyclone. Often called an easterly wave.

Tropics: Area from latitude 23.5 degrees north, the tropic of Cancer, to latitude 23.5 degrees south, the tropic of Capricorn. Sometimes called the "Torrid Zone."

Trough: In the Northern Hemisphere, an area of marked cyclonic or counter-clockwise flow of air where pressure generally reaches a minimum. Air flow is clockwise in a Southern Hemisphere trough.

TUTT: See **Tropical Upper-Tropospheric Trough.**

Typhoon: The regional term for a tropical cyclone in the Pacific Ocean west of the international date line and north of the equator, with sustained wind speeds of 74 miles per hour or more.

Vortex: Any circular flow of air around a discrete center.

Vortex message: A detailed report on the conditions and structure of a hurricane's eye, including observed minimum pressure, maximum temperature, location of center, shape of the eye, and peak estimated winds in the eye wall and the location where these winds were measured. Often includes remarks on peak winds measured at flight level by Hurricane Hunters when penetrating a hurricane's eye wall.

Wind: Air in motion. Types of wind relating to tropical cyclones: "extreme" refers to the fastest gust (see **peak gust**); "maximum sustained" refers to the fastest sustained wind in a tropical cyclone; "sustained" in the United States refers to 1-minute average speed, and internationally to a 10-minute average speed.

Wind shear: Any sudden change in wind speed or direction. In relation to hurricanes and other tropical cyclones, it usually refers to differences in the speeds or directions of winds at various levels of the atmosphere.

INDEX

ILLUSTRATION CREDITS